MOMENTS OF SILENCE

MOMENTS OF SILENCE

*The Unforgetting of the October 6, 1976,
Massacre in Bangkok*

Thongchai Winichakul

University of Hawai'i Press
Honolulu

25 24 23 22 21 20   6 5 4 3 2 1

Library of Congress Cataloging-in-Publication Data
Names: Thongchai Winichakul, author.
Title: Moments of silence : the unforgetting of the October 6, 1976,
massacre in Bangkok / Thongchai Winichakul.
Description: Honolulu : University of Hawai'i Press, 2020. | Includes
bibliographical references and index.
Identifiers: LCCN 2019050498 | ISBN 9780824882334 (cloth) | ISBN
9780824882341 (paperback) | ISBN 9780824882860 (epub) | ISBN
9780824882877 (kindle edition) | ISBN 9780824882853 (pdf)
Subjects: LCSH: Thammasat University Massacre, Bangkok, Thailand, 1976. |
Collective memory—Thailand. | Psychic trauma—Thailand. | Political
activists—Thailand—History—20th century. | Thailand—Politics and
government—20th century.
Classification: LCC DS586 .T578 2020 | DDC 959.304/4—dc23
LC record available at https://lccn.loc.gov/2019050498

University of Hawai'i Press books are printed on acid-free
paper and meet the guidelines for permanence and
durability of the Council on Library Resources.

Cover art and design: Ben Winitchakul. *When I Was 8 Years Old.*

Contents

List of Illustrations

Preface

The Making of the Book

This book has been one of my life's missions. It is about an atrocity that took place on Wednesday morning, October 6, 1976, in Bangkok, an event that Thailand has tried not to remember but that I cannot forget. Since then, not a single day has passed without my thinking about that morning.

This book took too many years to finish. In many ways, it has been a shadow following my intellectual journey and academic career. As a historian, my dream has always been to tell a "good" story, that is, an engaging or absorbing one that is provocative and imaginative. To me, a good story commemorating my lost friends and dedicated to them must reckon with the cruelty of Thai history as well. Given my involvement in the massacre, I resisted writing a book that focused on an explanation of what happened because some might see such a book as an excuse for my actions (and inaction) on that day. I preferred to let history judge. Instead, I decided to undertake a subtler, more difficult path, one that demanded my best efforts in research, thinking, and imagination. The result was my first book *Siam Mapped* (University of Hawai'i Press, 1994). I still wanted to write about the massacre, though, which I knew would be just as difficult. But I did not know how.

As the years passed by, my hope for truth and justice about the October 6 massacre that I had witnessed faded, and the silence surrounding it increasingly troubled me. Thailand did not seem to care about its past. People tried to bury it. Justice was irrelevant. I strongly believe, however, that the silence about the massacre speaks loudly about Thai society in ways that go beyond the incident itself: about truth and justice, how Thai society copes with conflict and its ugly past, about the ideas of reconciliation, the culture of impunity, and rights, and about the rule of law in the country. All this made me want even more to write about October 6.

The waves of memory studies in the 1990s in relation to com-memorations of the Holocaust helped me understand my experience and the memory of the October 6 massacre. Reading other studies helped me personally, too, in coping with the painful past. In 1996, on the twentieth anniversary of the massacre, I initiated a commemoration of the massacre in Bangkok. I wrote an article for the occasion, which was published in English in 2002. To avoid seeming to be an excuse for my past, the article focused on the memories of the event rather than what happened and who did what on that day. Many people encouraged me to turn the article into a book.

After more research and reflection, I realized that the article had covered less than half of the whole story. More stories were there for the telling about the changing memories of the massacre. The more I thought about it, the more it became my life's mission to finish. By 2006, my ideas and research had been largely sorted out. Then Thailand plunged into political crisis. My book project was caught up in the turmoil given that the former radicals of the 1970s played many parts in the downward spiral of democracy. I put the book aside to see how the story of the former radicals would unfold. The unfinished manuscript sat idly on my desk for some years. Sadly, after the dust had settled in 2010 Bangkok had seen more death and yet another massacre. A few years later, I saw the ending of the book. I had a chance to reconceptualize the entire project in early 2015, and found the urge to finish the book too strong to contain. I gradually lost interest in my regular teaching duties because my mission was to write this book. I decided to retire from Wisconsin in 2016 so that I would have the time to get it done.

Although the excitement of the cultural studies of memory has been winding down, my personal mission remains: to leave something in this world to remember my lost friends by and to bring them the justice they deserve no matter how long it takes. Part of me is still the political activist who organizes memorial activities, as I have done several times over the years. Part of me is the historian who wants to leave a scholarly contribution in the hope that it will be taken down from its shelf from time to time so that the October 6 massacre will be known for years to come. It is a privilege to have the opportunity to erect a memorial to friends in the lasting form of a good book, something that is very close to my heart as a historian.

That privilege, nevertheless, comes with a burden—writing this book was very difficult for me in many ways. Anyone who knows

Thailand will realize that the draconian lèse majesté law (Article 112 of Thailand's Criminal Code) could pose a problem given the dubious role of the monarchy in the incident. But possible trouble is beyond my control given that the law has been applied arbitrarily anyway. All I can do is to try to walk a fine line in my expression. The passing of King Bhumibol in 2016 and the growing deification of him posthumously, however, did not affect the writing or timing of the publication of this book in any way. The most difficult aspects were personal and intellectual. The emotional toll was beyond words. It is probably the main reason why the project has taken so long, for I needed many breaks along the way, sometimes for months at a time, before I could take up my writing again.

Intellectually, the contradiction of myself as the writing subject has been a major difficulty and challenge. I did not want to write a personal memoir, whether in a melancholy mode, a heroic mode, a guilt-ridden mode, or a vengeful mode, let alone cast blame on other people. As a historian, I wanted to write a critical study of the changing memories of the atrocity. However, I am not an outsider of the historical subject I am writing about, nor an objective historian of the event I study. Even my acts of studying and writing about the incident have been a part of changing memories of the event. In a nutshell, the author's position is problematic. I am a protagonist of the event I was trying to write about as a scholar. The solution was not merely carefulness and self-critique. There was no easy middle path or compromise either. The only way to navigate the space between being a witness or participant and being a historian or analyst is to make it productive and original, allowing the tensions and paradoxes within the author's position to play themselves out in the thinking and writing of the book, producing lines of inquiry, questions, analyses, and interpretations that are unique and insightful.

To anyone who might say that this book is not purely academic, so be it. Part of my soul is in this book. Nevertheless, for anyone who thinks that academic and activist lives cannot be combined, I beg to differ. The result in this case is a unique genre, an academic work with a touch of memoir. The traces of dual authorship are manifest in many forms throughout the writing process and in the text of this book. It is in the story, the tone, the voices, even in the use of pronouns—we or they, ours or theirs, and so on—not only when I discuss the perpetrators, but also the victims, who are sometimes friends, other times companions but also the subjects of my critical observation. In this book, pronouns are mostly reflexive rather than a calculated device.

Despite the unconventional approach due to the tension in the author's position, nonetheless, I hope readers will find this book to be the serious and critical reflections of a historian about an incident he witnessed and the memory changes he has been part of. Writing this book has been a fulfilling experience. I may not ever be satisfied with this book because the atrocity and the loss of friends are beyond my ability to express. But I am grateful that I have finally been able to tell the world the story that it should not forget. I trust the memory of the massacre will continue as long as this book remains on a shelf somewhere in this world.

Thongchai

Winter 2018

Acknowledgments

I am grateful to many people during the long journey of this book. First are those who have given me support and encouragement even when I went through difficulties and thought that I could not finish. Susan Friedman and Steve Stern in particular have provided inspiration to me throughout the years. Carol Hau, Junko Koizumi and colleagues at Kyoto University, and Takashi Shiraishi and the Institute of Developing Economies (IDE-JETRO) in Japan helped me get time to work on this book in early 2015 and in 2017–2019. I owe thanks to the Institute for Research in the Humanities at University of Wisconsin–Madison and the Asia Research Institute at the National University of Singapore for the time to work on the earlier stages of the book.

I presented various versions and parts of the manuscript at Chiang Mai University, Thammasat, Chulalongkorn, Wisconsin, Cornell, Ohio University, SOAS, North Carolina, UC Berkeley, UCLA, York, NUS, and at the conference in Cebu organized by Maria Diokno and Kiichi Fujiwara. Thank you to all for comments and encouragement at those presentations. Thanks also to Charnvit Kasetsiri, Kasian Tejapira, Chaiwat Satha-anan, Prajak Kongkirati, Charles Keyes, Craig Reynolds, Dan Doeppers, Michael Cullinane, Paul Hutchcroft, Alfred McCoy, Anne Hansen, Katherine Bowie, Robert Bickner, David Streckfuss, Florencia Mallon, Leigh Payne, Tyrell Haberkorn, Thak Chaloemtiarana, Prasenjit Duara, Hong Lysa, Sinae Hyun, Taylor Easum, Francis Bradley, Shane Strate, and Thanapol Limapichart for their contributions in many ways that they may or may not realize. Thank you to students in my seminar class in Spring 1996 in which the very first ideas for this book were formed; to Niti Pawakapan for our conversation that led to the title; and to Puangthong Pawakapan for attentive comments on many issues throughout and for her dedication as the manager of the digital archives, the "Documentation of October 6" (www.doct6.com). Penny Edwards and Tamara Loos read the entire manuscript and offered valuable comments, conceptually and in details, that help improve it significantly.

Thanapol Eawsakul was an amazing assistant who helped in indescribable ways, intellectually and practically, for two decades. He always went beyond my requests, including the discovery of the archival trove at the museum at the Attorney General Office in Bangkok. I am grateful to Mrs. Em-orn Tanthian, the librarian and curator of the museum in the early 2000s, for allowing me and Thanapol to work on those documents when nobody else knew them yet and even before they were catalogued. Wanchai Tantiwitthayapithak gave me the opportunity to try the first article in Thai in the *Sarakhadi* (Feature) magazine in 1996, which was the beginning of this long journey. Peter Ungphakorn, Jariyaporn Krabuansang–the editor of *Sarakhadi, Fa Diaw Kan (Sameskybooks)*, and Thammasat University Archives gave me permission to use their photos. Pamela Kelley, who is familiar with my "Th/English," carefully edited the first draft of the manuscript. She is the reason I returned to University of Hawai'i Press for this book.

My sister, Ben Winitchakul, was enthusiastic when I asked her to design the cover. Her impressive designs reflect, I believe, not only her artistic gift but also her memory of that morning at home. My wife, Somrudee, understands in ways nobody else could what this book means to me. Thank you for listening to my thinking aloud, sharing my grief when I was overwhelmed, and delightfully supporting me in every way.

No words can be enough to express my gratitude to those who lost their lives on October 6, 1976. This book is for them. It is worth little, however, compared to their sacrifices that allowed others, including me, to live on. In the spirit of this book, the silence after this sentence is not emptiness and not an ending, but is full of the indescribable memories, instilled with hope, dreams, courage, and so much more that their sacrifices have inspired me.

Thai Language Conventions

This book adheres to the phonetic transcription for most Thai words but does not use tonal marks. This practice follows the "General System of Phonetic Transcription of Thai Characters into Roman" devised in 1954 by the Royal Institute in Bangkok. Moreover, because of the constraints of typesetting, the superscript and subscript marks of certain vowels and consonants are not shown. Exceptions are those names that have been transcribed by various other systems or perhaps no system at all. In the case of a name known widely or a name that can be checked, the owner's transcription will be followed. Otherwise, the spelling follows the system of romanization mentioned above. The English names of certain Thai royals, such as Chulalongkorn, Bhumibol, and Vajiralongkorn, have been adopted rather than the lengthy official titles. The official ranks and positions such as king, prince, prime minister, major general, captain, admiral, and so on are given in the first reference to each but omitted after that. Finally, as in conventional usage, Thai people are referred to by their personal names and Westerners are referred to by their family names. In the bibliography, Thai names are therefore entered by personal (first) name.

Acronyms

BPP	Border Patrol Police
CPT	Communist Party of Thailand
Doct6	Documentation of the October 6 digital archives (https://doct6.com)
ISOC	Internal Security Operation Command (the military's counterinsurgency agency)
NARC	National Administrative Reform Council (the 1976 coup group)
NCPO	National Council for Peace and Order (the 2014 coup group)
NSCT	National Student Center of Thailand (the leading organization of the student movement from 1973 to 1976)
PARU	Police Aerial Reinforcement Unit (the counterinsurgency force of the BPP)
TU	Thammasat University, Tha Phrachan campus, Bangkok
VOPT	Voice of the People of Thailand (the CPT's underground broadcast)

Chronology of Major Events

1932	End of absolute monarchy in Siam
1947–1973	Thailand under military rule with brief periods of elected government in 1949–1951, 1955–1957, and 1968–1971
1960s	Vietnam War brings seven US bases and troop deployments to Thailand
1973	Paris Peace Accords bring gradual US withdrawal from Vietnam and Thailand
1973, October 14	Popular uprising ends military rule; dictators go into exile
1975	Communist revolutions in Cambodia, Vietnam, and Laos
1976, October 6	Morning massacre, evening coup by the NARC
1976–1977	Thanin Kraivixian government
1977, March 26	Failed coup, its leader executed
1977, October 20	Coup led by Kriangsak Chomanan
1977–1980	Carter administration (US) advocates for human rights
1977–1978	October 6 trial
1978, September 16	Amnesty for the Bangkok 18 in October 6 trial
1978, December	Vietnam ousts Khmer Rouge
1979–1991	Sino-Vietnamese war
1980, April 23	Prime Minister's Order no. 66/2523 dramatically changes counterinsurgency policy in Thailand
1979–1982	Students gradually return from jungles, the collapse of the CPT

1988, July	Chamlong controversy during election of Bangkok Governor
1989	End of Cold War; fall of the Berlin Wall (November)
1991, February	Coup
1992, May 15–17	Popular uprising against military rule
1995	Fiftieth anniversary of the end of World War II and the Holocaust
1996, October 6	Commemoration of the twentieth anniversary of the 1976 massacre
1997	Financial and global economic crisis begins in Thailand
1999, July 28	Dr. Puey Ungphakorn, rector of Thammasat University, dies in England
2000, October 6	Inauguration of October 6 Monument
2001, October 14	Inauguration of October 14 Memorial Building
2001 and 2005	General elections bring landslide victory of Thaksin Shinawatra
2006, September 19	Coup topples elected government and begins a period of political crises
2010, April 10 and May 17	Massacres of Red Shirt protesters
2014, May 22	NCPO coup
2016, October 6	Commemoration of the fortieth anniversary of the 1976 massacre

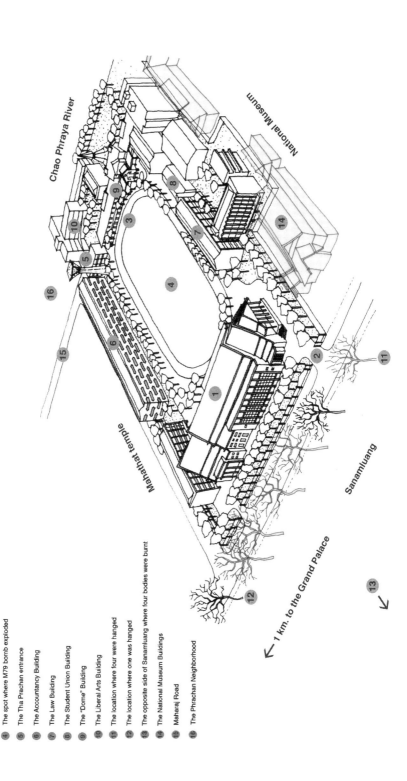

Chao Phraya River

National Museum

Mahathat temple

Sanamluang

← 1 km. to the Grand Palace

① Grand Auditorium
② The main entrance of Thammasat campus
③ The speaker's stage / platform
④ The spot where M79 bomb exploded
⑤ The Tha Prachan entrance
⑥ The Accountancy Building
⑦ The Law Building
⑧ The Student Union Building
⑨ The "Dome" Building
⑩ The Liberal Arts Building
⑪ The location where four were hanged
⑫ The location where one was hanged
⑬ The opposite side of Sanamluang where four bodies were burnt
⑭ The National Museum Buildings
⑮ Maharaj Road
⑯ The Phrachan Neighborhood

Prologue

OCTOBER 6, WEDNESDAY MORNING

"Please, my Police brothers, please stop shooting. Please. We gather here peacefully and unarmed. Our representatives are negotiating with the government right now. No more bloodshed, please. We beg you. Please stop shooting."

I remember that I kept repeating those words hundreds of times that morning—the same words, over and over, so that I did not need to think, because I could not think. From the back of the stage, as the voice of the demonstration, I tried to keep some semblance of order alive as long as possible. I could not think of anything else to do.

It was the most significant public speaking event of my life. But it was also the most irrelevant one. As I later learned, my disembodied voice was meaningful to thousands who were trapped inside Thammasat University (TU) under constant heavy fire. My voice did not help them at all, however.

I did not feel brave. I was terribly frightened. Only my awareness of those thousands under siege inside Thammasat kept me from abandoning the stage and running away.

....

At the time of the massacre I was a second-year student at Thammasat. I had been an activist since high school, joining a group of rebellious students who were dissatisfied with the state of Thai education. I became the leader of a national organization of high school students in 1974. Throughout my high school years, I spent more time at

1

protest sites, political demonstrations, printing shops, and meetings than in classrooms.

I was part of a circle of student leaders at TU in my freshman year in 1975 and became vice president of the TU Student Union in my second year. By 1976, I was a member of the leadership collective for the national-level student movement that organized many major protests, including the fateful one on October 6.

In early 1976, I was assigned by the leadership collective to be the main speaker in charge of controlling the crowd at major protests. On October 6, 1976, I was on the stage in front of the protesters throughout the night before the killing. It was my voice they heard during the final morning hours under siege.

....

Around midnight, the campus security post at a main entrance of the campus was torched. During the next few hours, flashes of light mixed with the sound of explosions of small homemade bombs erupting from time to time. Around 2 a.m., our security guards informed us that the campus was surrounded not only by the usual paramilitary groups like the Red Gaurs, but also by the police. As the night wore on, the gunshots intensified.

About 5:30 a.m., a very loud, high pitched sound frightened me. Boom! The ground shook. I could see several bodies on the ground in that area and realized what had happened. Shortly afterward, I was told that four people had been killed instantly and dozens with serious injuries needed to go to the hospital. I was enraged. Our thought may be deemed radical, but our protest and actions had been peaceful. We never used violence, never hurt anybody. We had talked about the possibility of a violent suppression by the state. But we could not really envision it. Sure, right-wing goons had attacked earlier demonstrations. But we knew how to deal with those kinds of attacks. We were aware of the worsening political situation. But we never anticipated the horrific and cruel raid that had just begun. Those kinds of things happened in other countries.

....

It was only a few days after my nineteenth birthday. To this day, I vividly recall how terribly shaken I was when I pleaded in tears to the crowd for vehicles and volunteers to take injured people to the hospital. How angry and frustrated I was when I learned that the vans with injured people were lined up at the campus gate because the police refused to let them out to go to the hospital. I wept like mad. I still do not understand why they did not let the injured out. Even in war movies, the injured are allowed medical care. But somehow, when it comes to conflicting political views, opponents are no longer human and can be slaughtered. . . .

. . . .

We gathered in the soccer field because the buildings surrounding it would protect us from small-scale attacks by goons outside. It did not occur to us that such a semi-enclosed site would be easy to blockade, that we could be trapped. And those buildings were not enough to protect us from an M79 grenade attack. Worse, inexperienced as we were, as the attacks increased, all we could think to do was move people from the open field to the buildings for shelter. We did not foresee that in doing so people would become easier targets for the shelling that continued for hours that morning. A site chosen for safety turned out to be fatal.

At first, just after midnight, the firing from the outside had been occasional, a few shots at a time. From 2 a.m. on, it turned into an occasional round of automatic fire with long intervals between rounds. Around 4 a.m., the firing became more frequent and intense from several machine guns at a time. At dawn after the deadly M79 explosion, the sound of automatic weapons became overwhelming. It was almost nonstop, with only ten-to-fifteen-second intervals every five minutes or so. The shooting lasted for several hours, though it felt like forever to me.

. . . .

I can still recall how I felt, begging repeatedly hundreds of times. I felt embarrassed. Throughout the demonstration the night before, we had criticized the state and its apparatus as dictatorial and oppressive. Our rhetoric was combative and aggressive. However, that morning the only thing I did was beg the police to spare our lives, as though I were crawling at their feet. At that moment, I felt ashamed.

Despite that, I continued begging them, hundreds of times, to stop shooting.

I learned afterward that some friends were upset that I gave in and begged for mercy. But I could not urge people to continue to fight. I hoped that the police might let up, that some negotiation between our organizers and the government might bear fruit. That was my thought—a desperate and false hope. . . .

Looking out from the stage at the edge of the soccer field, on the opposite side from the battlefront, I saw a few of our security guards on the ground. They were not moving any more. I saw people trying to break into the buildings, trying to hide. One was shot down. Looking to the right, I saw a man trying to run from a building toward a path and escape. But he did not make it. I saw with my own eyes hundreds of helpless lives. Angry and bitter, fearful and desperate, I could not lift anyone's spirit when I myself was too dejected and dispirited. Hope-less-ness.

All I knew was that if the voice from the stage stopped, people might despair even more. It did not matter what I said. I did not utter any spirited words or combative slogans. I did not help anyone who got shot either. We were a few lives sitting hopelessly together behind the stage. We were only half alive.

....

Crash! A loud noise came around 7:30 a.m. That was the last time I recall looking at my watch. I learned later that a bus had smashed the gate of the campus main entrance, allowing the police and a huge group of angry people to storm onto campus while a frenzied crowd waited outside. Once inside Thammasat, the police advanced slowly.

At first, I could see that they crawled while shooting at students who were trapped inside the buildings. Later, probably realizing that no one was offering any significant resistance, the police got up on their knees, taking more shots as they lined up in two rows along the small road in front of the Law School Building. Later, probably realizing that there was absolutely no resistance, the police got to their feet and walked confidently, firing freely at various targets they could see.

....

We took shelter in the building behind the stage, I wept for a long while. Finally my brother, Ngao, who had been with me behind the stage all night, told me we had to leave. He and I followed the last group of people to exit the building. We ran across a garden and got into the river, where a lot of people were walking along the shallow bank toward the Tha Phrachan Gate. It was the only way out. Most got up from the river at the Liberal Arts Building next to the gate. Many people ran safely out before the police could arrest them. But many others were not as lucky: they were rounded up and forced to lie face down in the street alongside the Mahathat Temple, adjacent to Thammasat.

By the time we got to the Liberal Arts Building, the gate was closed. Suddenly a police officer appeared briefly at the pier nearby, spraying our group with bullets. When he left, we jumped into the river and got out at a narrow lane beside the river. I had lived in one of the shop-houses there since I was born. I wanted to go home. Ngao told me to keep running. I was confused, but I followed him. I learned later that the police had searched my house looking for me. They took away everybody who had taken shelter there, including another of my brothers. After hitting him with a rifle, they took him to prison even though he hadn't been involved and was at home all night. . . .

. . . .

We ran to an empty market space. . . . Dozens of people were there before us. One way out was toward the street where police waited to round us up. The other was to jump into the river.

With a small group of people, I walked slowly in the water under the riverside houses lining the bank. After only a short distance, two Border Patrol Police on shore pointed their M16 rifles at us, ordering us to get out of the water and surrender. One man in our group trod on some sharp object in the water. He could not pull himself up. One of the policemen yelled, about to fire his rifle at him. We were all shocked, screaming frantically, and helped push the man up on shore. All the men were ordered to take off their shirts and surrender all their belongings, including glasses. We had to follow along a small lane lined with dozens of Border Patrol Police with heavy weapons until we got to the main street. There, the police forced everybody to lie face down, bare chested, on the asphalt street that runs alongside one of the best-known Buddhist temples in the country.

Then a policeman came near shouting the names of Pichian and Thongchai.[1] Pichian was not at Thammasat that night. Me—I was there. On my right, my brother Ngao put his arm over my head and shoulder. Then the man on my left, whose face I did not see, moved closer to me and put his arm over my other shoulder too. Both tried to prevent me from responding to the call. I stayed still, not because I was smart, but because I was not in a state to respond to anything.

....

After the shooting was over, we remained in the street for what seemed like a long while, although I'm not sure how long it really was. . . . It took a long time for the bus to take us from the street near Thammasat to the prison on the outskirts of Bangkok. When we got off the bus, the police lined up, throwing punches and kicks at each of us. But I did not feel anything. I was still numb. My mind must have wandered. Perhaps shame gripped me. Why did I leave Thammasat?

Ngao stayed with me all the way to the prison cell. For a few days, I did not cry even once. I cannot remember much about those first few days in prison. No fear or anxiety. Nothing. I could not re-member talking to Ngao or anybody else during the first few days in jail even though a few people told me years later that they had been glad to meet me in prison during those few days and know I was alive. One told me that he had given me his glasses before he was re-leased on bail. I could not recall meeting him, though I realized after a few days that I was wearing somebody else's glasses.

The police called everyone in for registration and interrogation. For unknown reasons, my cell was the last one the police came to, three days after our arrest. Then they finally found out, "Thongchai's been arrested!" as one newspaper headlined it the following day, even though I had been in their hands the entire time. A few days later, in the middle of the night, a number of us—the alleged ringleaders—were taken from our cells in pairs, loaded into police vans, rushed to somewhere far away. I thought that was the end for me. As it turned out, we only spent one night away, at various places under police de-tention, before we were transported back to the prison the following day. Throughout those initial days in prison, I was not afraid any-more. No, I did not feel brave. Rather, I did not feel anything. Perhaps nothing could be worse than being in Thammasat on that Wednesday morning.

....

For a few years after the massacre, I was vengeful. I dreamed of a Communist Party victory, a just outcome after the state's cruelty. This probably helped me suppress the guilt I had been feeling about leaving Thammasat that morning. But it was just another naïve and pitiful hope that eventually evaporated. . . .

In mid-1996, a friend called from Bangkok, informing me about a plan to visit the parents of Jaruphong Thongsin, a good friend who had carried out his responsibility to clear people out of the Student Union Building until it was too late for him. But his parents did not know about his death and still hoped for his return. I did not know what to say to them. What could I say about why Jaruphong did not return home and I did?

History is so cruel, in every sense of the word, and utterly irrational too.

Thongchai
Early Fall, 1996

Chapter 1

THE UNFORGETTING OF OCTOBER 6

For decades, the most heinous event in modern Thai history remained foggy in the awareness of the Thai people. During the carnage, news and information about it was tightly controlled as state propaganda ran rampant. Rumors and sensational stories swept across the country. Even a few decades later, despite a more open political atmosphere, the subject remained too sensitive to discuss in public. The massacre is difficult for Thai society to remember in any meaningful way for many reasons. The witnesses—be they victims, perpetrators, bystanders, or observers—were uncomfortable articulating their memories in either public or private settings. For those who did, their memories are difficult for the public and the younger generations to believe because the brutality was unprecedented. Photos and more facts emerged over the years. Yet Thai society remained ambivalent. Hence, for the first twenty years, the massacre stayed largely in the shadows, recognized and talked about in public only in a limited fashion. Ambivalence has persisted. Memories have changed. Thai society still refuses to fully confront the dark history of what took place on October 6, 1976. Silence, relatively speaking, is still in place.

This book is about the silence surrounding the tragedy. Its focus is not on what happened, but on the reasons and conditions behind the continuing ambivalence and on the changing memories of the massacre over the four decades that followed.

The most obvious and straightforward reason for the silence is political. As I explain in chapter 2, the monarchy and the Buddhist order (the *sangha*) were involved in the conspiracy that led to the kill-ings. To speak the truth about the massacre could be devastating to Thai society because the damage to these two most important spiri-tual institutions could have unimaginable repercussions. Besides, anyone who speaks the truth would be subjected to the draconian lèse majesté law, severe punishment without due process.[1] The truth about the massacre is thus both suppressed and self-censored. Silence is prescribed by law but is also voluntary, in fear for oneself and con-cern for the country. Under the present political system, Democracy with the Monarchy as the Head of the State, as it is officially called, the memory and history of the massacre of 1976 remains in the realm of the unspeakable. This political situation is nonetheless the easiest reason to understand.

In this book, I argue that silence about the massacre is attribut-able to more complex factors, namely, the "chronopolitics" of mem-ory (that is, the changing politics and discursive conditions that affect memories), the ideological and cultural factors that are pervasive in Thai society, and the dominant public discourse at various times. The conflicts that ultimately led to the massacre were products of the Cold War, especially the domestic one, which lasted into the early 1980s. The post–Cold War conditions have rendered the memories of October 6 from the communist and anticommunist perspectives ob-solete. Ideological factors have contributed significantly to the am-bivalence and silence about October 6, namely, Thai historical ideology, nationalism, the peculiar notion of individual rights and rule of law, and so on. Buddhism in particular is an important source of concepts that facilitate, shape, and limit the comprehensibility and meanings of the atrocity as well as how to deal with it.

Silence, this book argues, is not forgetting. Instead, it is a symp-tom of the inability to remember or forget, the inability to articulate memories in a comprehensible and meaningful fashion, or to depart from the past completely. I call this condition between remembering and forgetting the "unforgetting." This book is about the unforget-ting of the October 6 massacre in Bangkok in 1976.

MEMORY

This book has been informed by and benefited from the political and cultural studies of memory in many ways that I elaborate in this chapter. First, different types of memory of past atrocity, as Lawrence

Langer suggests, are helpful to identify, understand, and conceptualize the various memories of those involved in the October 6 massacre, including their social and political status, how they relate to one another, and their symptoms.[2] Nevertheless, as Langer himself admits, those types are actually nuanced and fluid. One's memory, individually and collectively, includes the traits of more than one type. Although I use the conceptual and methodological tools of others in dealing with the memories of the October 6 massacre, I am not interested in the neat or precise classification of those memories because the nuances and ambiguities can be helpful.

Among the first issues most cultural studies of memory try to establish is the distinction between history and memory, especially in the collective sense, because our interest is also in "how societies remember."[3] The fundamental distinction most studies agree on is that memory suggests the personal—often emotional—recollection of the past, whereas history is instead typically—at least nominally—an evidentiary recounting. According to Susan Crane's account, one of the best expositions on this issue, they are different forms of historical consciousness, separated by "a confusing or hair-splitting fine line" between them, and do not necessarily contradict or oppose one another.[4] Memory is based on or drawn from lived experience, whereas history is mostly the knowledge of the past constructed from evidence that the historian did not experience. As Maurice Halbwachs, one of the most prominent scholars of memory, suggests,

> history starts only when tradition ends and the social memory is fading or breaking up. . . . the need to write a history of a period, a society, or even a person is only aroused when the subject is already too distant in the past to allow for the testimony of those who preserve some remembrance of it.[5]

Thus memory is admittedly subjective, whereas history is supposed to be objective even if objectivity is impossible. Memory belongs to someone who remembers because it is meaningful to the owner, whereas history's meanings are impersonal and do not belong to anyone in particular.[6]

These contrasting attributes are, however, not definitive. Most scholars agree that memory and history are overlapping rather than neatly delineated. For instance, I was a witness of the massacre, am aware of my own limited memory, and am a historian trying to write a history of the memories of the massacre from a critical distance and with scholarly methodology. Moreover, as this book shows, individual memory is usually also shaped by history and ideology rather than personal experience. In this sense, memory is not truly individualized, but instead, or also, shaped by others and the collective experiences as well. Memory never denies the point of view or perspective of the one who remembers. History, on the other hand, is also a construct from certain perspectives despite its claim to objectivity.

Often, one's memory is in fact the recollection of something one learns indirectly, especially in the case of memory of a public event. The word "memory" is also used when the account of a firsthand experience is transmitted in an intimate fashion as to family members, even a later generation, even though this generational memory is not free from lapses and changes, and often interpretations. Memories via public experience and generational memory are not quite history either because their origin is based on contemporary and personal experiences, not impersonal evidence. At this point, the line between memory and history is blurred.[7] Sites of memory, as Pierre Nora suggests, can impart memory for generations, long after the lived experience has gone. Likewise, a commemoration, a ritual, or a representation of the dying memory are no longer the lived experience. These kinds of memory, distant from the lived experience, probably overlap with the realm of history.

Despite these distinctions, history and memory overlap and are undistinguishable in many respects. For an ambivalent memory, such as those of the October 6 massacre, the contrast between the two can be misleading. In this book, I use the words "memory" and "history" loosely, sometimes intentionally signaling the blurred line between them. This does not mean, however, that I do not recognize their differences in important respects, especially an individual's memory based on firsthand experience and empathy for such firsthand experience on the one hand, and a study and writing about the past with critical distance on the other. I am careful about the choice of words when the distinction is clear.

Memory of any public phenomenon is always multiple: any event can be viewed from different layers or scales—local, national, transnational—that interact and inform, contest and complement one another, often with varying implications for the present.[8] The memories of the October 6 massacre contend not only with oblivion but also with one another. Memory based on firsthand experience does not guarantee the reliability and accuracy of the account. A firsthand memory may be affected by ideology or the memory frame. It can change over time as well, just like second- or thirdhand accounts. Like primary and secondary sources for a historian, each must be handled with particular care, criticism, and skepticism.

COLLECTIVE MEMORY

What is the relationship between individual and collective memory? Some might assume that individual memory is a discrete fragment of the collective memory. It is not clear, however, how they come together—by combination, assimilation, conglomeration, contestation, domination and subordination, or something else. Collective memory, in this view, is the rich totality of lived experiences, in contrast to a historical construction that would reduce, select, and discard some of those elements for the sake of meaningful coherent narrative. Such an assumption is simplistic and usually not the case.

Collective memory is the shared experiences of a group of people (neighbors, a school class, a community, a nation). Only those experiences that are, Maurice Halbwachs suggests, "of concern to [a great number] of members" will be remembered; the ones that are not will be dropped.[9] However, the notion of sharing something or of having a common experience are inexact. A collective memory is often a broad stroke of narrative that leaves aside the differences and multiple perspectives within it. Because of this, not despite it, collective memory has the capacity to accommodate the varying individual memories that may fit despite their differences. The most important point here is that the relationship between the individual and collective memory is not that of the part to the whole. Instead, in selecting certain elements and making them meaningful while dropping others, collective memory provides a structure or a frame for the individual ones, recognizing some as more meaningful and some less so, and even not recognizing some. As Susan Crane succinctly puts it, "individual memory can only be recalled in the social framework within which it is constructed."[10] Or, in Elizabeth Jelin's words, "individual memory is, thus, always socially framed. . . . The social is always present even in the most 'individual' moments. . . . Anything that does not find a place or a meaning in that framework is material that can be lost and forgotten."[11]

Steve Stern explains the relation between individual memory and its frames in his own terms, that is, a "loose memory" is not intelligible until it fits the larger frame of the "emblematic" memory shared by the collectivity or community. For the memories of an authoritarian past, he suggests four types of emblematic memory that help makes sense of the individual ones: salvation memory, typically for a perpetrator who believes that he saved the country as required by the necessity of the situation at the time; unresolved rupture or the unhealed wound, for the victim whose memory remains unsettled and who has not yet come to terms with the past; resolved but painful memory, for the victim who lives an in-between life, with hurt and hope, stigma and strength, with or without closure, who is willing to move on even though the pain has not gone; and closed box memory, for anyone who considers the past as divisive, troubling, dangerous, and thus better put away and forgotten because it could destroy the peace and normalcy of family, society, or the nation.[12]

Collective memory is a social phenomenon. An articulation of memory is first and foremost facilitated by language. Halbwachs reminds us of this fundamental truth, "there are no recollections to which words cannot be made to correspond. We speak of our recollections before calling them to mind. It is language, and the whole system of social conventions attached to it, that allows us at every moment to reconstruct our past."[13] Language is a social convention—socially formulated, socially reproduced, and socially transformed. Language, in its connotative sense, includes the vernacular discourses and texts shaped by a particular history and culture of a society. In this book, I explain how a number of particular discourses and ideologies that are pervasive in Thai society provide the "language" that makes some individual and collective memories comprehensible and others not.

First, Thailand has a long history of authoritarianism over the past hundred years, from the absolute monarchy before 1932 to several periods of military rules since then to the present day. National security has always been a higher priority for the state than anything else. The state's power often overrides those of individuals and the freedom of assembly and expression. These are the political conditions that have effectively shaped the language in which memories are understood.

Second, nationalism and a royalist historical ideology are pervasive and strong in Thailand. Historical ideology is significant to the

framing of memory of the massacre given the lack of any concept of
state crime in Thai historical ideology. The official history of Thailand
that its citizens have been indoctrinated in for generations is a saga of
the unity under benevolent monarchs against foreign threats. A massacre by the state, especially one of extreme brutality, does not fit
neatly with the royal-national narrative. Thus it is more difficult for
the memories of the massacre to find an appropriate narrative frame.
Third, Buddhism is another important resource for "language" or
concepts relevant to dealing with a traumatic past, namely, the no-
tions of history, truth, reconciliation, forgiveness, and justice. These
ideologies and cultural determinants deeply affect how individuals
respond to atrocity, and how to remember—or not remember—the
controversial and painful past.

Finally, memory of an event, even an incomplete one, takes the
form of a narrative. Like historical knowledge, the construction of a
narrative form is far from an unmediated articulation. Because we
usually do not realize that memory requires a narrative form, this
book directs attention to the factors that affect the formation of a
narrative of the massacre, such as the precedent and available modal-
ity of the expressible narrative to which a memory must be shaped
lest it be rendered incomprehensible.

MEMORY CHANGES AND FORGETTING

This book is about the changes of memories. We often talk about
how memory fades, as if time itself is an eraser of memory. In fact,
time itself does not cause forgetting. We know and remember many
historic events but often forget what we had for breakfast just two
days ago. Everyone can remember the biographical milestones of
childhood but tends to forget more recent days and months that pass
by without remarkable events. A society remembers events that mark
its history, sometimes even the ones historians have proven did not
take place. Yet it lets the memory of other events fade into oblivion
even though some individuals still remember them. "Time" is in fact
an encompassing term for all actual factors and conditions that affect
and change memory or induce amnesia.

As a social phenomenon, the individual and collective memory
can be affected and changed by many factors: be it a rumor or hearsay, a popular film or book, a historical study, an ideology, or a particular social and political environment. For a political incident, the

obvious factors that usually come to mind are power (political partisanship, authority, threat and intimidation, law suits, censorship, and so on) and benefits (potential gain or loss, job security, cost, effects on family and property, and intangible ones such as reputation and fame). In this book I deal with these obvious factors that affect the memory of the October 6 massacre. I pay attention, however, to the less obvious ones as well.

We usually think memory changes because of a newfound fact or truth. This is sometimes true. A change in framing or the rearticulation of a collective memory affects individual memories and the memoryscape even more.[14] Studies on this matter are numerous. For example, the changing relations between the United States and Japan, adversaries in the Pacific War who turned into close allies after the war, altered how Japan's role in the war was remembered. The contesting frames of Japan's role as aggressor or victim render the collective memories of the war divergent and thus ambiguous. Economic miracle and material prosperity in the immediate decades after the war shaped the war's memory in Japanese society.[15] Carol Gluck conceptualizes it succinctly: "every country had its own 'chronopolitics' of memory, in which changes in domestic and international politics over time created the conditions for changes in the memory-scape."[16] In other words, memory changes under the political climate of subsequent times. The chronopolitics of memory also plays a role in the ups and downs of influences of those contesting ideologies and public discourses too. Throughout this book, we see the explicit and implicit impacts of chronopolitics on the memories of the massacre.

The October 6, 1976, massacre was a culmination of the ideological conflict of the Cold War in Thailand. How it was initially understood and remembered in the wake of the massacre was shaped by Cold War tensions at the time. Its consequences, however, as explained in this book, led to drastic changes to the state as well as the Communist Party of Thailand (CPT), and resulted in the beginning of silence from around 1978. In Thailand, the end of the domestic Cold War came in the mid-1980s, a little earlier than the global one. The political climate changed dramatically after that. Ideological antagonisms became less of a factor due to the collapse not only of the Soviet Union but also of socialism as a counter-ideology to capitalism. These changes had an enormous impact on how individuals and the society remember the atrocity. In the new era, in which human rights and democracy became common in public discourse, it was difficult for many to understand the intense antagonism between communism and anticommunism and why it had been pursued to such a deadly extent. In the changed atmosphere, what had seemed reasonable became ridiculous, pride turned to foolishness, courage to nonsense, sacrifice to empty loss, and vengeance to guilt, self-doubt, and moral dilemma. Thus almost two decades of ambivalence and silence followed. During that period, the memories of both the victims and the perpetrators of October 6 shifted tremendously. The voiced became silenced and vice versa.

However, the political legacies of the Cold War propelled Thailand into new conditions of hyper-royalism, thus perpetuating, perhaps intensifying, fear for oneself and concern for the country. Despite the partial breakthrough in the silence in 1996, thanks to the movement that year to commemorate the tragedy, public knowledge and discourse about October 6 has been restricted to a limited extent since then. Over the past twenty years, given all these factors and more, memory has changed. So often even a little slippage of some facts in the narrative can change the meanings and consequences of such memories. The passage of more than forty years is not long enough to declare all the memories dead, either the individual or the collective ones, or to make the October 6 massacre an event from the remote past, to make it history. But it is long enough for the memories of lived experiences to decline, shift, and alter through chronopolitics of memory and other conditions. It is long enough for the millennial generation to have acquired their secondhand memories from their elders and from living under the consequences and legacies of the massacre.

The younger ones live in the new conditions of the twenty-first century. Their memories come with certain generational perspectives that may or may not correspond to those of the previous generation. Memory shifts and slides are common. They are usually treated with scorn as the failure to remember, as symptoms of forgetting, as the decline and loss of authentic memory, or as falsehood. What we often do not realize is that generational memory is a form of memory production. For the memories of October 6, different generations interact and exchange their memories in the public sphere via public discourse that affects the memories of individuals across generations. This book is not interested in what is correct or false, authentic or otherwise, so much as how memories alter, how the shift occurs, and the meanings and implications of those changes.

In many studies of memory, the opposite of memory is forgetting. Jelin suggests three types of forgetting: definitive forgetting, an attempt to erase recollections of facts and processes of the past; evasive forgetting, an attempt not to recall the upsetting memories after an atrocity; and necessary forgetting, the feeling of unburdening oneself from the weight of the past and moving on to focus on the future.[17] People may also willingly forget, or not care to remember, for various other reasons as well.[18] In the case of the October 6 massacre, efforts were made to definitively forget, though they were hardly successful even decades later. Those efforts were enabled in part by the chronopolitics of memory but to a greater degree by the discourse of national reconciliation, forgiveness, and national interest. This book discusses those conditions that try to foster forgetting. Evasive forgetting has been common among the victims but is also common among members of the public who were aware of the possible repercussions of memory. The last kind of forgetting has been explicitly encouraged from time to time in the name of national interest and the future. To call for the necessary forgetting in the case of the October 6 massacre is like citing Ernst Renan's maxim—"forgetting and . . . historical error is an essential factor in the creation of a nation"—in the wrong context, making it an excuse for the crime.[19]

However, the most serious problem with the memory-forgetting dichotomy is not that it is wrong, but that it is, as Stern puts it, "insufficient—profoundly incomplete and in some ways misleading."[20] This book argues that it is misleading on two counts. First, memory does not necessarily fade into forgetting. It may slide into another version of memory of the same event. Second, and more important, between the binary opposition of memory and forgetting is at least another condition of memory. Stern calls it "memory impasses." I call it the "unforgetting."

SILENCE AND UNFORGETTING

Is silence always forgetting? Is such a binary between memory and forgetting misleading? Earlier studies of memory usually take silence as a mark of forgetting, either a sign of or a precursor to amnesia. This is not entirely wrong but it is not always right either. Silence is usually the result of the conscious effort to suppress memory, either by power or authority (being silenced) or voluntarily (being silent). Silence, however, is also a symptom of obedience to authority, especially in an authoritarian society such as Thailand. In such cases, being silenced and voluntary silence, being censored and self-censoring, are hardly distinguishable.

I argue, however, that between memory and forgetting is an active silence, which is not forgetting. In music, silence is the interval between two sounds. It is an integral and active component of the musical sound. The absence of sound in music is neither failure nor inaction; it is part of the production of sound, making sound by not creating it. In literary works, not only is silence the space between words, it is also often a device for literary effects, such as a pause in a conversation or stream of thought or a mute character. In films, silence is as prominent as dialogue. If memory is like music or a visual image, silence is the nonvocal or invisible part of memory, adjacent to memory, and vice versa. To put it another way, silence is defined by the sound, the conversation, the visual adjacent to it.

Scholars of memory and silence of the authoritarian past have argued convincingly that silence is not necessarily forgetting, not the absence of meaning.[21] It is the memory that is marginalized or unrecognized, suppressed, unvoiced, or unrepresented. Silence is the memory we fail to hear or see, located adjacent to the expressed and voiced one. It is the realm of the unforgettable or unvoiced but not forgotten memory. It is inarticulate memory. Or it could be the memory whose owner tries to avoid, bury, and not recognize, to forget but without success. As I explained earlier, I call it "unforgetting," a term I use synonymously with "silence" on many occasions in this book. If dark matter makes up a significant part of the universe and if mute sounds help make music what it is, unforgetting must also make up the totality of the memoryscape. This realm may be enormous if we can train our eyes and ears to see and listen to it.

Generally speaking, memories are contested but not all memories are equal. Some are dominant, more powerful, more acceptable or tolerable; others are harder to believe or accept, or even threatening to the well-being of an individual or the status quo of a society. Memory of a political event can be controversial and involve high stakes if it can jeopardize the position or livelihood of one person or another. In these situations, some memories are promoted, publicized, or allowed to circulate, yet some are condemned to obscurity or marginalized into the adjacent realm of silence. The unpleasant, painful, and dangerous ones are avoided. Such memories often are not articulated, are not able to be articulated, and thus have no voice, no narrative, no story, and no history (yet). This is exactly what Michel-Rolph Trouillot calls, in spatial metaphor, the edge of the voiced, a story that is hard to comprehend and is often explained away or forced to fit existing narratives.[22]

Stern notices a similar condition of unforgetting in his study of Chile's memory of the Pinochet regime. Calling it "memory impasse," he describes it this way:

> The idea of . . . forgetting . . . is useful to a point, but it simplifies the Chilean path of memory struggles. . . . The problem turned out to be more subtle and . . . more horrifying. . . . [like the] famous phrase by Mario Benedetti, "oblivion is filled with memory" . . . Memory of horror and rupture also proved so unforgettable or "obstinate" . . . What emerged instead was impasse. [The memory impasse] remained too strong for Chile to take logical "next steps" along the road of truth and justice. The result was not so much a culture of forgetting, as a culture that oscillated—as if caught in moral schizophrenia—between prudence and convulsion. [T]his was a "moving impasse."[23]

Whereas "memory impasse" implies a passive state of memory, I call this condition the "unforgetting" because it is alive and could be actively resisting oblivion.

Silence is not a void; it is a countersound. "The look of silence," as suggested by Joshua Oppenheimer in his 2014 film of the same title, is full of memories that try to be articulated, heard, and seen.[24] This book is about the unforgetting or the memory impasse of an atrocity in Thailand, contemporary to Augusto Pinochet's Chile but much less known to the world. The October 6 massacre, too, proved "so unforgettable," but has been caught between memory and forgetting because the country cannot take the next steps along the road to truth and justice. The book shows the causes and conditions of the unforgetting, how they survived and changed over four decades, and the effects and implications for the country even today whether people are aware of them or not. Silence is not a passive realm of memory but one of counter or resistant memory. If memory can find its site in places, monuments, and commemorations, the unforgetting too, as the book shows, registers in monuments and commemorations that reproduce the unforgetting.

Another common assumption is that silence is not good, is unpleasant, is a condition of something bad, something gone wrong.

This is not necessarily so. Such simplistic assumptions usually imply that forgetting and silence are a wrongdoing that benefits powerful people. This is not necessarily so either. This book visits some examples of voluntary silence that came about for good reasons. For some, silence was a way to keep memory and hope alive. For many, Buddhism also contributes to virtuous silence. It provides a comprehensible explanation for incomprehensible event and offers guidance for how to overcome the painful past in order to live on in the present and move on to the future. Silence is also a way to make a loud noise of discontent, as in the case of a well-known victim, the former rector of Thammasat University. "Put simply, being silent does not mean being silenced."[25] The former is a choice of action; the latter is the denial of freedom. The former can be a form of resistance, even a way of communication, the latter a form of repression and the death of expression.

Ambivalence and silence are not always indicative of absence, erasure, or degeneration either. They can be productive as well. The unforgetting of the October 6 massacre has generated various political and social phenomena, even a few concrete memorials and monuments that bear the marks of traumatic ambivalence. It has produced a narrative of an event that never occurred, a collective false memory of the massacre, yet the one that Thai society can accommodate and has lived by. Memories of the massacre can even produce political identities of individuals and civic groups based on nothing but the shared memory of the radical past, preserving both the positive—idealism, inspirations, shared experience, connections, a network of people, and so on—and the not-so-positive baggage of such memories into the new millennium.

AN OVERVIEW OF THE BOOK

Given this understanding of memory and silence, the cultural logic of memory can be summarized as follows. First, memory responds to, and serves, the present, although it claims to re-collect the lived experience of the past. Second, memory is always a perspective, a view of the past from a selected angle. Whose perspective is it and how is it adopted or selected? For every memory is always a competing or contested memory. Third, therefore, memory (something kept alive) always indicates forgetting (something lost). It is productive (something created) and circulative (something exchanged). Fourth, apart from experience, the material of memory, the meaning and intelligibility of memory, are affected and shaped by ideology, the narrative of relevant history, available frames, prior text, or narrative precedents. This book observes these understandings in examining the silence of the October 6 massacre.

Chapters 2 to 6 are chronological, marking the chronopolitics of memories and silence of the massacre, from the beginning of memories in 1976 and the beginning of silence in 1978, to the two decades of silence and shifts of memories up to the breakthrough of silence in 1996. Chapters 7 to 9 discuss different kinds of silence of the victims and the perpetrators and explain the conditions of memory slides over generations, especially after 1996. Chapter 10 returns to the chronopolitics of memory from the late 1990s to the present day.

Chapter 2, "The Massacre and Unanswered Questions," is the only one in the book that deals with what happened in the morning of October 6, including the larger historical context, the pretext, and the immediate situation before the killing. Because many facts about the incident remained unknown, the chapter raises thirteen major questions that still need answers, from the roles of the monarchy and the Buddhist sangha, the United States, the Communist Party of Thailand, to the identities of the perpetrators, the reasons for the brutality and the desecrations of the corpses, and other critical mysteries. Not only do these facts and mysteries serve as the setting for the remainder of the book; they have also contributed in many ways to the unforgetting and the changing memories afterward.

Chapter 3, "The Beginning of Memory," argues that the official narrative put forward by the state immediately in the wake of the massacre was the beginning of collective memories of the massacre that endured for several decades. On the other hand, the immediate reactive narrative by the radicals and the Communist Party became the frame for a counternarrative. Instead of gradually taking shape out of diverse individual memories, as one might assume, the dominant discourses of the perpetrators and the victims were put forward immediately in the public sphere by protagonists on both sides. The collective memories influenced and shaped the individual memories, which made themselves meaningful by aligning with the collective ones.

Chapter 4, "The Trial and the Beginning of Silence," explains the unfolding political situation during the two years after the massacre until the beginning of silence. The focus is on the October 6 trial in the context of the political changes that took place because of a major shift in the counterinsurgency strategy of the Thai state. The potential fallout from the trial that could hurt the state was turned into the cornerstone of a new strategy that called for reconciliation with the leftists, resulting in the 1978 amnesty bill that absolved all wrongdoing on October 6, 1976, and ended the trial. The reconciliation, which had strong public support, necessitated silence about the massacre.

Chapter 5, "Silence after 1978," demonstrates the changing and fluctuations of the memories of the massacre between 1978 and 1996. Thanks to the greater degrees of democratization and liberal politics, the perpetrators' heroic victory turned into a shameful episode in the eyes of the public. However, the radical movement did not benefit from this but instead collapsed in the early 1980s. The October 6 tragedy became an empty loss, a sacrifice for a lost cause. Justification and pride in their memories evaporated. Silence prevailed. Silence was common among other witnesses and observers of the 1976 massacre too. The traces of these changes surfaced in political controversies, in writings such as novels and memoirs, and in a stalled monument project.

Chapter 6, "Commemoration 1996," explains conditions in the mid-1990s when former radicals collectively launched the first major commemoration of the massacre on its anniversary in 1996. The chapter describes why and how breaking through the silence surrounding the October 6 massacre was a historic, cathartic moment for many former radicals, individually and collectively. However, some memories were even further marginalized, and the perpetrators remained silent, so it was only a partial break in the silence. Limitations for the discourse about the massacre remained. The ambiguity in the public memory of the massacre also persisted. Silence—the unforgetting—also perpetuated and was illustrated in monuments of the October 6 massacre and related events.

Chapter 7, "Good Silence," tells the stories of those who voluntarily chose silence. Their reasons vary. A father chose not to end his memoir of the search for his son in order to keep his son alive in his memory. His hope lived on as long as his son's body was not found. Sadly, the truth broke down his hope and ended the false memory. For some pious Buddhists, silence is a way to overcome hatred and vengefulness. But what are the implications of these beliefs for truth, remembering, and justice? A third case shows how a medical affliction that brought silence to a victim of the massacre became a thoughtful soliloquy that reminded people of the atrocity and its consequences. Are these good silences?

Given the extended period of ambiguity and relative silence, despite the partial breakthrough, Chapter 8, "Sliding Memory," explains how the memories of the massacre shifted over the generations to produce a different memory. The dominant ideology of Thai history and other relevant ideological elements (truth, justice, and so on) has tamed the subversiveness of the unforgetting of October 6. The hyper-royalist politico-cultural conditions also contributed to memory slides. Not only were the dangerous memories quarantined; these ideological effects also modified the narrative of the October 6 massacre to the extent that it generated a false memory of a massacre that never occurred. The new narrative that emerged serves all the dominant ideologies and discourses, including the royal-nationalist narrative that the Thai state celebrates.

Chapter 9, "Silence of the Wolf," traces the changing and unchanging memories of the right-wing perpetrators by the 2000s.[26] In addition to using their testimonies to the police shortly after the incident, I have tracked them down and had face-to-face interviews with many former adversaries, including the notorious ones. It was not surprising that none of them showed remorse. Despite that, the encounters produced many surprises, including who the actual killers were. Above all, most have been unable to avoid the chronopolitics of memory after the Cold War either. Many felt betrayed by history, politics, and the public. Hence, stigma and silence. Yet, some right-wing royalists remained very proud of what they did in the past and adamant that they would do it again if necessary.

The cathartic breakthrough in 1996 enabled the return to politics of the former 1970s radicals under the political identity of the Octobrists (*khon duan tula*). Chapter 10, "Praxis of Memory: The Octobrists," explores the rise and fall of this identity in dialogue with a recent book on the subject. Although the memory of the massacre that forms the basis for the Octobrist identity came with many positive attributes, it also entailed the negatives and insurmountable limitations that made the Octobrists unable to operate successfully under post–Cold War political conditions. The former radicals live on, but the Octobrist identity is dead.

In lieu of a conclusion, the epilogue—"Haunting"—shows how the unforgetting of the October 6 massacre is like a phantom in every corner of Thai society today. Writing a story about different moments of silence is a history of the phantom, of the traces of memory that are still alive, wandering around in various forms because they have not yet found a visible form or an intelligible voice. The silence is elusive, phantasmagoric, and haunting. The realm of silence could be a transient moment between memory and amnesia, the birth and death of history, words, and oblivion. It is definitely not yet dead or forgotten, however. It can be fantastic. This book strives to capture such liminal moments of memory—the moments of unforgetting of the October 6 massacre.

WRITING A GHOSTLY SILENCE

Moments of Silence deals particularly with the unforgetting and silence of past suffering that remains unsolved and without closure. It is a particular kind of memory and silence. In the words of Jelin, who has studied Argentina's Dirty Wars, writing about this kind of past is like "the representation of something that has been erased, silenced, or denied. . . . the presence of trauma is indicated by the coexistence of an impossibility of assigning meaning to past occurrences, [and] by the inability to incorporate it in a narrative. . . . [The] wounds imply great difficulties for constituting meaning and building its narrative."[27] It is like a ghost, Trouillot says, because this past was in a state of liminality.[28]

Writing about a ghostly silence also confronts the limits and problems that many scholars have addressed in the study of Holocaust memories. First, writing about a traumatic past is unavoidably inadequate. A historical explication cannot overcome the limitations in understanding and representing the enormity of an atrocity that cannot be represented in words.[29] The second problem for a historical representation of a ghostly silence, as raised by Dominick LaCapra, is whether a history should, has to, or can be objective and fair to all protagonists in an atrocity. A historian should not and cannot avoid being implicated in the process of writing about it, yet he also has the scholarly responsibility to do so.[30] Or as Valentine Daniel muses in his writing on the violence in Sri Lanka, if he writes in a straightforward way, the story would be full of naked violence; if he theorizes, it would "flatten reality"; if he does not write and does nothing, he violates his own ethics; and if he does not do his job well, he might offend the people he writes about and bring trouble to himself.

Ultimately, he is not sure what "language" he should use in writing this kind of story.[31]

I am aware of these concerns. If the memory and the unhealed wounds of a past atrocity are like a ghost, writing about it might have been easier because a horror story is a well-developed genre. But this is writing at the interstices of many realms, not only between memory, unforgetting and forgetting, but also between the act of writing and the unrepresentable enormity of the past. Despite that, ghostly memories need not be hidden in the abstraction of theoretical jargon because they are concretely identifiable at various moments in which memories remain stuck in ambivalence, unable to be articulated. The factors, reasons, and situations surrounding those moments that produce silence are concretely historical as well. We must try as best we can, cliché though that may be.

I am in both a better and worse position to write about the 1976 massacre in Bangkok than others. No reader should expect impartiality from me because I lost friends in the carnage. In writing this book, I do not make any pretense to objectivity. I have made my involvement in that Wednesday morning clear. Despite that, I proudly accept the challenge of writing a good history as only a historian can. That LaCapra has raised his question to any historian of an atrocity suggests that the dilemma is not mine alone. It is a challenge to anyone with moral decency who tries to write about a ghostly silence. I was fully aware and conscious of the enormity of the tragedy even before I began to write. If words are inadequate to represent it, it is not because I am not aware of that fact or because I have tried to trivialize the weight of the past. I understand the burden of writing about this ghostly past: it is not just another story to captivate a historian, it is my life. Part of my soul is in this book.

To me, writing and history are the best way to share the memory of the tragedy and my lost friends to the world. A rigorous scholarship demands my utmost effort as the offering to those in the heavens; if successful, it could be a lasting dedication on their behalf to the world of knowledge to fight ignorance and cruelty.

Turning the ghostly silence into words is a unique challenge for a historian and a survivor of the massacre. So many times I lost the words, and vice versa, because the unforgetting is much more, though sometimes less, than words. Nguyen Viet Thanh also remarks on writing about the memory of war that speaks to this book on the October 6 massacre.

When it comes to war, the basic dialectic of memory and amnesia is thus not only about remembering and forgetting certain events or people. . . . A just memory demands . . . a final step in the dialectics of ethical memory—not just the movement between an ethics of remembering one's own and remembering others, but also a shift toward an ethics of recognition, of seeing and remembering how inhuman inhabits the human. Any project of the humanities, . . . should thus also be a project of the inhumanities, of how civilizations are built on forgotten barbarism toward others, of how the heart of darkness beats within. No wonder, then, that . . . remembering is a *ghostly verb*. Memory is haunted, not just by ghostly others but by the horrors we have done, seen, and condoned. . . . The troubling weight of the past is especially evident when we speak of war and our limited ability to recall it. Haunted and haunting, human and inhuman, war remains with us and within us, impossible to forget but difficult to remember.[32]

Chapter 2

THE MASSACRE AND
UNANSWERED QUESTIONS

In the early hours of October 6, 1976, police and paramilitary groups surrounded Thammasat University, where four to five thousand people had gathered peacefully overnight to protest the return of a former dictator ousted by popular uprising three years earlier (see map). The morning was tense. Two weeks earlier, two activists had been hanged while putting up protest posters. Two days before, a student skit that reenacted the hanging of the activists had been targeted by the military propaganda machine, accused of mocking an effigy of the crown prince (figure 1). Students never had an opportunity to rebut the allegation.

At 5:30 a.m., a rocket-propelled bomb was fired into the crowd inside TU (map, #4). Four people were killed instantly. Dozens were injured. The massacre had begun. That bomb signaled the beginning of a nonstop barrage from military weapons that lasted several hours. A news photographer described it: "this was not a battle; it was the killing of defenseless people."[1] Neal Ulevich of the Associated Press, who had spent four years as a photographer in the Vietnam War, described the shooting as more bedlam than battle.[2] The protesters' security guards carried only personal weapons, suitable for protecting the demonstration from goons but not for fighting the police.[3] Their weapons could slow down but not contend with the onslaught for long. After a bus smashed through a university gate at 7:30 a.m., the police led the paramilitary groups into the campus. Ulevich adds, "all the shooting was directed [at] the building in which the students sheltered."[4] Most of the victims died from gunshot wounds or explosions

27

Figure 1a. The controversial hanging skit, allegedly mocking the crown prince at Thammasat on October 4, 1976. © Thammasat University Archives. Reproduced with permission.

inside the campus but some were lynched by the frenzied crowd that stormed onto campus after the gate was smashed (map, #2).

News clippings and dozens of photos showed incredibly barbaric lynchings both inside and outside the campus. Inside TU, a few dead bodies bearing the marks of gunfire and grenades were dragged along the soccer field by pieces of cloth wrapped around their necks. One was a friend of mine, Jaruphong Thongsin (figure 2). On the outside, a person was beaten before a group of men gleefully hanged him to death. Another was chased down, kicked, and punched. His dead body was hanged. In a 1977 Pulitzer prize–winning photo, a dead body hanging from a tree was beaten with a folding chair by an angry man (figure 3). Another man then took a turn. Altogether five bodies were hung from the trees encircling Sanamluang, the huge public space that connects TU with the Grand Palace, only a ten-minute walk away (map, #11, #12).[5] Six corpses were laid out on the ground, after which a man nailed wooden stakes into their chests, as if it were some kind of satanic ritual in a foreign film. A female student was chased until she fell. It is not clear what happened to her next. The photos show her naked on the ground, a stake placed on

Figure 1b. Front page of *Dao sayam* in the afternoon of October 5, 1976 (the advanced edition of October 6, 1976 issue). © Fa Diaw Kan.

Figure 2. Jaruphong Thongsin's body was dragged on the ground. Photographer unknown.

her body. The crowd of onlookers did nothing to help and some appeared to enjoy the spectacle. In another photo, a young boy, probably ten years old, urinated on an unconscious body. On the street in front of the Ministry of Justice, on the other side of Sanamluang opposite TU, four bodies were piled up with tires, soaked with gasoline, and set afire (map, #13). These brutal murders and the desecration of bodies took place in full public view. Many spectators, including young boys, clearly enjoyed the display (see, for example, figure 3).

On that Wednesday morning, the shooting deaths may have been the least painful and most civilized of the murders. It is not certain when the shooting and the murderous spectacle ended, sometime between 9:30 to 11:00 a.m.[6] The police rounded up the protesters who sought shelter inside the buildings, forcing them to run through two lines of policemen who kicked, punched, and beat them with their rifles. The police then ordered them, both males and females, to take off their shirts and lie face down on the ground, whereupon the goons were allowed to walk over their bodies.[7] Afterward, all the arrested students were herded onto buses and taken into custody.

Meanwhile, at the Royal Equestrian Plaza, a few kilometers from TU, right-wing groups gathered. They demanded that the government take decisive action against the communists, both those at TU and allegedly within the government. The elected government, too, was a target of the turmoil. Although this gathering was not directly involved

Figure 3. Neal Ulevich's 1977 Pulitzer Prize–winning photo of the hanging outside Thammasat on October 6. © AP Images. Reprinted with permission.

in the massacre, it was undoubtedly part of the day's plan to oust the elected government and perhaps democracy as well. In the afternoon, the right-wing demonstrators marched to Government House. The government retreated, making an official statement at 2 p.m. that blamed the students for lèse majesté and the protesters for using heavy weapons and causing casualties among the police and people outside TU. The statement also announced that the students were already in custody. Prime Minister Seni Pramoj appeared in public for the first time since the turmoil, repeating the official statement almost verbatim.[8] This responsive gesture had little effect. At 6 p.m., a military coup by the National Administrative Reform Council (NARC) was announced.[9]

According to the police, forty-six people died. Forty-one of them were on the "student and the accused" side. Five were on the "police" side—two police officers and three people who joined the attacks.[10] Several hundred were wounded. The missing were not reported. The police rounded up more than three thousand and put them in jail. Even though the number of dead was small relative to many atrocities and massacres in the modern era, the brutality of the killings and the dehumanized desecration of the dead made the

October 6 massacre stand out as particularly heinous. Our minds and sense of moral decency reject the reality of the event, which remains incomprehensible to many. Despite repeated calls by civic groups over many decades, no official investigation has been undertaken into the incident to this day. Only the unfinished October 6 trial in 1977 and 1978 and a few efforts by academics and political activists have shed any light on the massacre.[11] Otherwise, unconfirmed and confusing facts, hearsay, and many questions about it remain.

CONTEXT OF THE MASSACRE

Thailand's absolute monarchy ended in 1932 in a revolution by the People's Party, a group of civilian and military commoners. That historic moment is considered by many the beginning of democracy. In fact, democracy has hardly taken root in the country today given the long history of authoritarian rule by various undemocratic forces since then, namely, the monarchists and the military.[12] In 1947, an army coup marked the end of the People's Party and the beginning of the military rule that lasted until 1973, broken by a few intervals of elected government (1949–1951, 1954–1957, and 1968–1971) that did not last long until another putsch and yet another military regime.

The monarchists, however, were undeterred. Over time, they rebuilt the revered monarchy to become the highest moral authority in the land, vested with enormous unofficial political power, unlike most constitutional monarchies in the world today. After a failed attempt to return to power between 1947 and 1951, the monarchy began to revive gradually in the 1960s, in tandem with the support from the United States, which saw the monarchy as an important anticommunist element in the country.[13] The turning point was in 1973, when people's dissatisfaction with military rule over the years reached a breaking point. The student movement that had begun only a few years earlier turned to politics and demanded an end to military rule. The regime responded by arresting the student leaders, triggering a demonstration at TU that eventually led to a general uprising against military rule on October 14, 1973. The palace took the opportunity to assert itself as the promoter of democracy, forcing three leaders of the junta into exile and ending the violence after seventy-two people had died. The monarch then appointed the president of the Privy Council to be the interim prime minister. Thailand's democracy began (again). It was a parliamentary democracy headed by the monarch as the supreme authority and the sole source of political legitimacy. In retrospect, the October 1973 uprising, regarded by experts and the public alike as one of the historic leaps forward in Thailand's democratization, was the beginning of the monarchy's political ascendency as well.[14]

The 1973 uprising sparked a euphoria and energy for political freedom and social change. From 1973 to 1976, social movements for various causes erupted, demanding dramatic reforms in virtually all aspects of Thai society and undermining the power of some established institutions.[15] For instance, in 1974–1975 labor strikes occurred, on average, twice a day.[16] The thirst for new ideas was insatiable, especially for those that had been forbidden under military rule such as Marxism and Maoism. Many individuals and movements—of students, labor, and farmers—became radicalized. They demanded radical changes in democracy, land reform, worker's rights and welfare, education, capitalism, and so on. In the view of those in power, and increasingly of the general public too, these abrupt changes brought chaos and disorder. One crisis broke out after another, both within parliamentary politics and on the streets. Tensions intensified in almost every sector of society affecting people in all walks of life.

In 1975, communist revolutions took place in Vietnam, Cambodia, and Laos. Thailand was seen as the possible next domino in the regional stack to fall. The Thai state, particularly the monarchy and the army, was consumed by such anxieties. To them, the communist threat was not merely a factor of international geopolitics, but also an intense domestic battle. They had a great deal to lose. From mid-1975 forward, the student movement led by the National Student Center of Thailand (NSCT) was dominated by leftist radicals. In response to the growing radicalism, those in the establishment—the monarchy, the military, the state bureaucracy, and big businesses—organized anticommunist movements and paramilitary groups to counter the radicals.[17]

These groups embraced the right-wing (*fai khwa*) label to fight against the left-wing (*fai sai*) radicals. Ideologically, the right wingers propagated slogans of nation, religion, and monarchy, regarded as the sacred pillars of the country and which the communists were allegedly trying to destroy. Among the most notorious right-wing groups were the Red Gaurs (*Krating daeng*), the Nawaphon, and the Village

Scouts. As discussed in chapter 9, the military agency for counterin-surgency—the Internal Security Operation Command (ISOC)—orga-nized, financed, and orchestrated the actions of the first two right-wing groups and a few others. The palace's patronage of the Village Scouts, a popular movement with ultraroyalist and anticommunist leanings, was never a secret to the Thai public.

The right-wing movements grew rapidly beginning around 1975. Political polarization intensified and tensions often turned violent. The Red Gaurs in particular were notorious for their intimidations and skirmishes at almost every protest and demonstration. Their at-tacks became increasingly violent over time, sometimes resulting in fatalities. From mid-1975 to October 1976, almost a hundred leaders of radical civic groups and left-leaning political parties were assassi-nated.[18] Not a single perpetrator of these crimes was ever found. Electoral politics became fragile, unable to cope with the acute situa-tion. The public became weary of endless turmoil.

Throughout this time, the police and military took no action to stem the violence. Instead, they helped escalate the polarization. In addition to the ISOC operations, military propaganda forcefully tar-geted the radicals, labeling them "scum of the country" (*nak phaendin*), lackeys of the communist aliens (mainly of Vietnam), and the enemy of the nation, the religion, and the monarchy. The military also prepared to take advantage of the turmoil. When violent inci-dents with a few fatalities took place at demonstrations in March, June, July, and August 1976, rumors about a putsch swirled and they no longer seemed far-fetched. Yet despite such rumors and specula-tion, my recollection of the period is that a horrific massacre was still unthinkable. We were familiar with coups, which in practice were mostly intra-elite affairs. We had experience with an uprising, such as the one in October 1973. Still, the carnage of October 6 was unimag-inable at that time.

PRETEXT OF THE MASSACRE

The pretext began on September 19, 1976, with the return of General Thanom Kittikhachon, the dictator who had ruled the country from 1963 to October 14, 1973, the day he was forced into exile. Thanom returned in the robe of a Buddhist monk, pleading to the public that he merely wanted to return to make merit for his dying father. He went straight from the airport to the Bowornniwet Royal Monastery under the full protection of a military motorcade. This well-orchestrated return was undoubtedly intended to provoke the public and the student movement, thus intensifying political conflict and destabilizing the elected government. Even though it was in crisis from factional infighting, the government realized that Thanom's return threatened its survival and the young democracy that had begun only three years earlier. The radical movement, too, was aware of this tense situation and tried to prevent a coup. The NSCT carefully organized a few demonstrations at various places around the country. Then, on September 29, two labor activists were found hanged in a public space with marks of police handcuffs on their wrists.[19] Despite assassinations and violent attacks during the previous three years of confrontations, public hanging was unprecedented. The public was horrified. A few days later, the NSCT called for a major demonstration in the afternoon of October 4 at Sanamluang, a huge public ground outside TU (see map, #11, #12), to protest Thanom's return and the hanging. They demanded that the government of Seni Pramoj take decisive actions to end the attempt to restore the military rule.

October 4, 1976, at noon, student groups at TU performed a public skit to protest the hanging and to encourage students to join the demonstration later that day. The skit included a mock hanging that ended without controversy (see figure 1a). The gathering in the afternoon went as planned until dark, when the NSCT decided to continue the protest until its demands were met. The gathering, however, was moved from Sanamluang to the soccer field inside the TU campus because, as the thinking went, buildings around the field could protect the demonstrators from any attack by right-wing goons using small firearms and explosives (see map). A gathering on a campus with a few entrances was safer and easier to manage. But choosing to do so suggested that the NSCT did not anticipate the entrapment. Even though a coup might be foreseeable, a massacre by the state's armed forces was still beyond anticipation.

The demonstration continued to the next day without major trouble. Then, in the late afternoon of October 5, a right-wing royalist newspaper, *Dao sayam,* headlined that the student protest had included a mock hanging of Crown Prince Vajiralongkorn (now king). A photo from the October 4 student skit accompanied the article to show that the face of the hanged actor indeed resembled the crown prince (see figure 1b). Meanwhile, the military broadcast network, which controlled the radio airwaves across the entire country, began its propaganda, accusing the NSCT of lèse majesté. Within a short time that afternoon, the photo had shifted political focus from Thanom's return to the mock hanging. In the anticommunist fervor of the time, the alleged mock hanging reaffirmed the belief that the students were communists who planned to overthrow the monarchy. About 9 p.m., the government ordered the arrests of those involved in the hanging skit, possibly trying to curb the rapidly rising pressure from right-wing royalists and to rein in the protest movement at the same time. The NSCT was alarmed. Yet they, and I as well, believed that they could explain ourselves to the public given that the accusation was baseless. At 9:30 p.m., the NSCT held a press conference denying the allegation and introducing the actors to the public. Unfortunately, the NSCT's explanation to counter the military's propaganda was too late; the earliest this information could have reached the public would have been the next morning.

The situation at TU was extremely tense throughout the evening and night. At Sanamluang, the angry crowd of agitators, including the paramilitary groups, gathered in increasing numbers as the hours went by. At midnight, the university's security post at the main entrance went up in flames (see map, #2). The police appeared with heavy weapons outside the campus around 2 or 3 a.m. A few hours afterward, they began firing into TU campus. The NSCT scrambled to obtain the government's guarantee of safety but succeeded only in getting an agreement for their leaders to bring the students who had performed in the skit to meet with Prime Minister Seni at his residence in the morning. As the government prepared for the students to turn themselves in, the NSCT leaders sought a safe conclusion to the demonstration. When they eventually left, after 6 a.m., the NSCT party did not realize that during those morning hours the government had been losing power. When they arrived at Seni's residence, instead of meeting with the prime minister, the police took them into custody.[20]

At Thammasat, the carnage began at 5:30 a.m.

UNANSWERED QUESTIONS

Putting aside several absurd allegations, such as that the demonstrators were Vietnamese rather than Thai, or that there was a secret tunnel in TU to stockpile heavy weapons, many questions about the massacre remain unanswered and perhaps will not be.[21] These mysteries have contributed in various ways to the ambivalent memories and silence about the massacre over the decades that followed. Here I discuss only thirteen significant ones.

First, was the violent suppression of the radicals prepared in advance or an unanticipated opportunity for the right-wing factions? Given the fear of communism and the intensified and violent political polarization, months before the massacre the leader of a conservative political party suggested that the right wing should eliminate the left (*khwa phikhat sai*—literally, the right kills the left).[22] A Buddhist monk claimed that the killing of communists was not considered a serious religious sin (*kha communit mai bap*) because it was akin to killing the Evil One in a Buddhist fable.[23] Notorious songs, such as *Nak Phaendin*, which characterized the radicals as scum of the country, could be heard from many broadcasts everywhere and every day.[24] A poster reading "All Socialists are Communists" (*sangkhom-niyom thukchanit khu kommiunit*) appeared across the country in early 1976. The intense anticommunist atmosphere definitely contributed to the rage of the crowd and the heinous acts during the massacre. Despite all of this, the question remains whether the massacre was planned or anticipated by the establishment or whether the situation got out of control.

Nevertheless, evidence exists that the idea for a coup had been hatched in February 1976, though, in the words of the US ambassador to Thailand a week after the massacre, "it was not until last week that the elements essential to a final decision were brought together."[25] Kukrit Pramoj, a former prime minister, made a similar observation to David Cole, the British ambassador to Bangkok at the time: "It was the coup they planned against me last February; they just took it out of the cupboard again."[26] In February 1976, King Bhumibol was informed about the plot for a coup, both ambassadors reported, but he opposed it. An elder statesman confirmed this information, that Admiral Sa-ngad Chaloryu, the supreme commander of the armed forces at the time, had had an audience with the king. Sa-ngad raised the possibility of a coup as the king listened attentively. Sa-ngad told the king that he could not find a candidate for the prime minister afterward. The king then named a staunch anticommunist judge, Thanin Kraivixian.[27] On October 6, 1976, Sa-ngad was the head of the coup group (the NARC). A few days later, Thanin was appointed prime minister. The king, in the words of the American ambassador, "apparently approved" the coup.[28] "It is inconceivable that this latest [coup] could have gone ahead without at least the knowledge of the king's acquiescence," the British ambassador observed.[29] Scholars David Morell and Chai-anan Samudavanija state that "the fusion of royal legitimacy and military power had [allowed] the army to act once more in national interest."[30] When did this fusion begin? Given that the plot of a coup was prepared many months in advance, was the massacre in the morning part of the plan for the coup in the evening or it was an unanticipated opportunity?

Second, who conspired for Thanom's return and for what particular goal? A journalist concluded a week after the massacre that the conspiracy turned out to be the single stone that killed two birds, namely, the end of the radical student movement and the fall of the elected government.[31] The eventual outcome did not, however, necessarily mean that the conspiracy was designed for those outcomes. The unfolding situation and public reactions involved many factors that were probably unanticipated and beyond anyone's control or plan. But it was not beyond the ability of those who prepared for the coup to take advantage of it and to turn it to serve their scheme.

Thanom had attempted a return once before, in December 1974. It sparked swift and widespread protests, causing him to head back to Boston, Massachusetts, only a few days later. Then, in August 1976, General Prapat Jarusathian, another dictator who was forced into exile at the same time as Thanom, returned to the country as well. The NSCT protested and clashed with the Red Gaurs, prompting the government to take swift action forcing Prapat out. Prapat left the country only after he went to the palace, although the role the palace played in this incident was unclear. Nevertheless, Prapat's return took place only a month before Thanom's. Was the former a test run for the latter? To this day, we know some more about the massacre but not much about these pretext events.

Third, the Bowornniwet temple that took in Thanom was among the top royal monasteries in the country. It is also the headquarters of the Thammayut sect, which was founded by a monarch of this dynasty about 1830, and thus every monarch of this dynasty was a patron of this sect and this temple. Bhumibol himself was ordained here in 1956. In fact, the partner and personal facilitator for the king when he was a monk, Phra Yannasangvara, was the abbot who ordained Thanom in 1976. Yannasangvara later became the supreme patriarch of the Thai sangha, which position he held from 1989 to 2013. The monk who was the facilitator for Thanom in 1976 was the abbot's secretary. He was later an outspoken leader of an ultraconservative Buddhist group, Pariantham Samakhom. Was it by chance that Thanom was ordained at this temple and facilitated by these monks? To what extent (if any) were the palace, this revered monk, and the sangha establishment part of the plan for Thanom's return in a monk's robe? (Thanom quit the robe only a few months after the massacre, and his father did not die until 1980.)

Fourth, the biggest elephant in the room and the most troubling question for Thai society was the role of the palace in the right-wing movement, in Thanom's return, and in the massacre. King Bhumibol was often cited with high praise for his mediation to end the political violence in 1973 and 1992. The 1976 massacre is conspicuously unmentioned in most biographies of him.[32] No evidence indicates that the king even tried to intervene to end the massacre. Evidence to the contrary, however, is ample. In the words of British ambassador Cole on November 5, 1976, "The King . . . has been involved in recent events to a very deep extent. . . . [However] the actual events of 6 October had taken everybody by surprise."[33] Paul Handley makes a detailed implication of the palace in the buildup of the right-wing movement and in the situation that led to the massacre and the coup, although their involvement in the killing on that day was not clear.[34] The king's silence that day was conspicuous, and he has remained silent ever since.

Despite the general misperception that the Thai monarchy is above politics, it was in fact active in politics throughout Bhumibol's reign (1946–2016).[35] The monarchy has played a significant role in the counterinsurgency since the 1960s, thanks to the support by the United States and the royalist junta at the time.[36] In regard to the right-wing movement, given the anxiety after the communist revolutions in Indochina in 1975, every member of the royal family was active in the mobilization of the Village Scouts in 1975 and 1976.[37] Bhumibol, writes Katherine Bowie, "was clearly the single most important personage fostering the movement's expansion. Royal patronage facilitated support from both the government and the private sector."[38] The British ambassador wrote, "[As] I have remarked before on the Queen's Marie-Antoinette complex . . . her obsession . . . with security and anti-communism . . . she has become closely, even too closely, associated with the right-wing organizations. . . . The last conversation I had with her . . . centered obsessively on the right-wing Village Scouts as the salvation of the country."[39] Around that time, the politico-cultural condition that I have called "hyper-royalism" had just begun as part of the anticommunist atmosphere.[40] A number of anticommunist songs composed by the king filled the airwaves of military propaganda and became theme songs of the right-wing movement.[41] On October 6, 1976, the active crowd at Sanamluang and at the Equestrian Plaza was mostly the Village Scouts.[42]

As to Thanom's return as a monk, the question might be whether this farce would have been a laughing matter had his ordination and residence not been at the Bowornniwet temple by the abbot who was very close to Bhumibol. Did it take place without the king's knowledge? Two days after Thanom returned, the king and queen made an unscheduled visit to the temple.[43] The lady in waiting to the queen emphasized in her press conference that they came to meet the abbot (that is, not Thanom). Nevertheless, she relayed the queen's concern that vicious people were attempting to burn down the temple and to destroy Buddhism, thus the queen urged people to help protect the temple, and thereby Buddhism as well.[44] She did not name the enemy, but perhaps there was no need to do so.

During the massacre, one of the main police forces that stormed into TU with heavy weapons was the Border Patrol Police Aerial Reinforcement Unit (PARU). It had been created in the early 1950s by the United States as a special force for counterinsurgency operations. The king and the queen had had a long association with the Border Patrol Police (BPP) and the PARU since then, thanks in part to the proximity of a palace and the PARU headquarters, and in part to US efforts to increase the monarchy's role in anticommunism. Since the 1960s, the entire BPP had been brought under the royal patronage of the royal family, especially the princess mother of King Bhumibol.[45] Although the BPP is officially part of the police command, it enjoys relative autonomy, thanks to its special relationship with the palace. On October 6, the PARU got the order around 2 a.m. to move from their base more than two hundred kilometers away to arrive at TU around 6 a.m.[46] At 2 a.m., heavy shooting at TU had not yet begun. Was the order to enter TU made with the advance knowledge of what was going to happen in four hours? Why use a force from a distance instead of a unit in Bangkok? Why the PARU, given that Bangkok is not at the border, nor did the operation at TU need an aerial unit? Or was it the most trusted unit by and under command of whoever made the order? Who gave the order? To be fair, no concrete evidence pointed to the palace. In fact, who ordered the PARU at 2 a.m. to go into TU remains a mystery.[47]

The same day, October 6, the king and the crown prince went to visit the abbot of the Bowornniwet temple again. A newspaper also showed a picture of them among the Village Scouts at the Grand Palace.[48] At 5 p.m., shortly before the coup, the king advised the governor of Bangkok, who was a leader of the Village Scouts who gathered at the Government House, to end the demonstration. The crown prince was present at the gathering, telling the Scouts to end their demonstration.[49] On the following day, Princess Sirindhorn and her sister went to visit the injured police officers at the hospital, praising them for their sacrifice to the country. On October 20, the two princesses presided over the funeral of a Village Scout who had died in the incident, honoring him as an example whom other Village Scouts should follow.[50] As we see in chapter 9, this scout was active in a paramilitary group created by ISOC.

These facts about actions (and inaction) by the royal family raise the question of what exactly was "a very deep extent," as the British ambassador put it. Were they part of the atrocity? Did they know in advance? What did they think after it had taken place? Did the absence of the royal intervention to stop the killing reflect their inability or complicity? Unfortunately, the subject of the palace and the massacre remains taboo in Thailand. Most Thais are either ignorant about it, or are willing to turn a blind eye to the elephant in the room.

Fifth, who ordered the siege at TU? The government of Thanin Kraivixian said that the Seni government ordered the arrests of students (and is thereby responsible for the massacre). Seni issued a formal statement clarifying that his government ordered only the arrests of those involved in the alleged mocking-the-crown-prince skit. It did not order the arrests or suppression of the demonstration.[51] To this day, it is unclear who ordered the operation at TU in the middle of the night. Neither is it clear by whose order the six students who went to meet Seni at his residence were taken into custody. Had they met, would it have been possible to stop the carnage?

Sixth, why did the Seni government take no action throughout the morning? Did they know the actual situation at TU? Were they in fact still in power when the shooting began? One thing was clear about the government that morning: it was scrambling for its survival. According to the memoir of a cabinet member of the Seni government, the prime minister called for a special meeting that morning to declare a state of emergency. The goal was to disperse the right-wing gathering at the Equestrian Plaza. The cabinet members who opposed the emergency were the right-wing politicians, Chatichai Choonhavan (later prime minister from 1988 to 1991) and Praman Adireksan (deputy prime minister in numerous governments from 1975 to 1987). Chatichai brought in Charoenrit Chamratromran, deputy chief of the BPP and cofounder of the Village Scouts, to support his argument. Another police general, Chumphon Lohachala, reported to the cabinet in tears that students were heavily armed, resulting in heavy casualties among the police. Charoenrit and Praman urged that it was an opportunity to eradicate radical students. The national police chief, on the other hand, apparently not being part of the conspiracy, reported to the cabinet that no police were dead and only a few were injured. The cabinet also learned that police found only three light pistols among the demonstrators.[52] In the end, the cabinet could not agree to a state of emergency.[53] Throughout the day, the government did nothing except issue a statement over Radio Thailand at 2 p.m., blaming the students for the violence in the morning. According to the statement, it appears that the government even accepted the hearsay about the arms stockpiles in TU despite knowing it was untrue. This showed either how far those in government would go to save themselves or how powerless they really were. Thus they did absolutely nothing.

Seventh, apart from the police and the PARU, who were the perpetrators, especially those who committed the heinous acts? Their identities remain formulaic and generic. Two specific issues that merit attention are, first, the presumption that the state's forces that morning were the army and the police, and, second, the formulaic mention of the triplet paramilitary groups in the massacre: "the Red Gaurs, Nawaphon, and the Village Scouts."

On the first point, the army's propaganda was definitely responsible for the false accusation regarding the skit and the anticommunist hysteria. The ISOC was behind the deadly right-wing groups. However, army personnel did not actually participate in firing at the demonstrators. The armed force that morning was the police.[54] According to the top police commander that day, about four hundred police were deployed at TU.[55] They came from four main branches, the local police from various districts in Bangkok, the Crime Suppression Command, the Special Operation Command (the so-called Riot Suppression Police), and the PARU.[56] Given political confusion and possibly several coup plots under way during those hours, it is unclear whether these police forces were coordinated or represented various contesting political opportunists and coup plotters.

For the paramilitary groups, almost every writing about the October 6 incident mentions the triplet—Red Gaurs, Nawaphon, and Village Scout—as the perpetrators. Among them, it was not clear who did what during the massacre. Because the Red Gaurs were already notorious, crediting them with the brutality was convenient. However, as we see in chapter 9, they denied it with a legitimate alibi. My research found that the deadliest perpetrators were the fringe groups of goons who were much less known and mentioned only in passing in writings about the massacre.[57] Except for the Village Scouts, to this day we know very little about these right-wing groups, let alone the goons.

Further, many accounts of the right-wing groups seem to be recycled, that is, circulation of the same information from only a few original sources. The case of Nawaphon, allegedly the "biggest and most influential right-wing organization" at the time, is a good example.[58] Nawaphon features prominently as a major right-wing group in every writing about the massacre. Yet the descriptions of Nawaphon in most of them are similar.[59] Founded in 1974 and funded by ISOC, it is said to be a huge anticommunist civic group with more than a million members across the country, including officials and business people in provincial cities who provided more funding.[60] Its prominent members included a privy councillor, a few army and police generals, two TU professors, and a notorious Buddhist monk. A political operator named Watthana Khieowimol was the group's public face. Most accounts say Nawaphon focused on psychological warfare with activities such as meetings, several large gatherings, and setting up the local anticommunist cells and networks across the country. Some said it had assassination units as well.[61] Morell and Chai-anan provide Watthana's background based on an interview with him. They tell us about a gathering of Nawaphon as well, though it does not mention the source other than Watthana.[62] Handley describes a rudimentary structure (upper and lower levels) of the group.[63] Despite its intimidating image and Watthana's boastful press conferences, news was scant and photos few about Nawaphon's activities at the time. Its large gatherings were not known, except the highly publicized meeting of fifteen thousand local leaders in January 1976 that was repeatedly mentioned. Other public gatherings that Watthana boasted about and claimed as Nawaphon's were the ones in which the right-wing crowd was mixed and indistinguishable.[64] The only different image of Nawaphon is from a recent book, which says the US agencies at the time suspected Watthana's credentials, and described the influence of "shadowy" group as "minimal," "light-weight," and "opportunistic."[65]

In my view, Nawaphon was probably a phantom organization intended to inflate the image of the right-wing movement as a popular movement and to intimidate the radicals. Its "mass base" and local cells were the same people that the ISOC had organized around the country for years as part of its counterinsurgency operation.[66] They could show up as Nawaphon's people for seminars and photoops if the ISOC ordered them to. The assassinations, if true, could be the dirty work of any anticommunist group, especially military personnel under the ISOC, only giving credit to Nawaphon. In other words, Nawaphon was probably only the public face of the anticommunist functionaries who operated as the deep state, independent of the fragile elected government. Apart from the ISOC, Nawaphon did not have its own mass base or organization. No million members and no assassins. Only Watthana and his mouth.[67]

Eighth, did the United States play any role in the massacre? Did the American government know about it beforehand, provide assistance, endorse it, or help cover it up? Given US support for many dictatorial regimes throughout the world during that period, including deadly ones in Southeast Asia and Central and Latin America, these questions are legitimate.

Judging from the evidence, especially the cables between the embassy in Bangkok and Washington, DC, the United States followed the critical situation closely at every step but seemed content to stay on the sidelines. It might have anticipated a coup, as most keen observers had, but not a massacre. It only analyzed and explained after the fact, as most observers did. It did not intervene in any way and did not condemn the atrocity. In mid-1977, the US Congress held a hearing on the situation in Thailand within the regional context of the communist advance in Southeast Asia.

The explanation for US inaction in 1976 despite concerns about the communists in Southeast Asia is beyond the scope of this book. The US retreat from Southeast Asia began even before the Indochina revolutions in 1975 and sped up after that. It quickly scaled down the number of personnel and began to leave its bases in Thailand as well. The region, Thailand in particular, suddenly became a lower priority for both the US government and academic inquiry, as it is today.

Nevertheless, the indirect US role in the massacre should not be overlooked. Almost all the deadly functionaries of the state that operated on October 6, 1976, were the products of the US counterinsurgency—namely, the ISOC, the BPP, the Thai military, and so on. Even the monarchy, which had been crippled by the end of its absolute era in 1932, was revived and promoted to power by the United States in the 1960s.[68]

Ninth, one of the most intriguing conspiracy theories is about the skit that triggered the royalist rage. What explains the resemblance between the student actor in the photo and the crown prince (see figures 1a and 1b)? Some suggest that either the skit or the photo, perhaps both, were part of the plot for the massacre and the coup.[69] On the other hand, a few observed that the massacre was a blessing in disguise for the Communist Party of Thailand (CPT), raising a theory that the skit might have been the work of the CPT.[70] People who were involved with the skit categorically denied these theories.[71] These suspicions are retrospective speculations based on the consequences of the photo. To this day no evidence supports any of them.[72]

Let us lay out and consider the facts. The skit was produced by TU's drama club. The NSCT did not know about it and was not involved in any way. It was performed in public on October 4 to an audience of a few hundred people. Two actors, not one, took turns playing the hanged victim. The skit did not mention the royals. No one in the audience suggested that any actor resembled the crown prince. After it ended, the skit was not mentioned at the ensuing demonstration until the controversy broke out a day later. The black and white photo of the skit was published on the front page of several newspapers in the morning of October 5, including *Athipat* (the NSCT's newspaper) and the *Bangkok Post*. None of them had a caption that related to the royals, or a hint at lèse majesté. In the early afternoon that day, however, a woman filed a charge against the NSCT based on the picture she saw in the *Bangkok Post*. The army broadcast then spread the allegation that the NSCT had staged a mock hanging of the crown prince. The allegation spread like wild fire. That afternoon, *Dao sayam* printed a large photo of the alleged mock hanging on its front page with the headline, "Crown Prince Hanged in Effigy. The Country Erupted. The NSCT Crushed the Hearts of All

Thais" (*Khwaen kho hun muan chao fa chai. Phaendin duat. Sun yiap huachai thai thang chat*) (figure 1b).

Right-wing royalists undoubtedly believed the allegation. Their opponents tended to believe that the photo was doctored.[73] So did Seni Pramoj.[74] In 1988, twelve years later, the *Bangkok Post* issued a clarification for the first time denying all allegations. It said that after the publication on October 5, 1976, the Special Branch Police (Santiban) came to confiscate the negatives and the prints.[75] In the issue on October 7, 1996, twenty years after the massacre, a longer clarification appeared on its front page.

> Apart from a clarification issued in 1988, we have chosen to remain silent, not wishing to revive this painful episode . . . hoping that the accusation will fade with passing time. . . . Silence has been interpreted as admitting [the allegation].
>
> The photo in question was not in any way doctored. The negative was not tampered with. . . . [This has been verified by the police.] The film was developed in our dark room. Prints were made in the same room. When they were presented at the news conference, none of us saw that the actor in the mock hanging looked like a member of the Royal Family. The decision to use the photo was straightforward: it was the best of the day.
>
> Those of us responsible for making the decision about the presentation of news and photos feel deep sorrow about the carnage. . . . But we were never part of [the killing] deliberately or otherwise.[76]

After the publication, the editorial continues, the *Bangkok Post* received several threats from right-wing elements. The paper insisted that there was no collaboration whatsoever between the *Post* and *Dao sayam.* In 2000, I interviewed several people at the *Post* office who were involved with the publication of the photo and the reporting of events in 1976. They insisted that they did not see the resemblance of the actor and crown prince, either on the scene at TU or in the photo. Nor did they see it at the editorial meeting when they chose the photo for the front page of the October 5 issue. Had they seen it, they argued, they would definitely not have published the photo because they could have been charged with lèse majesté.[77] A *Dao sayam* journalist also denied the suspicion that the film or the photo were doctored.[78] Ji Ungphakorn and Suthachai Yimprasert considered the original photos that the police collected from the *Bangkok Post* and *Dao sayam* and also conclude that neither the film nor the photo were doctored.

Could the resemblance be a happenstance, a truly tragic one that was unanticipated even by right-wing groups, *Dao sayam,* or the coup plotters?[79] Could the resemblance be the result of the power of suggestion, similar to the mental trick that makes us see a rabbit on the moon every time we look at it simply because we are told to see the moon that way? So many conspiracy theories about the skit and the photo exist because it is difficult to accept that such a deadly coincidence or human fallacy could have caused such a tragedy, but it cannot be explained any other way. Somsak Jeamteerasakul reaches the same conclusion, that the photo was not doctored, and *Dao sayam* did not suspect anything about the photo before the allegation spread in the afternoon of October 5.[80] *Dao sayam,* the right-wing movement, and the military seized the opportunity only to deal the NSCT a knock-out blow.[81]

Despite its repeated denial, the allegations about the *Bangkok Post* will be hard to dislodge because it is difficult to accept that a tragedy of such magnitude could be triggered by happenstance. When a controversy erupted again in 2000, a political activist and *The Nation,* the rival English daily, alleged that the *Post* was part of the conspiracy that led to the carnage.[82] The doubts will probably remain forever.

Tenth, why did the NSCT not end the demonstration on the night of October 5? In retrospect, this question is valid. But only in retrospect.[83] It was a common belief at the time that a demonstration should not end late at night for safety concerns, given the lack of public transportation and potential problems with right-wing goons. Remaining on a compact campus with a few entrances, such as TU's, was deemed safer. Of course, we (here I speak as one of the former leadership collective) did not foresee being trapped.[84] In fact, the situation was tense but no more so than anticipated before the police surrounded the campus. To end the demonstration after midnight without transportation could have triggered disorder. The heavy firing began about 4 a.m., at which point dispersing the crowd without safe passage could also have led to bloodshed. This was why NSCT leaders tried to secure the government's promise of safety before ending the demonstration. This explanation might be unconvincing to some. But it was truly our thinking and reasoning at the time. The truth was also that we had no experience of a siege or a massacre.

Our response to the immediate problem that arose was always a step too late.[85]

Eleventh, after the massacre, two thousand to three thousand students joined the CPT in its armed struggle against the Thai state.[86] That the CPT grew the most and the most quickly during the few years after the massacre prompted some to wonder whether it had anticipated the massacre but willingly let it happen to induce students to join the armed struggle in the jungles. Moreover, it was revealed later that, before the massacre, the CPT had withdrawn a number of its operators from Bangkok to its strongholds in the jungles. This revelation raised doubts about whether the CPT knew in advance what was going to happen, yet tacitly blocked the effort to end the demonstration.[87] But if the CPT had an inkling of the massive suppression to come, why was the radical leadership of the student movement, who were either in contact with or under the influence of the CPT, caught completely off guard?

> the CPT had infiltrated the [student movement] leadership and chose to employ such an incident to engender just the kind of emotional reaction from the right that did occur on October 6. Party leaders could have reasoned that massive violence against the students rallying at Thammasat was exactly what was required to induce a sizable number of potential student cadres finally to reject parliamentary reform and join the party's revolution in the hills. This was indeed the result, though it need not imply that the hanging incident had been consciously staged by the CPT as a calculated move to anger the rightists.[88]

This allegation led to further rumors and allegations—that the mock hanging was a conspiracy by the CPT, or that the extremist faction among the students refused to end the demonstration while the moderate faction tried to ease the situation by negotiation with the government.[89] It also cast doubt on me personally. According to one allegation, I was part of the CPT's plot to not end the demonstration in order to let the massacre take place and result in the student exodus to jungles.[90] I can only categorically deny this.[91] Besides, in my opinion, the accusation assumes an extraordinary ability of the CPT to manipulate every step of the situation and to foresee or control the outcomes as well: first, the skit that did not cause any suspicion of lèse majesté until the photo was published in several newspapers and the allegation was fanned by the military broadcast and by a right-wing newspaper; second, the siege by the angry crowd and the police, the deployment of the PARU, and the inaction by the government; third, the unprecedented level of brutality; and, fourth, the decisions of so many individual students to seek vengeance by joining the armed struggle. The allegation gives too much credit to the CPT to foresee precisely how events would unfold.

The CPT certainly played a crucial role in the increasing radicalism of the student movement and contributed to how the student leadership thought and made decisions in crucial situations. In those days, as far as I can say, none of the student leaders could foresee a massacre in concrete terms. It remained theoretical to us, because we learned from reading about the experiences of other student movements. Any talk of a massacre before that day was abstract. By the time it took place, we could only react to the immediate situation at hand. We were unable to think a step ahead, let alone three steps to boost the CPT's armed struggles.

Twelfth, even today, we do not know much about the victims of the massacre—who they and their families were or how they died. Their families deserve to know more about the deaths of their loved ones and deserve recognition for the silent suffering they endured given public sensitivities about the massacre in Thailand. But a thorough investigation is unlikely any time soon, perhaps forever.[92]

For years after the massacre, it was not clear how many people had been killed, who they were, how they died, how many were injured, and how many missing. Many believed that more than a hundred died.[93] Reliable information was limited because all media were either shut down or strictly controlled for months afterward. Instead, hearsay about rapes, drownings, and tortures spread widely. Subsequently, during the period of silence, the dead, known only vaguely and collectively—not as individuals with names, faces, families and personal lives—were overlooked. Even former radicals remembered them collectively as tragic martyrs rather than as individuals. More reliable information came to light only after my assistant and I found the autopsy reports in 2000.[94] Yet a number of unanswered questions about the deaths remain to this day.

The autopsy reports are helpful, but they are not entirely reliable. Many pages of the reports are misplaced, causing confusion due to the mismatches of the photos and the medical examiners' records of several individuals. This problem took me years to solve, but it was not among the most difficult puzzles, such as the six "unidentified Thai males" (*chai thai mai sap chue*). Three have been identified since then. Three remained unknown despite photographs and descriptions of their bodies.

Next, most people who know about the October 6 massacre have seen only one hanging victim, the person in Ulevich's photo. Autopsy reports report two, thus I had thought for years that there were two.[95] In 2016, after careful research based on the autopsy reports, photos, and news clippings, the research team for the digital archives of the incident, the Documentation of the October 6 (Doct6) project, confirmed four hangings, plus one unconfirmed. Of these, we can identify three of them. The remaining unidentified hanging victim is the person in Ulevich's 1977 photo whom people have seen the most (figure 3).[96] More than forty years later, despite the photo's worldwide distribution, we still do not know the identities of the two protagonists in the photo: the man with the chair, whom I would call the Chair Guy, and the victim.

To this day, we do not know the identities of the four bodies that were burned. Was the remaining unknown hanging victim among them? If not, his body disappeared. Even if he was one of the four, who were the three others? Will these remaining unidentified victims ever be known?

The final question, the thirteenth, why such brutality? The answer to it would not help solve any unknown about the massacre. But the answer is probably more meaningful than any of the previous ones. A brutal massacre can occur when opponents are seen as less than human. My Lai, Rwanda, and many war-time atrocities took place after hatred and fear had brewed for some time, making the opponents less or nonhuman. This first stage of dehumanization is common to all atrocities. So it was to the October 6 massacre.

Some of the heinous actions on that day were to kill or to torture victims to death; but most were the desecration of dead bodies, as if the victims were animals, devils, witches, or satanic creatures, namely pounding a stake into the chest, hanging and burning, dragging a victim along the ground, and urinating on the bodies. Based on the autopsies and photos, only one of the four or five hanging victims was hung to death. The rest died by gunshots and explosives before their bodies were hung. Only one of the four burning victims might have been burned alive. The bodies impaled through their chests were dead ones. My friend Jaruphong died before his body was dragged along the ground.[97]

For Watcharee Petchsun, who was left naked on the ground with a stake on her dead body, the autopsy report states that she died from a gunshot wound with no trace of rape or a stake piercing any part of her body before her death. If the report is accurate, the removal of her clothes and the placing of a stake on her naked body near her private parts were acts staged for public spectacle. It was the cruelest of acts because it not only degraded her humanity but also humiliated and destroyed her femininity to the utmost degree. As the photos show, the abusers and the onlookers were all men and boys. No male victims were sexually mutilated either. Although both male and female protesters were ordered to take off their shirts after the arrests, the television commentators made fun of the shirtless females with sexual innuendos that females could have hidden weapons under their shirts (see chapter 3). They did not make fun of the shirtless males. The dehumanization was gendered.

The third stage of dehumanization was the evident pleasure participants and bystanders took in committing those acts and in participating in the spectacle, as if they were at a communal festival or a ritual performance.[98] How could people stage the raping of a dead woman or enjoy watching it? An artist reflects on the Pulitzer Prize–winning photo of a hanging:

> It is not just the bloodied victim hanging from the tree, and not just the madness in the face of the man in safari suit who is gleefully slamming [the] lifeless body with a metal chair. . . . what has haunted me is the crowd of spectators at the scene. Herein lies the horror: their faces, some of them mere boys, some smiling, some laughing, many seeming to cheer on the lynching, some fearful, some hysterical.[99]

It was the pleasure of conquest. The barbaric acts not only were justified because the victims were subhuman or nonhuman, animals, or devils, but also induced pleasure because they were the ritualistic performance of the conqueror, like a victory parade with the victim's head displayed as a trophy. The performance had to be public for the spectators to enjoy the communal triumph, and it served to terrorize the enemies at the same time. The conquest over femininity was, literally and figuratively, the ultimate conquering performance for male satisfaction.

Was this third stage of dehumanization the inevitable outcome of extreme hatred, anticommunist hysteria, and ultraroyalist fever?

What do the acts of public desecration tell us about Thailand, its people, culture, and politics? What do they tell us about humanity?

Who was Chair Guy who repeatedly slammed a folding chair against a hanging body, who added more newspapers to fuel the fire burning a pile of corpses, who then sat on the naked body of the dead woman? Was he a trained agent provocateur who was assigned to incite the crowd by committing those acts, or was he an ordinary person turned into a desecrator by events of that morning? As time went by, as decades passed, did he regret his acts? Did he brag about them? How did he remember what he did? I wish I could track him down. I would like to meet him, to ask him those questions, without vengeance and with the promise not to interrupt his answer. In a similar vein, did those men and boys still enjoy the spectacle the day after? As time went by, did they regret being part of the spectacle? I wish I could meet them. I wish to learn how they remember that Wednesday morning of October 6, 1976.

Chapter 3

The Beginning of Memories

Even before the shooting ended at Thammasat University, the airwaves began to echo the jubilance among the perpetrators of the massacre. The broadcast that day not only misinformed the public but also justified the atrocity, just as standard propaganda would. Perhaps unbeknownst to the perpetrators, it also established a narrative of the massacre, a collective memory that framed many individual ones and the public discourse of the massacre for years to come. Perhaps like the big bang theory of the universe, the initial moment was tremendously important because it was the beginning of memory and would have a lasting impact on the perpetrators and the public alike, regardless of its falsehood and unreason. The victims and their sympathizers and the opponents of the state belonged to communities of different collective memories that were suppressed after the incident. Their silence in the public sphere, however, did not mean that their memories had been wiped out. Rather, most of them found alternative spheres beyond the state's control and surveillance, namely, the underground, the jungles, and within the limited spheres of families and friends. For the radicals, their bitter memories led them to embrace the Communist Party of Thailand (CPT)'s armed struggles against the government in Bangkok. But the radicals' and CPT's memories were not the only alternative. Many other victims found different communities of shared memories, and those who could not live on in silence. The post-massacre period provided the conditions for the beginnings of these memories.

OCTOBER 6 AS THE VICTORY OVER THE COMMUNISTS

On October 6, 1976, television and radio broadcasts in the country were mostly under army control. In Thailand, then and now, all airwaves belonged to the two main agencies of the state: about half of them to the Department of Public Relations (DPR) and the other half to the armed forces. Private operators get concessions or rent airtimes from them for commercial or similarly justifiable purposes. The DPR operated Radio Thailand and its branches in every region and province. It also owned the rights to two of the four television channels at the time. It set up a semigovernmental company to operate one channel and gave the concession to a private company to operate the other. The rest of the airwaves belonged to the military, allegedly for national security reasons. Then and now, the army owned one television broadcast, TV5, and gave the concession for the other to a private company. The various regiments, branches, and districts of the armed forces throughout the country own and operate particular bands of airwaves for commercial radio broadcasts. This military fiefdom has not changed, even in democratic periods, since the beginning of radio broadcasting in Thailand.

During the rise of the right-wing movement from mid-1975 to October 1976, these military broadcasts coordinated into a unified network under the command of then Lieutenant Colonel Uthan Sanidvongse, who was the broadcast master at the Armor Broadcast Services (Yan Kro). A unified network meant that every military broadcasting service in the country would relay the programs from Yan Kro, controlling literally half of the nation's airwaves alleged to be critical to national security at any moment. The name Yan Kro thus became synonymous with the entire military network. The protest against Thanom's return was one such critical moment. The unified broadcasts from Yan Kro went to work again, without which the massacre might not have happened. The army also used TV5 for propaganda. The entire country fell under the spell of its propaganda.

As the carnage at TU was unfolding, Yan Kro and TV5 worked in tandem, broadcasting live throughout the morning. Their main task was to justify the massacre on two related grounds: first, the mock hanging of the crown prince was extremely hurtful to the Thai people, hence the students must be punished; second, the student movement and the demonstration were part of a communist scheme to overthrow the monarchy and destroy the nation. The protesters at TU were called the rioters (*phukokan chalachon*), the deceived (*phulongphit*), the trouble makers (*phukokhwam mai sa-ngop*). They were Yuan, the broadcast repeated several times throughout those hours.[1] "Yuan" is a Thai pejorative term for Vietnamese. In the anticommunist fever of the times, it was not merely a slang term for an ethnic Other, a non-Thai, but also a dehumanizing term for an enemy of Thai-ness.

On TV5, the hosts provided comments, explanations, and excuses for the actions they saw on television. They repeatedly said that the shootings were from inside TU targeting the police and the crowd outside: "hundreds of police officers were injured and dead." Students had to be stripped to distinguish them from the ordinary people who helped the police. The hosts commented many times on the size of the patriotic crowd, "hundreds of thousands" of people, both outside TU and at the Equestrian Plaza. They were voluntary, active, and willing to take risks to fight "the commies" inside TU. The hosts were overwhelmed, proud, and delighted by the popular support. They seemed to enjoy what they were seeing and doing, as when one quipped that those arrested could not speak Thai and thus must be Yuan; then they all laughed together. The nonsense about female students, that they "took off their own clothes out of fright—nobody ordered them to do so . . . they were not naked; they still have bras on," was a kind of sexual jest among the all-male commentators.

At the end of the operation at TU, as the police corralled the students onto the buses that would take them to prison, the television hosts were in a jolly, celebratory mood. They boasted how great their mass supporters were. Some of whom, according to the broadcast hosts, had asked for arms and explosives to spearhead the raid into TU while the police were waiting for the order at the beginning of the carnage. On the other hand, the hosts and their guests, the first six policemen who had led the crowd into TU a few hours earlier, made fun of those arrested and of the victims of torture and hanging. At one point, their conversation became a sarcastic joke.

A police guest, "Those who were hanged and burned cannot speak Thai, can they?"

The host, "Oh, they must be the Yuan."

A police guest, "They couldn't speak Thai, but not sure they were Yuan, either."

The host, "If they were Lao, [Thais] should be able to understand them. But if (they were) Yuan, we couldn't."

This light-hearted exchange probably took place when the television screen showed the hanging and burning of humans.

Around 10:30 a.m., the DPR televised the massacre briefly with a different view on its channel. Its news editor, Sanphasiri Wirayasiri, a legendary pioneer of Thailand's television, could not stand the military's propaganda. He singlehandedly filmed and reported the brutality as it unfolded. The DPR broadcast was taken off the air shortly after. That evening, the coup regime issued an order, announced nationally, to sack Sanphasiri from the DPR and the company that operated the television.[2] Other than this one rebellious act, information about the incident at TU was almost completely under army control. Its view turned into the dominant narrative of the event. Even the government folded into the right wing's narrative, as reflected in its official statement and Seni's press conference that afternoon.

One of the earliest orders of the National Administrative Reform Council, the military junta that seized power that evening, was to shut down all daily newspapers and to censor every magazine and news publication before it went to print. Some dailies closed only for a few days, but many did so indefinitely.[3] The tight media control remained in place for more than a year. Except for the October 6 afternoon prints of a few dailies, the published information, explanations, and excuses followed the state's narrative of the incident. In fact, the censorship was not officially lifted for some years and the massacre remained one of the most sensitive items for the authorities for many more years. In 1979, for the first time in Thailand, the news magazine *Lok Mai* (New World) published a few horrific photos of the massacre. It was swiftly shut down and the printed copies taken off the market.[4] People in Thailand heard but only vaguely about the massacre.

Nevertheless, no control was complete or total. On that day, foreign journalists and photographers took the risk to inform the world of the carnage in Bangkok, despite the scary situation that almost took the life of a United Press International journalist. Neal Ulevich, an Associated Press journalist and photographer, managed to wire a dozen photos to the Tokyo office, then to the world. Given the technology at the time, which was slow and available only at the government's Central Post Office, the authorities might have found out and intervened at any time.[5] Fortunately for these foreign journalists, authorities did not pay as close attention to them during the chaos as to Thai journalists. For some years, apart from word of mouth, these foreign sources of photos and reports were circulated illegally within small circles such as university campuses as alternative information about the massacre.

The first announcement of the coup group on October 6 in the evening reinforced Yan Kro's narrative of the incident, that is, that the protest was a communist plot, in cooperation with communist Vietnam, to destroy the nation and the monarchy. The authority's actions, which were never described clearly, were necessary to restore law and order. This political and overwrought account was the first narrative of the massacre to reach the public sphere; it was also the only one allowed for some time. Soon after the incident, the coup group organized a concerted propaganda campaign—a small booklet, a film, and an exhibition about the incident at TU.[6] The propaganda emphasized that the violence committed by the radicals against ordinary patriots and the police on that day showed evidence that the students were communists, such as the flag and symbol of the People's Republic of China and leftist publications that proliferated from 1973 to 1976, and displayed numerous heavy weapons allegedly found at TU as proof of the planned insurrection. Fortunately, it suggests, the radicals were defeated by those hundreds of thousands of patriots outside TU and at the Equestrian Plaza that day. The propaganda also asserted that the Seni government had been weak and indecisive in dealing with the communists, hence the necessity for the coup, "which had not been planned beforehand," but was needed to prevent further bloodshed and the destruction of the country.[7] The coup government also sent the right-wing demagogue, Samak Sundaravej, on a world tour to provide the world with the state's version of the massacre.[8] For many months, daily newspapers followed this narrative, castigating the students as villains, the ousted government and many professors as their enablers, and so on. Meanwhile, another dictator in exile since 1973, Prapat Jarusathian, returned home to a warm welcome in January 1977. In an ostentatious press conference, he condemned the student movement as having been communist since 1973, when it led the uprising against his regime.[9] Thanom left the monkhood the same month and demanded the return of all his assets confiscated after the 1973 uprising.[10]

THE RIGHT-WING COLLECTIVE MEMORY

Despite its distortions and falsehoods, the military's narrative was the first collective memory of the incident and would frame individual experiences and memories. Evidence of the effects of this emblematic memory are the testimonies of the witnesses to the police in November and December 1976, part of the preparation for the charges against the ringleaders in the October 6 trial.[11] Among the 244 witnesses were seventy-two police officers, eighteen military officers, forty-six faculty, staff, and security guards at TU, fifteen faculty and staff from other universities, fourteen journalists and media photographers, two alleged leftists who turned against the leftists, and about thirty people from various right-wing organizations. Among the most prominent names were Seni the ousted elected prime minister and Uthan the broadcast master of Yan Kro. Some of them were expert witnesses, such as weapons experts from the military, medical examiners who performed the autopsies, managers of the banks that had the NSCT accounts, and so on. The majority, including fifteen TU professors known for their right-wing views, members of right-wing-groups and labor unions, and a majority of the police officers, especially those from the Special Branch (Santiban), or political police, all testified against the students. Eventually, the prosecutor chose eighty-two of the 244 to be the prosecuting witnesses in the October 6 trial in 1977 and 1978.[12]

Let us take for granted that these witnesses had individual memories of the massacre, each with different experiences at various spots and moments during that morning. By the time they talked to the police in November and December that year, their accounts showed the influences of the right-wing collective memory. For example, several mentioned encounters with protesters who did not speak Thai, implicitly or explicitly offering testimonies that fit the narrative of the Vietnamese or communist plot.[13] Apart from police officers, many also testified that they saw or heard gunfire from inside TU—that is, by students—toward the police, one claiming to have witnessed heavy casualties among the police and the right-wing crowd because of "the powerful fire power of the students."[14] One went as far as to claim not to have seen or heard the police shooting, but to have witnessed shooting and brutality by students.[15] In contrast, many heard shooting in both directions, or were confused as to who did the shooting, and only one dared to say the shooting was primarily from the outside.[16]

Some of the strongest testimony against the communists came not from the goons or the police but from the right-wing professors. Some claimed to have recognized on the spot that the skit portrayed the mock hanging of the crown prince, rather than later from the photo.[17] They offered the police the names of the alleged communist professors and students along with damaging information about them.[18] Some provided materials they had collected to help the police prepare their case.[19] They described their opponents in a coarse and ugly fashion, and some information was blatantly false and outrageous. The testimony against Dr. Puey Ungphakorn (figure 4), the liberal TU rector who sympathized with the students, is a case in point. The right-wing professors told the police that Puey raised funds to help students stockpile weapons, that he and some others were behind the labor strikes. One even testified that Puey once said that a left-wing labor leader "was a son to [Puey's vice-rector] who was my son, therefore [the labor leader] was my grandson."[20] Another said that anyone who opposed Nawaphon must be Yuan. One said that it was good that the October 6 incident had occurred because it had stopped the communists and restored peace to the country.[21] They signed their names to all these statements. Given the overwhelming anticommunist fever of the times, the language and rhetoric in which they expressed their views and false information were probably fairly typical.

Witness no. 141 probably epitomized the nearly complete blending of individual memory and the collective narrative of the right wing in those days. She was a food provider at a canteen in TU that was close to the river but some distance from Sanamluang and the soccer field. Despite that, she claimed to be able to move around the campus rather freely and that she had witnessed several actions around the campus that morning, including the ones that occurred near Sanamluang. She testified that she heard the police tell people to leave the campus, but "a guy in long hair like a Hippy stayed at the gate to attack, kick, beat people who wanted to leave," that she saw a protester who tried to escape get shot in the water by students, that she wanted to get out too but was blocked by students. She saw students fire at the police who waved a white flag trying to negotiate a ceasefire, but did not see the police fire any shots. The students' security staff then ordered her and other people at the canteen to move into a room on the upper floor. They took the valuables from people, including 18,000 baht in cash from her. When she refused, they slapped her in the face and injured her left eye. She saw a number of students take three boxes full of hand grenades, six to seven handguns, and bags full of documents to hide them near her food stand.

Figure 4. Dr. Puey Ungphakorn. © Peter Ungphakorn. Reprinted with permission.

One of them threatened her not to tell anyone or she could be dead. She identified one student from the photos of the arrested as provided by the police. She insisted that she remembered others as well but whose photos were not among the ones she saw.

The testimony of witness no. 141, however, was undercut by witness no. 142, another food provider who was with no. 141 most of the time. Witness no. 142's testimony was a far more plausible account of the same happenings, without embellishments from the right-wing collective narrative. Simply, she tried to get out via one gate but met students who said she should not do so because they could not guarantee her safety. She then returned to the food stand without venturing anywhere else, let alone near Sanamluang on the other side of campus. Given the sound of heavy fire from the soccer field, she and others hid in a room upstairs. She saw two students hide weapons, and they threatened her not to tell anyone. She identified the same student as witness no.141 did.[22] That was all. No announcement by police. She witnessed no one killed by students in the water or anywhere else. She did not witness the shooting of police with a white flag who tried to negotiate with students. This action was told by a police officer via Yan Kro that morning and reported by a few dailies subsequently. If it was true, it took place near Sanamluang.[23] It was likely that witness no. 141 picked up the heroic story of the police later and incorporated it into her memories as well. The shooting, killing, and brutality by students with heavy weapons such as boxes of grenades could have been added to make it fit the collective memory during the months after the massacre.

Similar suspicious additions also appeared in the purported eyewitness accounts, for example, of witnesses nos. 109, 219, and 220, whom I met and interviewed in the 2000s. Only witness no. 219 could recall a few of the actions he had claimed to witness, far fewer than those in his sworn statement. Witness no. 220 confirmed that he had witnessed one hanging but insisted that he did not see much else because he was mostly at the fringe of the action. Witness no. 109 repeatedly insisted that he had observed the scene from afar and did not witness any actual event. Both 109 and 220 denied that they ever gave testimony to the police afterward. Perhaps such an ugly episode is not worth remembering. Perhaps they were truly on the fringe. Their individual memories were affected by what they learned from the media and the state's propaganda in the days that followed. They made their own memories fit the collective one to enhance their esteem as active participants in a historic event. Thus the collective memory was not a compilation of individual ones. Instead, it was a template through which individual memories could be remembered and communicated. If it were otherwise, memories that contradicted the conventional account would be deemed too idiosyncratic and negligible to be believed.

VENGEANCE FOR THE BRUTAL CARNAGE

The victims, their sympathizers, and the critics of the state naturally did not subscribe to the right-wing narrative and collective memory of the massacre. To them, October 6 could not be viewed as anything but a brutal crime by the Thai state. It was the day that, as the writer Wat Wanlayangkul put it, "the Wolf devoured the Lambs."[24] Under the repressive conditions after the massacre, how could they cope with their memories of the event? How could they deal with the anti-communist environment from which their memories dissented? Was there an alternative collective memory in which they could take refuge? How could the dissenting memories survive individually? The radicals, their sympathizers, other victims including the relatives of the dead, found their different ways to mourn and to remember, from joining the communists to living on with their isolated memories. The conditions of the post-massacre era also marked the beginning of these dissenting memories, which lasted for decades to come.

The reign of terror continued after the killing that morning. More radical students who were not at TU that night were arrested afterward, mostly at home. The police interrogated many families and searched many homes afterward, even the ones of those who died.[25] Most universities were closed for a few weeks and TU was closed for a month and a half.[26] Left-leaning publications were considered communist, and in that atmosphere the notion of the "left" expanded to include most liberal political and critical publications and even academic textbooks. In thousands of households around the country, people destroyed or burned their books. Sulak Sivaraksa, a prominent social critic who owned a book store, estimated that about a hundred thousand books were destroyed at his store and warehouse alone.[27] Even a nonradical victim, such as Sanphasiri, who broadcast the brutality, suffered from the massacre simply because of his professionalism, becoming persona non grata and went bankrupt trying to defend himself from false charges. He even considered committing suicide.[28]

A few days after the initial interrogation, the police searched my home as well. They brought me home in disguise, allegedly to protect me from the angry crowd who might recognize and attack me. Given that Ngao and I were in prison as ringleaders, my siblings were sent away from home to stay with various relatives for months after the massacre. This was typical for many, perhaps most, families of college activists, whether radical or not. Those parents were trying to shield their children not only from the police but also from their royalist neighbors. The anticommunist hysteria provided fertile ground for the proliferation of vigilantism. Like many others, my parents became targets of insults from neighbors for raising communists: college activists had become communist suspects.[29]

For the radical youths who were the direct targets of the suppression, the massacre was a critical turning point. Their stories, one after another, repeat almost the same sentiments—extreme grief and fear. The brutal killings and the loss of their friends were indescribably shocking to them. Feeling threatened, being followed or watched by the authorities, they were afraid of meeting one another even on campus, let alone outside it. Fear spread to all. Unsurprisingly, many felt vengeful. How could they return to school again or live a normal life in a situation that was so severely repressive, where they were considered enemies of the nation? To thousands of these radicals, the massacre proved that the CPT was correct—that the ruling class, the Thai state, the imperialists, the feudalists, the capitalists, and the junta were so brutal that they would kill people who fought for democracy and for a better society, and that peaceful struggle within urban areas had limitations. Armed struggle in the countryside, as advocated by the Maoist CPT was, they felt, definitely the correct alternative.[30]

For a few years before the massacre, the CPT had gained influence over the student movement from top to bottom. The extent of influence and domination of the CPT—whether it could actually direct the decision-making process of the student movement or could only influence their thinking—remains debatable.[31] It is fair to say, however, that the CPT's armed struggle and its rationale was known among the young radicals. In the post-massacre condition, it was not difficult for the CPT to assert itself as an option for them. Only one day after the massacre, on October 7, while three thousand were still in jail and many thousands more were in shock, the CPT issued a statement condemning the Thai state for its crime on October 6. It stated forcefully that armed struggle was the only viable option to combat the barbarous state, and that the CPT was in solidarity with the victims.

> In the areas under the reactionary [government's] control . . . the people's struggle for independence, democracy and a just society will never be extinguished. People will never surrender . . . The "Red" areas in the countryside are trustworthy and offer a strong supporting force.[32]

Perhaps the most impact was from the messages (in writings and via interviews) from the survivors of the massacre.[33] This is especially true of the statements by famous student leaders and public figures who fled to join the CPT, such as those who did on October 14, 1976, only a week after the bloodshed in Bangkok.[34]

> Young Thai people, school children and students had been peacefully struggling within the framework of the constitution and the country's laws . . . [But] our friends . . . had been barbarously terrorized, arrested, detained and killed one after another. . . . Our sincerity received . . . shameless slander. . . . [Our] peaceful methods were rewarded with grenades and hailstorms of bullets. . . .
>
> This is the end of our struggle within the framework of the laws written by the reactionary ruling class . . . The lessons we learned with much blood and many lives clearly point out to us that national independence and democracy cannot be gained by reform in a decadent and unjust society . . . peaceful efforts to create a new progressive state power of our people are impossible. . . . The people's state power can only grow out of the barrel of a gun.[35]

In the weeks and months after the bloodshed, the Voice of People of Thailand, the official broadcast of the CPT, pounded that message daily, including in an important CPT statement on December 1, 1976, the thirty-fourth anniversary of its founding.[36] The CPT called October 6 the "bloodshed incident" (*korani nongluat*), using adjectives such as barbaric (*pa thuan*), cruel (*hot rai*), torturous (*tharun*), and the like. They called the dead victims "the martyrs" (*wirachon*) who sacrificed for the struggle for independence from US imperialism for democracy and a just society. In the CPT's discourse of the massacre, vengeance by arms was explicit and justified. This became a collective memory, a powerful alternative to that of the state.

Despite their youthful age, the radicals faced a decision that would affect the rest of their lives. They were young men and women in their late teens and early twenties with hopeful futures. Most had never thought about making such a momentous decision before. Many recall the moment with similar sentiments—grief, fear, vengefulness, and reluctance to make such a life-changing decision under extreme pressure. Those who decided to go to the jungle were not necessarily committed communists who subscribed to Maoism. In addition to the belief that the CPT would provide a refuge for their radical idealism, the strong drive that led them to embrace the CPT was fear for their lives, revenge for their friends, and their need for a space where they could "cry and condemn the murderous madness as much as I want to."[37] They sought a community where they could embrace their memories of the October 6 massacre.

Sentiments of grief and vengeance are clear in many songs composed by students in the revolutionary zones. Following are the lyrics of a famous one.[38]

From Lanpho to Phuphan

The Dome of Thammasat stands tall in the battle.
It witnessed so much blood and so many lives that have ended.
October 6, our friends've gone.
So furious and bitter as if my heart caught fire.

We fought with bare hands when they raided.
Mad bombs and bullets stormed at us.
It sounded like a dirge announcing the death.
The field was flooded in blood.

They arrested us, killed us, and hunted us to our homes.
They threatened us wherever we went.
Try to endure, but it was unbearable.
Out fight must change . . . go to the mountain.

The embrace of Phuphan gives us a new life.
It is a university of the brave.
We'll be patient in our fight to kick out the dictatorship.
The US gang doesn't have a chance.

We will fight guns with guns.
With the guidance of the Party that shines brightly,
Guerilla fights will lead people to the new dawn.
Workers will eventually rule with dignity.

Today, Lanpho, Thammasat, may be quiet.
It is waiting for the new day.
The day the people's army declares victory.
We will then return to get their blood . . . to clean Lan Pho.

More than a year after the massacre, it was estimated that two to three thousand students had joined the CPT. Not only was the number quite high, but these young men and women were also the intellectual cream of a generation.[39] Thikan is probably correct in saying that "The group that benefited most from the political conditions under Thanin Kraivixian [the post-massacre period] was the Communist Party of Thailand."[40] Had the CPT won the war and Thailand turned socialist, the radicals' memory would have become the dominant collective memory of the massacre; the victims, the national martyrs, and the revenge of the young radicals would have been complete. But that did not happen.

NONRADICAL MEMORIES

Certainly, many young radicals did not join the CPT in the jungle for various reasons such as family, health, and so on. Many of them stayed to carry on the underground operation in urban areas after the massacre. Equally significant were the many student activists and the sympathizing public who did not even consider the jungles or the armed struggle an option because they did not subscribe to the CPT's ideology or methods.[41] They supported various radical causes, but their politics and activism were that of progressive liberal youth in the context of conservative Thai society, no more and no less. Nonetheless, they were in a movement that was undeniably under the strong influence, even ideological hegemony, of the CPT, which provided these disgruntled youths with the Maoist ideology and discourse to comprehend and articulate their views and idealism. Their turn to radicalism during those years was the result of a conjunction of factors that did not last long. These youths were as leftist as anyone in their late teens and early twenties can be, that is, they turned left fast but probably not deeply. They were "outsized" radicals, so to speak.[42]

The young radical movement was in fact ideologically diverse.[43] People of many other ideologies and convictions were influenced by the CPT's Maoism to various degrees. In the highly conservative context of Thailand, the liberal left and the committed Maoists were mixed. The movement was a refuge even for some radical conservatives, who were discontented with Thailand under the influence of the decadent American and Western culture, but who, given their young age, could not articulate their views on their own terms and therefore channeled their dissatisfaction by taking refuge under the Maoist umbrella. After all, the CPT's Maoism was also culturally conservative in many respects, such as anti-West nationalism and patriarchal heterosexism. Individuals in the movement were not invariably committed Maoists.

The view of the massacre held by nonradicals differed from both the state's narrative and the CPT's. Their collective memory was similar to the CPT's to some extent in the characterization of the incident as brutal killings. But it differed fundamentally in regard to the desire for revenge and the attitude toward armed struggle as a viable alternative. The nonradical collective memory was not as prominent, though it is not difficult to find either. For example, the memoir of a TU student describes her extreme fear and grief over the massacre: "I wish I could close my eyes and ignore the world," and the sad, scary, and grim atmosphere at TU under the control of the armed police for months after it reopened. She was with her close friend when he contemplated going to the jungle. She writes, "I understood what he meant, although I wished he would stay here with friends. . . . I told myself that I understand [her friend] but. . . . I was too weak and too young." She knew where they went and what they chose to do, "even though such action remains a mystery to me." "The communists," she writes, "are my dear friends, my respected professors, and many good people around me." She then describes at length many political activities in the post-massacre period that she decided to join in order to help revive the student's political activism.[44]

Among the radicals during the 1973 to 1976 period were the relatively influential Buddhists, who never subscribed to Maoism or the idea of armed struggle, but who advocated for radical spiritual changes including nonviolence. Loosely speaking, Thailand's radical Buddhist movement has been identified with a famous Buddhist social critic and writer-publisher, Sulak Sivaraksa. His ideas and social activism are the subject of several studies.[45] He has been influential among young activists from the late 1960s to the present day. Many radical leftists of the mid-1970s, including me, were initially politicized under Sulak's influence before turning left. Many remain committed and active in Buddhist clubs in universities and in civic groups for various social justice causes. They agreed with the leftists on the broad agenda for political and social changes for the poor and the oppressed, but disagreed on what actions to take.[46] In 1976, they were active in the protest against Thanom's return. Clearly, their memory of that morning was different from that of the leftist radicals. I discuss their view at length in chapter 7, regarding the Buddhist approach to the atrocity.

Beyond the radical students, the professional intellectuals—academics, journalists and publishers—were most affected by the massacre because they were also active participants and beneficiaries of the intellectual bloom between 1973 and 1976. The left-leaning liberal newspapers and news magazines, namely, *Prachathippatai*, *Prachachat*, and *Chatturat*, were shut down indefinitely on October 6. Hundreds of books, including several academic texts, were banned. Some academics and journalists were arrested, hunted down, interrogated, and publicly denounced as communists. Some who were active and prominent in the radical movement and who were part of the CPT's network before the massacre thus faced the same fate as radical students and also went to join the CPT in the jungle. Most, however, were neither part of the CPT's network nor subscribers to its ideology. Quite a number of them went into exile during the repressive year after the massacre. A few never returned. Unarguably, the best-known case was that of Puey, the rector of TU mentioned earlier. Although his actual experience on October 6 was unique, it is representative of the views and memories of the October 6 massacre among intellectuals.

As a former governor of the Bank of Thailand and a technocrat, Puey was widely and highly respected for his integrity. As an academic, he was known for his center-left views in a conservative country dominated by the military and the royalists. After the popular uprising in 1973, he was in 1974 the first rector of TU elected by faculty and students. During those tumultuous years, TU became known as the center of radical activism—hosting public forums, leftist publications, protests and demonstrations, even sheltering protesting peasants and workers. In fact, Puey faced tremendous pressure both from the radical students who treated him as part of the establishment, and the political right wing, who believed that he was a communist and a mastermind of the radical movement. This was the genesis of the nonsensical but widespread rumors that, for example, TU had stockpiled heavy weapons or built a tunnel underneath the river in preparation for a communist insurrection. He had been a target of military smear propaganda long before the massacre.

On October 4, during the students' skit about the hanging of two labor activists, the TU student union also called for the postponement of the examination period. Puey personally negotiated with the activists to end the protest out of respect for those who wanted to take the exam. Yet he was accused of being behind the lèse majesté skit. On the morning of October 6, according to his memoir, he was at a meeting outside TU. Unable to intervene and devastated by the carnage, he tendered his resignation. Meanwhile, the Yan Kro broadcast urged people to find him and punish him for being behind the communist plot to overthrow the monarchy. For safety, he decided to leave the country. At the airport, Village Scouts gathered calling for his head, so to speak. Salang Bunnak, a well-known right-wing figure and a police commander who had led his force into TU in the morning, showed up and confronted Puey, yanking the phone from his hand while he was talking and shouting at him. Puey was detained at the airport for three hours before an order from "the superior" permitted him to let him leave the country.[47]

For almost a year after the massacre, Puey actively campaigned to tell the world about the massacre.[48] His account of the massacre and the coup, written in exile on October 28, 1976, but circulated among his colleagues and followers in Thailand, was influential for several decades, thanks to the credibility of the author and to the lack of other critical accounts during the first few years after the massacre.[49] His writings, interviews, public forums, and testimony to the Subcommittee on International Organization of the Committee on International Relations of the US House of Representatives—were probably the most influential counternarrative to that of the state at a time when alternative accounts were either censored or circulated only underground.[50] To Puey, and likely to other nonradical intellectuals as well, the tumultuous years between 1973 and 1976 were the result of problems that had compounded during the long military rule since 1947. The student movement was not to blame for those problems. The blame more appropriately should go to those who had lost power, benefits, and privileges after the uprising in 1973, who then tried to rescind the democratic forces by any methods, including negative propaganda and violent measures. The student movement was an important democratic force, in his view, but students tended to be arrogant, inexperienced, and naïve. They fought every issue everywhere all the time, created enemies across every social class, and antagonized too many government agencies. They thought that the public was always on their side, but they were wrong because they had caused considerable political fatigue. Puey expressed understanding for the radicals who had joined the CPT, for the peaceful option of working within a democratic system had been shut down.[51]

In his view, the massacre was definitely not a heroic triumph over the communists but the opposite, because the number and quality of people who joined the CPT after the massacre was unprecedented in the party's history.[52] Puey's view was not leftist either. Although he expressed sympathy for students, he did not show even slight sympathy or support for the CPT, its ideology, narrative, or armed struggle. He was not overly ideological, seeing Vietnamese communists or US imperialists around every corner. Ideological jargon was nonexistent in his discourse. His prose is straightforward and almost rhetoric-free. His most ideological writing, the short essay "From Womb to Tomb," in my opinion expresses the basic social democratic ideal.[53] Decades later, for many reasons discussed in later chapters, he has become one of the most recognized victims. His views represent the collective memory of the massacre shared by many people, including former radicals who became disillusioned with the CPT.

SILENT GRIEF, FOREVER FEAR

Perhaps the most widely known writing that reflects a nonradical but sympathetic view of the radical students was the short story by Atsiri Thammachote, "Khunthong Will Return at Dawn" (*Khunthong chao cha klapma mua fasang*), which was first published in the reputed weekly news magazine *Sayamrath Sapda Wichan* (Sayamrath Weekly) in September 1977, under the repressive regime of Thanin Kraivixian.[54] It is the story of Mother, who keeps waiting at the dawn of every new day, looking forward to the return of her son, Khunthong.

The story tells us that he left without telling anyone on the day the incident occurred in the rainy season last year, with only one bag on his shoulder. He wept all the time. Mother knows he was angry, but she does not know at whom. She still wonders why he decided to leave the comfort of home to become an outlaw. But she is confident that Khunthong will return home one day and she will be ready to greet him. Even though he does not show up this morning, he will return.[55] This is obviously not the voice and memory of a radical but one of their sympathizers, who were waiting for the "new day." The short story was widely talked about when it first appeared. I recall it as a piece of exciting "news" delivered to us in the prison by our many visitors at that time. It probably represented a voice and collective memory that a large number of people shared but could not express at the time. Although both Mother and Khunthong were fictional, the story represented shared sentiments and memories that were all the more truthful because of the thousands of real mothers and real Khunthongs who could not speak out.

Although those nonfictional mothers waited eagerly for their children to come home, many in fact lost them that morning. They were also victims of the massacre by their association with the victims. These extended victims coped with their losses in different ways suitable to their individual conditions. One of the common, noticeable dispositions they shared was their silence in isolation due to the extreme grief and fear that overwhelmed them in the wake of the massacre. For many, grief and fear have still not dissipated.[56]

The grief of these parents and relatives was due not only to their senseless and unexpected loss, but also to how their children died and to the public response to their deaths. The degradation of their children to subhuman must be incomprehensibly cruel for them.[57] Unlike the typical practice among the ordinary Thais, who would keep the corpse for only a short period and then cremate it, some families were reluctant to cremate their children to avoid detection, or chose to keep their bodies quietly for more than a year, or to bury instead of cremating the body.[58] Moreover, in the wake of the massacre, according to almost every family, neighbors and ordinary people looked down on them, harassed them, accusing them of raising communists or of themselves being communists.[59] Not only were their children's deaths denied honor, they were also stigmatized for being the enemies of the nation. The brother of one victim told of going to the district officer to remove the name of the victim from his household registration. There, he met a relative of another victim. With the death certificates in their hands, they stood silent. They said nothing to one another, did not even share their grief. They realized that their loved ones had been branded "bad people" in the eyes of the public. They were not sure how people around them might react to the relatives of "bad people" from TU.[60] They retreated to their homes, to silence and isolation.

The departure of their loved ones was never clarified. No investigation was held, let alone justice dispensed. Worse than having no closure, the victims and their families were stigmatized. Most of these extended victims lived on quietly, trying not to let people know they were relatives of the massacre victims because they could be doubly victimized. It was therefore extremely difficult for most of them to come to terms with their loss. Most admitted that they have not been able to do so even decades later. Most did not attend any of the commemorations that have taken place every year since 1996. But they never forget either. Most continue to make merit for the massacre victims regularly, even every year, but they do so quietly and in isolation.[61] They do not seek a collective memory or a public commemoration.

Nevertheless, the silence of these extended victims actually reflects the various ways they individually cope with their traumatic memories. In most cases, silence was not a path to forgetting. Rather, it was a different way to keep the memories of their loved ones alive. Take the case of the family of Suphon Phan. Before 1976, Suphon was a conscripted soldier and indoctrinated to a "hate the students" mentality. His brother, Somtat, persuaded him to attend some student demonstrations and hear what they had to say. Suphon changed. Suphon was shot while driving the injured to the hospital in his van on October 6. A few days later, Suphon's mother, his elder sister, and Somtat, searched the hospitals to find him. When the mother found her son's body at a hospital, she lamented until she fainted. After a quiet cremation attended only by family members, according to Somtat, his mother still wept, alone, every day, for months. She gradually came to terms with the loss. As it turns out, Somtat himself was perhaps most affected by Suphon's death. He felt it was his guilt because had he not convinced Suphon to open his mind to the students, his brother would not have died, and his mother and the whole family would not have hurt. He never went close to any political activity again and never attended a commemoration. His younger sister, who was close to Suphon, however, still honors her dead brother regularly.[62] In this case, we can observe that the seemingly similar silence of three people in the same family who suffered the same loss is in fact the expression of different individual ways of coping with trauma.

Nonetheless, not every grieving mother stays in isolated silence. Lek Witthayaporn, mother of Manu, has been active in seeking out a community of shared grief. During the October 6 trial in 1977 and 1978, Lek attended the trial regularly. Her son was not on trial but she met families of the arrested ones in court. We may say that she joined the families of other victims to support the defendants who were friends of her son. She said in 1996 that she was very sad, of course, but she was proud of her son for who he was and what he tried to do. She wanted to fight until Thai society remembers the October 6 victims. In fact, she wanted to sue whoever caused her son's death, but could not find relatives willing to join her effort.[63]

Lek was a member of the only two families of the victims who have appeared regularly at the commemoration since 1996. A few others attended occasionally but did so quietly, never letting people know that they were relatives of the victims. It is not surprising that they would not join Lek in a lawsuit against the perpetrators. In 2017, when the Documentation of October 6 project contacted them for interviews, many declined. Apart from being hurt by their loss, they remain fearful. They do not want people to know that they were parents or relatives of the victims. Not only has the loss remained an open wound, but the stigma too remains in place. Forty years later, in 2017, many of them characterize the massacre as a sensitive (*la-iat-on*) issue and do not want to get involved in any way. It is not difficult to understand the reasons for their fear and what makes the issue still sensitive after forty years. The state's narrative of the massacre and the stigma it produced, and the fact that the two most sacred institutions in the land—the palace and the Buddhist *sangha*—had their fingerprints on the horrific events, are the two factors that continue to make the massacre a sensitive subject for public discussion.

Differences in memories of the massacre reflect the individual situations among the victors and the different kinds of victims. These differences and nuances were amplified by changing politics and changes in their lives in the following decades. As we shall see, the state's memory was so untruthful that it gradually lost credibility. People no longer believe it in Thailand, especially since the Cold War

ended in the early 1980s. Despite that, as subsequent chapters explain, its effects and legacy remain powerful and intimidating to
many today, bringing fear and silence among relatives and no doubt
the general public as well. Hence, silence reigns among these extended
victims.

Chapter 4

THE TRIAL AND THE BEGINNING
OF SILENCE

Most of the three thousand people who were arrested from Thammasat University were released on bail in the first week after the police interrogations. I remember that advice circulated in the prison about how to answer the police interrogations—to tell the police that we had gone into TU for free music and entertainment or that we had followed friends there. We all disclaimed political ideology or any active role in the demonstration and the radical movement.[1] Of course, about two dozen of the alleged ringleaders whose names were on the police list were denied bail. After a month, a few hundred remained because no one had bailed them out or they were too poor. Five months after the arrests, the police dropped all the charges for most people who were originally arrested, excepting the two dozen ringleaders, who included my brother and myself.[2] On the basis of National Administrative Reform Council (NARC) Order no. 1, all the cases considered a threat to national security, including the suspects from the October 6 incident, were under the jurisdiction of the military court, even if they were civilians. In addition, thanks to the Communist Act at the time, the police could keep suspected communists, including in this case the ringleaders, in custody for a year without charge or trial, rather than the eighty-four days applicable to any other crime. Six of the alleged ringleaders were put in Bangkhwang, the facility for serious criminals. The women were held at the women's prison. The rest, myself and my brother included, were at the Bangkhen prison.

In mid-August 1977, five of the alleged ringleaders, including my brother, were released after the police decided to drop the charges against them. The remaining eighteen, including myself, were formally charged on August 25 and appeared in military court for the first time on September 5, 1977, almost a year after being arrested.[3] The ten charges were revolt, treason, communist activities, assembling to use force that harms the public, killing policemen, possession of illegal weapons and military-grade ammunition, and more. The six who were arrested on the way to meet Seni were also charged with lèse majesté for their alleged involvement with the mock hanging of the crown prince.[4] Under the law of the military court at the time, we could not have a lawyer to represent us and we had no right to appeal. We were on our own. We, the prisoners, quipped that had we been penalized to the maximum for each charge, each of us would have been executed almost a dozen times in addition to receiving several life sentences. Another student took part in the skit but was not at TU that night. He was arrested after the massacre and put on a separate but related trial for only one charge—lèse majesté. The trial was called in Thai the October 6 trial (*khadi hok tula*) and was known worldwide as the Bangkok 18 or Bangkok 18+1 case.

This chapter describes the political changes during 1977 and 1978 that affected the October 6 trial and the memory of the massacre, and how the trial and memories of the massacre in turn stimulated more political change. The far-right royalist government became a major liability in the anticommunist efforts, which faced an unprecedented challenge from the growing Communist Party of Thailand (CPT). The coup in October 1977 marked a significant shift from the far right not only in national politics but also in the country's anticommunist strategy. Meanwhile, the October 6 trial was full of ironies that had unexpected impacts. Above all, it turned into a public testament of the massacre whose real perpetrators were not on trial. The amnesty of the Bangkok 18+1 on September 16, 1978, marked the fall of the anticommunist triumphalist discourse in public sphere. Yet it did not lead to the recognition of the victims' voices or memories. Instead, it marked the beginning of silence for the sake of reconciliation.

IN THE CAGE

The Bangkhen prison was officially not a prison per se. It was one building within the compound of the police training school, manned by police officers, that was used to detain illegal immigrants who were waiting for deportation to their home countries. For reasons beyond the scope of this book, most of the detainees had been waiting there for decades. Many had aged and died there because deportation was a remote possibility. It was a place of forgotten aliens, unrecognized even by the official prison system. Once the three thousands captives from TU joined these forgotten and ignored, the unofficial prison was officially turned into a "temporary" prison. (Since then, it has housed subsequent generations of political detainees.)

The conditions behind bars at Bangkhen reflected the changing political situations outside the prison. On October 6, 1976, when we got off the bus that had transported us from TU, we were living punching bags for the police, who lined up from the bus to the building entrance. In the first few days, before most people were released on bail, every cell was incredibly crowded and unsanitary. More than fifty people were confined in the three meter by five meter cell with me. The cell had a single open lavatory. It was horribly inhumane, perhaps a continuation of how we were treated at TU. In the immediate period after the massacre, angry police guards treated us as though we were the communist enemies of the country, the devils who had killed policemen. Their angry outbursts, beating and kicking at prisoners as if punching bags, were common. We, the ringleaders, thought that this was the end of our lives. We survived day by day. Time no longer mattered.

After the majority of the detainees were released in the first few weeks, we had more space, but conditions were still far from humane. During the first few months, angry police guards still called some detainees out from their cells at night from time to time for beatings.[5] A dozen of us ringleaders were put together in two cells separated from other prisoners because we were considered dangerous. We were denied visits for several months, so our cells remained locked day and night. Only the commander of the prison had the keys, so we were at least spared the guards' brutality. At one point, the police claimed that they had uncovered a plot for a prison riot. We the ringleaders were suspected and moved to another cell, where we were given only a limited amount of water each week. After the initial anticommunist hysteria had died down, life in the prison became quiet, even boring given that no reading or writing materials were allowed.

The failed coup in March 1977 brought sudden changes in the prison. Some of the coup makers joined us at Bangkhen. Most of them were rich and powerful. A few were famous public figures who were treated according to their high social status. The police even allowed the privileged detainees to bring amenities to their cells, even their own mattresses. We received windfalls, including a larger cell and more relaxed restrictions. The police allowed us to roam around on the same floor outside the cells in the daytime and gave us one hour every day for exercise in the open air on the roof-deck of the building. We were allowed weekly visitors, who could bring us outside food, far better than the prison food, and books such as romance novels and cartoons. In this more relaxed atmosphere, we befriended police officers, many of whom were part-time students to whom we offered tutorials. An experienced police sergeant at the prison explained to us candidly that the failed coup signaled a conflict within the military and the possibility that the ruling regime would be short lived. Political changes might come soon and, he joked, some of us might become their bosses in the future. Life in the cage became more humane.

After the coup in October 1977 that ended the royalist regime of Thanin Kraivixian, the political winds blew in our favor. The October 6 trial caught public attention domestically and internationally. Life in prison became much better during the second year. The weekly (and daily) visitor time was generous. Restrictions on outside food and reading materials were fewer or nonexistent. We subscribed to a few daily newspapers. We wrote letters to friends and later some essays and articles for publication as well.[6] We even convinced a police officer to bring in a small transistor radio for us. Our cell door was locked only at night, so we could exercise freely on the roof-deck and dry our clothes under the sun.

The sergeant had been right.

THE FALL OF THE RIGHT-WING ROYALIST REGIME

The Thanin government represented the extreme political far right at the time. A judge who rose to the Supreme Court before 1976, Thanin was a staunch royalist and an anticommunist ideologue who had written several books on the dangers of communism to Thailand and appeared regularly on an infamous anticommunist television program before the massacre. As mentioned in chapter 2, when the would-be coup leader raised the idea of a coup to King Bhumibol at a private audience in February 1976, the king hinted at Thanin for prime minister after the coup. After Thanin was toppled from power in 1977, the king appointed him to the Privy Council immediately, where he remained until the king died in 2016. Many key members of Thanin's government were notorious for their far-right, royalist ideology. Among them, the best known was Samak Sundaravej, a demagogue who was highly popular among right-wing elements for his blunt, provocative retorts to the radicals. He was rewarded by the coup regime with the powerful position of interior minister. Many critics believe that he played an important role in the massacre, though he has persistently denied it. Throughout his long political career, including a brief stint as prime minister in 2008, Samak never shied away from boasting about his right-wing political views and from making provocative remarks about the massacre, even as late as 2008.

Thanin's right-wing ideology and authoritarian rule were suffocating, for example, the twenty-year plan to return to democracy, the government's daily newspaper so full of propaganda, the anticommunist propaganda aired on television and radio and in print, and the many social restrictions and public mandates in everyday life that accorded to royalist conservative ideology. The government quickly became unpopular. Taking advantage of this sentiment, and given the rift within the military, a coup was attempted in March 1977. Although it was put out down swiftly, popular discontent with the far-right government continued, intensifying from mockery to hatred. Moreover, in the post-massacre conditions in which thousands of students, who had a large number of sympathizers, had joined the CPT, the far-right anticommunist politics were like fuel on a blazing fire. As Mallet noted with supporting statistics, "armed clashes have become more frequent as the guerrillas take bolder measures as measured by the significant rise in the death tolls of the [government] forces."[7] Given these factors, plus Thanin's growing alienation from the NARC, due partly to his confidence in the palace's support, another military putsch finally put an end to the far-right government that October.

Although the coup makers, led by General Kriangsak Chomanan, were mostly the same key members of the NARC, they were not as conservative or royalist as Thanin. Probably driven in part by the concern that they were losing ground to the CPT, several early measures and policies of the new regime were to remove the repressive measures that Thanin had put in place. One of the new regime's early orders was to amend the law of the military court to allow the accused to be represented by a lawyer.[8] Although the order did not mention the October 6 trial, we were without question the first beneficiaries of the order. The trial had enormous implications for many political stakeholders at the time, not merely for the country's stature in the international community, but also for the country's future in regard to the fight against communism and the prospects for democracy.

The Bangkok 18 Case

By the time the Bangkok 18 were charged in August 1977, dissatisfaction with the Thanin government had intensified. The hysteria against the radicals and communists had subsided, though the authoritarian NARC was still in control and fear of communism remained. The skirmishes with the CPT became a staple of everyday news. Stories and news about students in the jungles also appeared occasionally in public, but many more circulated informally on campuses and in the homes of thousands of educated families. The news of serious charges leveled at young students in their late teens and early twenties by the military court was a major event domestically and reported internationally as well. In the eyes of the world, the trial was cruel because it was a political trial of victims who had survived a brutal massacre. A week later, two petitions to the government regarding the October 6 trial were submitted by the Catholic community in Thailand, relaying the concerns of the international community. They suggested that the government move the trial from the military to a civilian court and urged the government to release us on bail.[9] Many more petitions followed from domestic as well as international groups.

The start of the trial in military court on September 5, 1977, opened up a space for public discourse. It was the first public political gathering since the massacre. The court room (inside the compound of the Defense Ministry) was crowded with journalists and ordinary observers; hundreds, perhaps thousands, more people flocked outside along the road into the ministry.[10] It appeared that even the Thanin government did not anticipate the crowd (neither did we, the prisoners) given that the NARC's ban on political gatherings was still in place. More ironies were to come because under both the 1976 and 1977 coup regimes political gatherings were forbidden but court attendance was allowed. After their first court appearance, the defendants requested that the court find a larger room at an accessible location to accommodate the public. By that time, the new government was in power. In the new political atmosphere, the court agreed, moving the trial to another military compound on the outskirts of Bangkok to a significantly larger room in a building surrounded by an open space that could accommodate hundreds of people.[11] Moreover, after the first appearance, many people, including Seni, the prime minister in 1976, began to speak out. The massacre, already a year old, was once again in the media, though references to it remained ambiguous and cryptic.

Many civic organizations called for justice at the October 6 trial. The most significant one was a petition by 632 people, many of whom were prominent public figures from various professions, organized by Buddhist activists on October 26, 1977. Rather than calling for a civilian court for the Bangkok 18, the petition called for the amnesty of all political prisoners, including the Bangkok 18 and hundreds of those who had been detained without charge or trial under the Thanin government for being, in its terms, "Persons who are Endangering Society."[12] The amnesty, it argued, was necessary for reconciliation of the country, which had been torn by serious conflicts and division for some time that had worsened under the Thanin regime. In addition, in late November 1977, the new coup regime announced an amnesty for all those involved in the March 1977 abortive coup. This prompted many more calls and petitions urging the government to do the same for the Bangkok 18 and other political prisoners.[13] Most of them cited common reasons, namely, national unity and reconciliation. The exhausted public seemed willing to let bygones be bygones.

Apart from the changing conditions of domestic politics, many international human rights organizations also took up the Bangkok 18 case. Further, several foreign governments expressed their concerns to the Thai government and sent representatives to attend the trial. In response to this attention, the government tread more carefully, wanting to avoid being seen as barbaric. In addition to allowing lawyers to represent us, the six of us from Bangkhwang no longer had to come to court in chains as if we were serious criminals. In early 1978, the Carter administration, which had notified the Thai government of its attention to the case since mid-1977, began to show stronger interest in the trial.[14] Staff from the US Embassy made regular appearances at the trial, and a special representative from Washington discussed the issue with the Thai government and visited the detainees in person (another huge factor in the improved conditions at the prison). The world's watchful eyes remained on the Bangkok 18 throughout the trial.

THE TRIAL AND ITS IRONIES

The ten charges in the indictment were drawn from specific actions. The first was communist activities, advocating the violent overthrow of the Thai state—the government, economy, and social institutions— while propagating the glory of the communist countries, particularly the People's Republic of China. The second was lèse majesté in the mock hanging of the crown prince. Third, the accused were charged in the deaths of two policemen and injuring a dozen more. The death of forty protesters in the same incident was not mentioned.[15] The indictment also did not mention the demonstration or gathering at Thammasat, let alone any hint of a massacre. The defendants, of course, denied all charges.[16] We argued at length that we were "democratic rebels against dictatorship," that the skit had nothing to do with the crown prince, and that we were victims, not perpetrators, of the "massacre" (*kan lom sanghan mu*). "The October 6 incident was a massacre . . . a most cruel and barbaric one, unprecedented in Thai history . . . [followed by] the arrests of the survivors," we declared.[17]

The prosecutor planned to call a total of eighty-two witnesses for the trial. Forty-four were police officers: nineteen from the local district of the Metropolitan police where TU was located, four from other districts, nine of the so-called riot police, eight Border Patrol Police (BPP), two from the Crime Suppression Unit, and two from the Special Branch or the political police. Fourteen were professors and lecturers from TU, including several right-wing ones. The remainder included four professors from other universities, two leaders of labor organizations, an expert from the Internal Security Operation Command (ISOC), three reporters, former Prime Minister Seni Pramoj and another minister from his government, and five medical examiners from various hospitals. Two witnesses were leftist activists who, based on their statements to the police in late 1976, would testify against the radicals.[18] During the twenty-nine court hearings between January 23 and 14 September 1978, only eleven appeared and testified in court: two labor leaders, the ISOC expert, a political police officer who kept records of the activities of radical students between 1973 and 1976, and members of the first police group that raided TU on October 6, all of whom appeared on TV5 that morning, including Colonel Salang Bunnak and two BPP officers.[19]

Only in rare instances did these witnesses mention any of the defendants. None of them recognized the defendants, except perhaps Sutham Sangprathum, the National Student Center of Thailand leader whose name frequently appeared in the daily media before the massacre. The police witnesses recounted how they had been attacked but said nothing specific about any of the defendants. Even the political officer who collected materials about student activities was unable to explain unambiguously which acts, talks, books or pamphlets violated the anticommunist law, let alone whether any of the defendants had participated in such acts. In fact, we learned how poorly the police spies did their job. Their notes from several public forums were incomprehensible, names were unrecognizable. Their records showed how superficial, disorganized, and perhaps unprepared the political officer was—making them more frightening rather than less so. On the other hand, given that most of the police witnesses had been in action that morning, their testimony was informative; we learned concrete details about what had happened. We learned, for example, that the BPP received the order to deploy during the night, many hours before the heavy shooting began. We saw in court many photos of the incident for the first time because they had been censored at the time. Many accounts that circulated informally or underground among the radical students were related in court and recorded by the judge. Most important, what we heard in the courtroom was also heard by the hundreds of people outside, as well as the public at large, who could read the same details the next morning because the testimony was reported by the media throughout the trial. Further comments and discussions about the testimony appeared regularly in the dailies and news magazines for many months in 1978. When witnesses described some of the photos of the heinous acts with remarks like "these were utterly cruel acts, incredibly horrifying acts," the public heard and read about them too.[20]

Although we, the prisoners, did not anticipate our release any time in the near future, as the trial slowly dragged on, with seventy more witnesses yet to testify, we became much more relaxed. In my view, the October 6 trial was an ironic commentary on Thailand's political conditions at the time in three respects. First, although the ban on political gathering had been in place since the coup in 1976 and continued after the 1977 coup, the gathering at the court was a stark exception. Thanks probably to the international pressures against a secret venue, the trial was open to the public in a space where hundreds of people could gather legally weekly or twice weekly. Although the location of the court house was not convenient (inside a military compound outside Bangkok that offered poor public transportation), people attended in large numbers. Most stayed in tents outside, enjoying the open political discussions that were prohibited elsewhere. It was safe too, given the military protection from the right-wing militants.

Second, given the fear of repercussions and the post-massacre repression, the October 6 incident was a highly sensitive topic and seldom discussed in public at the time. The trial became an occasion in which the incident was discussed legally, publicly, in great detail, and at great length. It was more informative than any other sources at the time and often critical of the state. Unlike the underground network of the radicals, the military court provided an open public sphere for discourse about the massacre that extended far beyond the courtroom due to media coverage of the trial.

Third, and most important, the October 6 trial became a public trial of the perpetrators of the massacre. Even though none of them was charged, and the massacre was not even mentioned in the indictment, the trial exposed some shocking facts, implicated unidentified perpetrators, and hinted at the narrative of the victims. Although court procedures were not suited to uncover a comprehensible narrative, the testimony suggested a counternarrative. It also confirmed the growing public perception that the state's narrative was untruthful, that the entire trial of the Bangkok 18 was unfair and evidence of injustice, that unspeakable wrongdoing had been committed by somebody else.[21] The more sympathy that arose for the Bangkok 18, the stronger the implication that the real perpetrators were elsewhere, and curiosity all built to know what actually happened and who did it on the morning of Wednesday, October 6, 1976.

"Had the defense witnesses," Tyrell Haberkorn writes, "given testimony, the prosecution, and the repressive parts of the state behind it, may have had a great deal to fear. The actual events of the morning of 6 October . . . would have been revealed."[22] In fact, the trial had not yet revealed much. Only eleven of the eighty-two witnesses for the prosecution had testified. But the ironies of the trial were probably too troubling and perhaps too dangerous to those in power, almost all of whom could be implicated in the massacre in one way or another.

THE AMNESTY

The idea of an amnesty was first floated in public by the petitions of civic groups. It was reinforced in late 1977 when the government granted amnesty to the prisoners of the abortive coup of March 1977. The defendants of the October trial, many argued, were probably more legitimate candidates for amnesty than the makers of the failed coup. In February 1978, when the second witness was testifying in court, Prime Minister Kriangsak raised the possibility of the amnesty: "If the court decides to punish those eighteen people, the government will be ready to pass an amnesty bill that day."[23] The idea gained momentum again in mid-1978, and it appeared that the government supported it. Then, in less than one week in mid-September, the idea suddenly turned into a draft bill that the legislative body read, revised, and passed in a single day, on September 15: "Amnesty for Those Who Committed Wrongdoing in the Demonstrations at the Thammasat University between 4 and 6 October 1976."[24] Prime Minister Kriangsak emphasized in the legislative council as well as in public that the amnesty was the king's idea and everybody should be grateful to His Majesty's benevolence.[25] The next day, the Bangkok 18 were brought to the military court for the last time to listen to the judge's reading of the amnesty bill. The trial was over. We were freed.

The maneuver for the amnesty was surprising to those of us in prison as well, though we were not kept in the dark as much as the public was. We the prisoners heard the rumor from a journalist a few weeks before it happened. Then, about a week before the bill was passed, the exciting rumor became real when a representative of Kriangsak came to visit us at Bangkhwang and Bangkhen. Phichai Watsanasong was a famous television personality at the time, respected for his knowledge and journalistic expertise in international affairs. But he had been brought to Bangkhen, then later moved to Bangkhwang, for his involvement in the March 1977 abortive coup. He was one of our privileged prisonmates at both places before his release in the amnesty of late 1977. As reported recently by one of the Bangkok 18 about their meeting at Bangkhwang, Phichai said, "the government wants to end the war with students," therefore the government will grant amnesty to those in the October 6 trial.[26] The meeting at Bangkhen was the same in substance. I recall, however, a few additional issues from that encounter. First, Phichai hinted at the difficulty Kriangsak was facing in pushing for the amnesty because opposition to the plan was significant. Second, he made a strong suggestion—almost a warning—that we must return to school and focus on our studies. We understood it as a warning to not join the CPT. In pushing for the amnesty, according to Phichai, Kriangsak had assured his opponents that none of us was communist, implying that if we did something that hurt Kriangsak's credibility, trouble might follow. Phichai's allusion to important opposition and Kriangsak's overemphasis on gratitude to the palace hinted at who the unnamed opposition to the amnesty was. Paul Handley mentions that King Bhumibol had stalled the proposed amnesty for a year.[27] Somsak Jeamteerasakul later revealed a note from the deputy royal secretary at the time, dated September 6, 1978, conveying the king's concern that the trial could drag on for years and could jeopardize the country's security. The king, according to the royal secretary, urged the conclusion of the trial and the punishment of the guilty ones as soon as possible (*tatsin longthot phuphit doia reio*), who should then ask for pardon from the king. Somsak argues that the king probably preferred the royal pardon after the sentence, rather than the amnesty without the ruling, which prevented the show of royal benevolence.[28]

It was not clear why an idea that had been around for months was suddenly taken up and speedily pushed through by a maneuver that seemed opportunistic rather than normal legislative procedure. It was as if the opening for this high-stakes political action was a brief one. Opponents to the amnesty appeared during the legislative deliberation. Only a few openly and furiously argued against it, but a larger number opposed it by walking out and not voting rather than voting against it. The bill was passed with only one negative vote, but amid a conspicuous silence from the military officers who formed the majority of the house.[29] Afterward, an anonymous call came in for the Village Scouts to protest against the amnesty, attacking Kriangsak as a communist who had tried to destroy the heroic legacy of the right-wing factions on October 6, 1976.[30]

Let us look closely at the amnesty bill. The preamble of the bill reads as follows:

Considering that the trial related to the demonstration[s] at Thammasat between October 4 and October 6 1976, has gone on long enough and would continue for a greater period, if the case proceeded until completion, it would cause the defendants to lose their educational and professional future. Considering also that the demonstration and other wrongdoings took place due to the failure to understand the true situation because of their youth and their lack of experience [immaturity]. In addition, this government is determined to foster harmony [*khwam samakkhi*] of people in the nation. Given all these reasons, it is therefore appropriate to forgive them for their wrongdoings. This would give the opportunity for those who had committed wrongdoing, both the ones who are being prosecuted and those who are still at large, to behave in the right ways and to return to act in the common interest for the prosperity of the nation.[31]

The most important substance is in Article 3:

Article 3: All actions by whomever, which took place or were related to the demonstrations inside Thammasat University between October 4 and October 6, whether they were committed inside or outside the university, and whether the actions were taken by a principal figure, a supporter, a person acting for another, or a person who was used, if the actions were unlawful, the person is absolved from wrongdoing and all responsibility.

In Article 4, the bill stipulated the military court to release all the accused, the Bangkok 18+1; in Article 5, the bill prohibited those amnestied to complain or demand any rights or benefits.

THE SPECTER OF THE MASSACRE

A close reading of the bill yields the following observations. First, the main reasons for the amnesty were on the one hand, the future of the accused, and on the other hand, national harmony or unity (*khwam samakkhi*). Second, the amnesty was for both the Bangkok 18 and those who were still at large. Third, the bill passed a firm and clear judgment, despite the unfinished trial, that the accused were wrongdoers. It inscribed into law that the radicals were guilty but were freed due to the mercy of the state. Fourth, the incident was, in the words of the bill, the "demonstration[s]" at Thammasat. The Thai language does not clarify whether a word is singular or plural. Only the period of between October 4 and October 6, 1976, covers the wrongdoings beyond the morning of October 6. Fifth, Article 3 makes it more clear that the demonstrations are plural, covering both the one inside and the one outside the university. Sixth, also according to Article 3, the wrongdoings were "all actions" and the wrongdoers were "whomever" in the broadest scope, even though the preamble specifies only the accused on trial. Seventh, the wrongdoing was only vaguely identified as the acts "related to" the demonstration or demonstrations. From its title to the last word, no explicit mention is made of any act of killing or the many deaths, let alone the massacre.

Eighth, whether it was meticulously crafted with a hidden agenda, or carelessly written to include numerous ambiguities, the amnesty bill actually absolved "whomever" killed, tortured, gored, raped, burned, and desecrated the bodies and committed other unforgivable acts during the massacre—which was not even mentioned, as if it never happened. Ninth, by giving an iron-clad guarantee that the perpetrators would be forever free from any form of retribution, Article 5, as Haberkorn puts it, "means both that the students who were pardoned could not claim compensation for wrongful arrest, but also, this perhaps also meant that they could not then accuse state officials of committing violent crimes at Thammasat University." As a lawyer of the trial remarked in an interview, "This case did not end with the charges being dismissed. Once testifying began, the 6 October amnesty law was passed and it ended everything. They claimed to forgive the students, but in actuality, they forgave themselves because a lot of students were killed. Everything ended due to the amnesty."[32]

Haberkorn has alerted us to the "hidden transcript" of the amnesty of the October 6 massacre. What was not said, she writes, indeed "reflects a sharp presence."[33] Although the Bangkok 18 were the apparent beneficiaries, the amnesty bill essentially provided impunity for the perpetrators and the state. In contrast with the proposition of hidden transcripts as an art of resistance to domination, the presence in absentia for this case were those disguised meanings and silence about the state's crime and its impunity.[34] History knows who the true beneficiaries of the bill were. It was an impunity bill.

In fact, as Haberkorn points out, two, not one, amnesty bills addressed the wrongdoings that took place on October 6, 1976.

On December 24, 1976, the NARC promulgated "the "Amnesty for Those Who Seized the Government Power of the Country on 6 October 1976 Act." It, like the 1978 bill, did not mention the massacre. In it also, again like the 1978 amnesty bill, the massacre's presence was strong despite its absence. No record or concrete information about the drafting process or the deliberations among the drafters in 1978 is available, only the final text of the bill. We do have detailed information about deliberations throughout the drafting of the 1976 bill, however. The following is the amazing story of the 1976 amnesty bill in brief.[35]

Article 29 of the NARC's interim constitution had granted amnesty to those involved in the coup in the evening of October 1976, yet concerns arose that its language provided only limited coverage, both in terms of which individuals and what actions, related to the seizure of power on that day. The deliberations during the drafting of this bill, then, were about the scope of the acts to be covered (what they were and when and where they took place), what the wrongdoings were, and who committed them. The main question revolved around whether the events in the morning of that day—the massacre and the demonstration against the elected government—should be considered part of the coup, thereby covered by the amnesty as well. Yet, at that time, only a few months after the jubilant victory over the communists, the drafters of the 1976 bill wanted to ensure that those behind bars would not receive amnesty. In both the deliberations among the drafters of the bill and the discussions in the legislative body, the massacre and the demonstration against the Seni government were discussed. In their view, all the events of that morning were related, and they were related to the coup in the evening as well.[36] Despite that awareness, the massacre was neither explicitly mentioned or suggested. The 1976 amnesty bill was put in place, but as time passed questions lingered in the minds of many who were involved in those events that Wednesday in 1976: did the 1976 bill ensure impunity for all "individuals from [the rank of] private on up"? Was the bill and its wording broad enough to protect everyone, as they had assumed?[37]

Because the bill in 1976 did not specifically mention the massacre and focused instead on the coup, these people needed another bill specifically to ensure immunity for their involvement in the massacre. Ironically, the perpetrators of the massacre appeared to feel so vulnerable that they needed altogether three pieces of legislature to protect them: Article 29 of the NARC interim constitution, the 1976 amnesty bill, and the 1978 amnesty bill. The last differed from the earlier ones on at least two counts. First, it intended particularly to grant amnesty to those on trial that the earlier bill did not want to include. Second, it concerned all the wrongdoing and all wrongdoers of the incident at Thammasat in particular, not just the coup.

Despite its specific attention to the incident at Thammasat, the 1978 bill was loaded with ambiguities and silence that spoke loudly on several matters. Most conspicuous was the absence of any mention of the massacre (killing, death, brutality, and so on). The perpetrators wanted amnesty for crimes they were unwilling to identify precisely and which they tried to banish into nonexistence. In doing so, and as a consequence, the massacre remained between absence and presence, erasure and recognition, and forgetting and remembering. It was in-between the states of presence and memory. It was a specter that haunted the entire bill. The irony is that the 1978 bill appeared to give amnesty to the Bangkok 18 for nonexistent crimes they had committed, it was in fact an amnesty for the perpetrators of real crimes that were not mentioned in the bill and that remained in oblivion.[38] After their victory by butchering people barbarically, they needed three laws to exorcise the specter of the massacre.

THE AMNESTY IN THE LARGER DOMESTIC CONTEXT

The trial and the amnesty took place at a critical juncture for the Thai state. The prosecution of the Bangkok 18 epitomized a conundrum the Thai state was facing in its fight against communism, namely, that its military-oriented counterinsurgency strategy had not only failed to stem the expansion of communist influence but had also actually fueled its growth. Observing that the CPT had grown exponentially, especially since the massacre, more people in the counterinsurgency community realized that the longer the persecution of the communists, which the October 6 trial essentially was, went on, the more it would benefit the CPT.

For decades during the Cold War, the United States and the Thai state believed and depicted the spread of communism as the infiltration by foreign enemies—namely, the People's Republic of China, North Vietnam, and "Red Laos"—that sought to colonize and destroy Thailand. Communists were not Thai other than those locals who were deceived. The alternative view—namely, that communism primarily stemmed from the domestic conditions (injustice, poverty, oppression)—had not yet gained broad acceptance in the security community, though that was growing with time. Accordingly, the dominant approach to counterinsurgency was to identify and locate the infiltrators and eradicate them by force (arrest, detain, and kill), or known as the military-over-political approach, in contrast with political and economic solutions to eradicate the conditions that provided fertile ground for communism, dubbed the political-over-military approach.[39]

In 1973 to 1976 period, the dominant point of view was challenged, the alternate view being that most communists were rural folks who were neglected and suppressed. They were victims of abuses by the authority.[40] Thus, the more abuses, the more communists. The student movement helped shift the scale of the two approaches, exposing the cruelty and consequences of hawkish methods and raising awareness of the conditions that fueled the growth of communism. The public perception of communists shifted. In this light, the massacre was both the culmination of and the colossal mistake in the war against communism because "this single event represented a great leap forward for the CPT, which gained over 3,000 of Thailand's brightest and best left-leaning students, teachers, labor leaders, and politicians."[41] The Thai state helped make the CPT stronger than ever. "At its peak," a study suggests, "it had 12,000 to 14,000 soldiers according to government estimates; according to other estimates, there were 20,000. Guerilla zones existed in more than 40 provinces and the CPT had influence in thousands of villages with a total population of more than 3 million."[42]

The military leaders and younger commanders who leaned to the political-over-military approach played key roles in the successful coup in 1977.[43] They began to turn the state's policies and measures against the communists. Unlike the ultraconservative Thanin government, the new regime treated the radical students not as proxies of the communist aliens but as their own ideological opponents. In early 1978, it ordered the state's universities to readmit any students who had disappeared after the massacre and now wanted to return to class. They even allowed, within certain limits, a resumption of student activism.[44] The about-face of the state's counterinsurgency efforts extended to those radical students who had gone to the jungles and to all the CPT cadres as well. As we will see in chapter 5, the turnaround was a key factor that contributed to the eventual collapse of the CPT and the radical movement in Thailand. In this light, the 1978 amnesty of the Bangkok 18 was a significant moment in the shift in the state's anticommunist strategy.

THE BEGINNING OF SILENCE

The day after our release, Prime Minister Kriangsak invited the Bangkok 18 to a lunch at his residence. He opened his home and went into the kitchen himself to cook, performing for dozens of reporters and television cameras.[45] I have three observations about this lunch spectacle. First, Kriangsak urged us, and by extension other student activists and the Thai public as well, to let go of the painful and divisive past. It had been a "nightmare" *(fan rai)*, he said, and we should start afresh for the sake of the unity and harmony of the nation. Second, he emphasized repeatedly that the successful amnesty was owed to the benevolence of the king and the crown prince. It was not clear whether he was trying to avert repercussions from opponents of the amnesty by citing the royal protection or trying to please them by giving them credit. Third, throughout the entire encounter, Kriangsak treated us as the wrongdoers, such as by telling us not to repeat past mistakes. This definitely reflected his view and possibly that of all of those in power as well. It was the same discourse that had been formally inscribed into the amnesty law. In response to this unwarranted verdict, Sutham, the leader of the Bangkok 18, insisted during those hours that "We are the Innocent" *(Rao khu phu borisut)*, not the wrongdoers. Even though it may have seemed of little effect at the time, Sutham's remark was a historic one, a simple sentence that crystalized the entire counternarrative to the state's memory.[46] It notified history that the perpetrators of the massacre were still unpunished, regardless of what the amnesty law said.

On the following day, September 18, the student unions from many campuses cooperatively organized welcome-back celebrations for the Bangkok 18. The biggest and central event was at TU in the morning before each of the eighteen would return to their campuses for separate events. Several thousand people packed the Lan Pho, a historic space on Thammasat campus where many political gatherings took place and revolts began, to welcome all the released prisoners and their families. Brief stories about the massacre were told with an emphasis on "We are the Innocent." Several speakers reminded people that the closure would not come for the massacre until the truth was known and justice served. Reports of the celebrations as well as some accounts of the massacre appeared in newspapers. Many of us, the Bangkok 18, had scheduled talks with student groups to tell them what had happened two years earlier. A plan was also in place for an even more special event on September 22 to celebrate the release and to discuss the amnesty. Then, suddenly, the celebrations and all conversations about the massacre were cut short.

After the celebration at TU, the government urged universities and student groups to scale back the welcome events. Citing Kriangsak and pressure from the government, Chulalongkorn University revoked permission to use its venue for the September 22 event. Student leaders had an hour-long meeting with Kriangsak the next day. The prime minister insisted that all celebrations be canceled. He said "this [October 6] incident is over, regardless of who was right or wrong."[47] A few days later, he urged the media to stop digging up information about the incident.[48] The only reason he gave for the shutdown was for the sake of *khwam samakkhi* (unity and harmony). He also added vaguely that for the country to survive (*yu rod*), the situation was not right for the celebration. The state tried to suppress any exposure or discussion about the massacre in the name of unity and reconciliation, urging people to forget the past to avoid social divisiveness.

Unity, harmony, and reconciliation became buzzwords. For the sake of reconciliation, silence was prescribed, arguably so that the country could move on. The call for reconciliation and the prescribed silence might not have been so effective if not for its timing. The country had been exhausted from several years of tense conflict and two colossal events of bloodshed, one of which was brutal beyond comprehension. The country had witnessed the rise and fall of euphoric democracy and then one of the most repressive authoritarian regimes in Thai history; it had seen the activism and demonstrations of both leftists and rightists. People were relieved when the Thanin government was ousted but probably were not eager to return to the years of radical activism either. Silence descended on the discourse of the October 6 massacre, perhaps not so much because people were willing to cooperate with the Thai state to forget, but because they were too exhausted to remember. The search for truth and the quest for justice were an uphill battle. The posttrial silence among the radicals and their sympathizers was reinforced soon afterward by disillusion among the radicals and the collapse of the CPT (see chapter 5).

For the perpetrators, the October 6 trial, which weakened the perpetrators' memory and strengthened that of the victims, proved almost a reversal of fortune for the triumphalist discourse. "Almost" because the state was able to buttress its verdict via the 1978 amnesty bill and their persistent public pronouncements that the students were the wrongdoers. The victims were able to claim a certain space in the public discourse, but not able to push any further in the wake of the silence following the trial. Nevertheless, Sutham's historic statement reflected the condition of memory in suspension: if we are the innocent, then who are the guilty? Despite the state's unjust verdict that the students were the wrongdoers, the public understood that the perpetrators of the massacre had not yet been held accountable for their crimes. The perpetrators, too, were aware that their version of events had lost ground, so they too avoided speaking about the massacre in public. Silence descended on everyone.

On the second anniversary of the massacre, a newspaper was censored for publishing a cartoon about the incident. The press officer gave as a reason that "this issue [has] already quieted down through the amnesty which most people, including the students, are satisfied with."[49] The public discourse about the massacre quickly came to a halt. In 1979, police confiscated and closed a news magazine, *Lok Mai,* which published several pictures of the massacre.[50] In the same year, Chulalongkorn University shut down the student union building to force the cancellation of the planned commemoration of the October events.[51] In October 1982, two opposing student groups at Ramkhamhaeng University organized separate commemorations of the October 1973 uprising and the October 1976 massacre. The leftists celebrated the heroism and sacrifices of the martyrs of both events. To the other group, however, the 1973 uprising was a cause for celebration, but it had been tarnished by the leftists whose mistakes and failure were to blame for the tragedy in 1976. When the tension between the two groups was reported, the minister of interior commented,

> [Why] is that damn thing about 6 October not over yet? It was many years ago. Isn't it over and done yet? . . . It shouldn't have any fuel left. Come on, [we] should help the country. We should look forward to the future. Why do we keep bringing back the past. Let's forget it. Only a small group of students is causing trouble [because] they have their heads stuck on October 6. The country is getting better now. Don't pull it back.[52]

The commemorations of the massacre were well attended in 1978, less than a month after the amnesty, and in 1979. After that, based on news reports, it faded quickly and dissipated in the early 1980s. A news report in 1983 remarked that the commemoration was "sleepy" (*ngoi*).[53] In most years, the only commemoration was a small, poorly attended one at Thammasat. It was undistinguished and not always held. The only exception was in 1988, and it was due to a controversy discussed in the next chapter. In 1994, while on a research leave in Thailand, I attended the commemoration on the morning of October 6. Two hands were all that were needed to count the number of organizers and attendees together.

The October trial as a mnemonic moment was a milestone in the history of the massacre. It was also the beginning of silence. Ambiguity about what happened, about who were guilty, remained for many years. The massacre became known by the blandest of terms—"the October 6 event"—a reflection of ambivalence in an atmosphere of reconciliation.

Chapter 5

DISQUIETING SILENCE AFTER 1978

Fortunately for the Thai state, the new ideas and policies for dealing with the communist insurgency were implemented at the right time. The serious conflicts among the communist countries in Asia erupted into the ousting of the Khmer Rouge by the Vietnamese forces in the final days of 1978 and the 1979–1981 Sino-Vietnamese war. These conflicts led to disarray in the Communist Party of Thailand (CPT). Simultaneously, it was an opportunity for the Thai state to exploit the hostility among the communist backers of the CPT: first, to implement a rapprochement with the Socialist Republic of Vietnam in 1979; and, second, to forge an agreement with the People's Republic of China in the same year to end its support of the CPT. The agreement exacerbated an internal crisis within the CPT, primarily between the old cadres and those who joined the CPT after the massacre. In 1980, the general amnesty, in the form of the Prime Minister Order no. 66/2523, extended to anyone who had joined the CPT at any time for any reason, from the rank and file to the Politburo. It allowed them to return home and take up their lives without even having to report to the authorities, let alone face arrest or charges. This order epitomized the new counterinsurgency strategy, which was based on the recognition that Thailand's communist problem was primarily a domestic and political one.[1] It was, as scholar and former Foreign Service officer Bob Bergin summarizes, "a successful strategy aimed at the core discontent and aspirations of the insurgents, particularly the idealistic student followers. Instead of a brute-force military campaign, the Thai government offered amnesty, repatriation, and jobs to communist sympathizers, and freedom rather than detention. [The state addressed], directly and compassionately, the discontent that fuels insurrection."[2] The conjuncture of these factors led to an increase in desertions among CPT cadres from 1978 to 1982, virtually ending the Cold War in Thailand by the early 1980s.

The new political conditions affected memories of the massacre among the victims, the perpetrators, and the public. In the mid-1980s, the anticommunist phobia had come to an end and the civic groups and nongovernmental organization movements were growing. Many of these civic groups were driven by people from the 1970s generation, including returnees from the jungles. Human rights became a common parlance in the political public sphere, thanks in part to the growing global awareness since the late 1970s. Given this context, public perceptions of the massacre changed too. From 1978 to 1996, involvement with the right wing between 1973 and 1976 was viewed as a disgrace. A controversy during the electoral campaign in 1988 provided a snapshot of this shift, in which the perpetrators of the massacre in turn became the retrospective victims of their past. Yet the massacre was never discussed directly or extensively in public and the perpetrators were never confronted.

During the same period, former radicals also turned silent for an entirely different reason. During the heyday of the CPT, their hopes for a just revenge and a new society had compensated for their sorrow for the loss of lives. However, the socialist revolution as an imagined alternative to the state had collapsed and faded away by the early1980s. The decline and fall of the CPT and radicalism affected their memories of the 1976 massacre tremendously. It gave them a different perspective on their younger lives. I shared their ambivalence to some extent and learned from many of them personally. The chronopolitics of memory took its toll on them as well.

In 1986, a Thai scholar observed that, in contrast to the studies of the October 1973 uprising, a silence about the October 1976 massacre pervaded academia. The incident, he explained, was a scar on Thai society in that it exposed a propensity to violence and intolerance, which contrasted with the self-image of Thai society as peaceful and tolerant. The discomfort of acknowledging that Thais can be as monstrous as any other people brought on silence, a symptom of the tension between truth (what actually was) and self-knowledge (what we think we should be).[3] In a similar vein, a famous Thai writer noted in an essay in 1988 that the incident was still a fresh wound that Thai people, both perpetrators and victims, were ashamed to talk about. Even the writer's personal feelings about it were paradoxical. On the one hand, he wanted to forget it, especially the brutality and inhumanity that took place, but on the other, he wanted to remember it precisely because people were trying so hard to forget it.[4] This paradox and its symptomatic silence is exactly what I call the unforgetting.

THE VICTIM'S AMBIVALENCE

For many radicals, the CPT was both an idealistic alternative to the Thai state and an opportunity for revenge. But the CPT and the entire radical movement collapsed only a few years after they went to jungles. Three major factors were involved. First, the revolutionary movement was dogmatic and totalitarian. The party, from the top down to local commanders, tried to control their lives, behaviors, and thinking, but refused any efforts to improve or reform the party. Students were forced to obey the party directives regardless whether they made sense. Many directives were misguided in that they dogmatically adhered to the Chinese revolutionary experience from a different place and time. From the first months in the jungles, the new CPT members were increasingly frustrated with the old cadres and the party.[5] Many of them challenged the party, from its analysis of Thai society and revolutionary strategy to the practical inefficiency and poor management of day-to-day living. The breaking point was the lack of any kind of democratic process within this allegedly progressive party. The students' proposed changes were received with indifference.[6]

Second, the Sino-Vietnamese conflict led to cooperation between the Thai and Chinese governments. This allowed China to supply arms to the Khmer Rouge via Thai territory in exchange for the shutdown of the Voice of the People of Thailand, the CPT's broadcast based in China, and an end to China's support, including logistical supply, for the CPT. The CPT leadership, which had tagged slavishly behind the Chinese communist party for decades, declared its unyielding support for China. The rest of the party, however, was jolted. Cadres at every level reacted strongly to China's selling out of the Thai revolution and to the acquiescence of the CPT leadership.[7] The perceived betrayal amidst the other brewing conflicts within the party sent the entire party into crisis as dissatisfaction spread like wild fire.

The leadership reacted to the dissidents with insults, distrust and, in some cases, malicious smearing. The conflicts almost led to mutinies in several CPT camps. Eventually, the party's overdue response was too little, too late.[8] In the midst of the turmoil, the turnaround of the Thai state in dealing with the communists was timely, especially the amnesties that opened the door for radical students to return. The disillusioned radical students took the opportunity offered by the government, leaving the jungles individually and en bloc. It was a homecoming in total defeat, however. Only a few years before, they had denounced the Thai state, determined not to return until the revolution succeeded. Now they returned in utter humiliation to the embrace of the state. "I am a historical ruin," declared Seksan Prasertkul, one of the best-known radical students, shortly after he turned himself in to the authorities only half a year after the 66/2523 order in 1980.[9] He later told us,

> From now on, my life is in all likelihood void of meaning. After having dedicated one's life for a cause, binding one's self-value to such a cause, the utter failure made all purpose in my life almost completely disappear. Life becomes meaningless. . . . People like me probably become captives of our own memories that we cannot escape.[10]

Seksan's dictum became characteristic of the returnees. A common sentiment among them was uncertainty and insecurity. How would people—friends, family, colleagues, employers, even lovers—react to their past, that is, the decision to join the CPT, their guerilla actions, their radicalism, all of which had turned out to be a waste? After dedicating years of their youth to the historic mission of forging a just society with lasting happiness to all people, most of them felt completely lost and were disenchanted because of their mistakes. The disillusionment with the radical cause took away their reasons and justifications for their earlier decisions. Feeling that they had wasted years of their lives for nothing, they brought home only stigma and malaria. In the middle of their twenties, a returnee remarked, they already lost two historic wars: one in the city ending with the slaughter of their friends, the other in the jungles ending with the loss of their idealism.[11] After such mistakes, after having to beg for clemency from the state they had denounced, why would they not feel humiliated and ashamed?

Those who remained in the cities working underground and witnessing the gradual collapse of the radical networks were similarly, though less severely, depressed. Some struggled to defend their socialist idealism, trying to launch new rounds of debates and activism. Eventually, they too abandoned the cause. Like their comrades from the jungles, they could not continue to look at the past in the same way.

It was not difficult for them to understand the past rationally. But rationality was no answer to ambivalence stemming from disenchantment. Many of them, especially the former student leaders, could not exonerate themselves from responsibility.[12] Many had been active in the movement that led to polarization and death. Some had actively recruited for the CPT, sending people to the jungles, many of whom never returned. Without pride in their past radicalism, suffering and grief due to the loss of friends in the massacre and in the revolutionary war turned into personal trauma that was hard to come to terms with and might never go away. The price for all those sacrifices seemed suddenly too steep, the loss beyond any justification. It should not have happened.

It was at this time that a returnee friend of mine introduced me to the song "Empty Chairs at Empty Tables" from *Les Misérables*. Every word of its lyrics and the emotions evoked story echoed our sentiments, as if the song were about the failed revolution in Thailand.

> There's a grief that can't be spoken.
> There's a pain goes on and on.
> Empty chairs at empty tables
> Now my friends are dead and gone.
>
> . . . don't ask me
> What your sacrifice was for . . .

The grief that cannot be spoken, the pain of moral ambivalence, and the burden of being alive will stick with these survivors, myself included, perhaps forever. Most of these former radicals did not deny or forget their past. What was their sacrifice for? The empty chairs and tables were not as painful as the emptiness inside. Further, people around them may never understand them. October 6 became a specter for these survivors. It was not a subject we could talk about without troubling reflections.

DISQUIETING SILENCE OF THE DISILLUSIONED

Kasian Tejapira, today considered one of the best scholars in the country, wrote two short memoirs telling his story as a returnee from the jungle.[13] A budding scholar since his college years, he may not represent all the returnees whose experiences and voices remain buried. His memoirs nonetheless provide a lens into the life and sentiments of the disillusioned radicals. Thanks to his thoughtful introspection and ability to relay it in writing, we can learn what these people went through during the 1980s.

His first memoir begins with his experience as a Thammasat University student during the turbulent years that changed him and how the massacre was an important factor for his decision to join the CPT's armed struggle. "I didn't feel like returning to school any more. It seemed pointless to study. I wanted to get as far away as I could, to weep and curse the killing as much as I wanted to. Then, it occurred to me . . . the jungle."[14] Despite knowing very little about the CPT and never having been to any jungle, Kasian was determined and dedicated. Like the majority of his cohorts, over time he became very critical of the CPT. Realizing that this was not the future he had hoped for, he grew disillusioned and returned, though he was not as bitter or angry with the CPT as some others were.

Kasian gives us a glimpse of how returnees felt at the time. He was alienated by most of what surrounded him and alienated from himself as well. He was annoyed every time he was asked about the jungle experience because he wanted to forget it. He felt discomfort when he saw people graduate, and he was not among them. "How I could maintain my self-confidence?" For a while. He fortified himself with books, reading voraciously in isolation, and enjoyed small successes such as good grades "to protect myself from the society's snub."[15] Nevertheless, he did not deny the past.

> If I were to return to those bloody years, I would make the same decision. . . . Why didn't anybody speak out in praise of the spirit of those thousands of young people who [left family and loved ones] and risked their lives in the jungles . . . that they were correct, that they were great?[16]

It did not matter what anybody else might think; he insisted that those young people (including himself) were great, for they had sacrificed for the benefit of the people.

In the second memoir, he elaborates more on how he and some of the returnees coped with their ambivalent memories and experiences, revealing the various strategies to deal with the alienation and come to terms with their new lives. First, try to blend in with the crowd (other students), avoiding anything that might call attention to oneself. Second, if confronted with a question about the past, be evasive or fib to escape the question because it's hard to tell the truth. (He does not explain why it was hard. Was the past too complex to explain or did the returnees not want to revisit the past, or both?) Third, leave the painful past behind altogether and move on. "I washed my hands. Completely. I am already to be reborn, without the past whatsoever," a friend said. Fourth, talk about the past to understand it, to find an explanation for the failure of the leftists and the CPT.

> It began as a soft conversation, then got heated into a serious discussion, mixed with satire and rising voices. One said black, the other said white. Nobody talked about grey. . . . After that, they stopped talking because there were too many disagreements. Since then, we've only talked about jobs and ways to earn money . . . Politics was painful.[17]

Fifth and last, Kasian describes the moment that he finally came to terms with the past. It was a memorable occasion in which he spoke to hundreds of students about his experiences, including the massacre. It was a cathartic moment for him.

> [The audience] was completely silent while I kept talking, talking and talking, as if I was insanely talking to myself. Only when I finished did I hear the audience clap their hands. . . . then, I saw a few friends shed tears. . . . I had been back for two years. But on the day when I saw my friends shed tears, I felt that I could finally be myself again.[18]

Despite their varied individual experiences, most of the disillusioned radicals shared these experiences to some extent. Most were able to move on with their lives and have decent careers. A few had similar cathartic moments, when friends or listeners supplied that kind of restorative recognition and respect. Most, however, never had occasion to openly share their grief and sorrow, and never experienced that kind of public respect for who they were and what they had been through. During the silent period between 1978 and 1996, they were probably not sure how to talk about their memories because they did not know how ordinary Thais might react. Certainly they did not want an awkward silence, let alone a rebuke. They did not want sympathy or consolation either. So they kept their traumatic memories to themselves. I tend to be relatively more outspoken about the massacre than others, but I, too, speak about it only when asked to. I rarely initiate such a conversation. I normally do not initiate conversations about politics to this day. It took me years to understand and be able to characterize my paradoxical memories of the massacre and my own past radicalism—humiliation, regret and guilt, yet pride and dignity at the same time.

Above all, the disillusioned radicals had lives to live. They tried to return to them–finishing school, holding jobs and careers, earning money and having families—like ordinary people. Many felt they had fallen behind because they had wasted valuable years, and they kept busy building their futures like normal citizens. The need to find a receptive audience so they could speak out about their traumatic past was not urgent. To many former radicals, the commemoration at the twentieth anniversary of the massacre in 1996 (discussed in chapter 6), would be the first and probably the most significant chance for them to come to terms with their painful past.

The Perpetrator's Ambivalence

Chapter 4 discussed resistance to the 1978 amnesty bill. Instead of opposing it straightforwardly, the opponents of the bill chose not to endorse it by walking out or by abstaining. Only a few argued openly against it, one of whom was the staunch right-wing novelist who also chose to walk off rather than voting against it. A call for a protest demonstration did not materialize either. Throughout the welcoming celebrations of the Bangkok 18, during which the memories of the victims were voiced in the open, the right-wing voice was silent. The absence of their triumphalist narrative pointed to the extent that the heroic memory of their behavior was no longer popular. But this did not mean that they had gone away. They still lurked in the background throughout Kriangsak's maneuver for amnesty.

Thai politics from the end of the 1970s to the early 1990s was a transformative period that has been dubbed by scholars and the public alike as semi-democracy.[19] The parliamentary system had become normalized, though it was still under the auspices of the powerful military and the hegemony of the royalists and the monarchy as the sole source of legitimacy. A few aborted coups were staged between 1977 and 1987, and a successful but short-lived one in 1991, which turned out to be the beginning of the retreat of military from politics for fifteen years.[20] On the other hand, social and political liberalism was on the rise during the period, as was a growing awareness of human rights. In this political atmosphere, several incidents indicated that the right-wing memory of the massacre was no longer acceptable in the public view.

In early 1981, Prem Tinsulanond, the prime minister at the time, appointed General Sutsai Hatsadin to his cabinet. One of Prem's long-time friends, Sutsai was infamous for being the "Father" of the Red Gaurs. Voices of disapproval filled the media. Sutsai's reaction was to say that TU should be grateful to him because on October 6, 1976, the Red Gaurs had tried to calm down the hysterical crowd that had been eager to kill the students inside TU. Thus, in his words, he helped "save" them and the university on that day. His remarks drew protests. Thammasat students called him a criminal and demanded his resignation. Several cabinet ministers distanced themselves from Sutsai. Others openly rebuked him.[21] Although the protest had no effect, the controversy pointed to the persistence but retreat of the right-wing memory of the massacre.

The most revealing evidence of the perpetrators' turn to evasiveness and silence during this period was the controversy that took place during the general election in 1988. Chamlong Srimuang was a retired army general and a former leader of the Thai Young Turks, a small group of military commanders who had controlled crucial army divisions during the coups in 1976, 1977, and 1981.[22] As a pious follower of a Buddhist sect known for its austere lifestyle, Chamlong became highly popular for his honesty and incorruptibility.[23] During the rise of his political career, he was elected governor of Bangkok in 1985 in a landslide victory. Riding on his popularity, in 1988 he found a political party, Phalang Dharma (power of Dharma or righteousness), whose platform was to clean up the political corruption. It was during the campaign for the general election in July 1988 that the controversy erupted.

One of the candidates of Chamlong's party, Chongkol Srikanchana, gave a public interview about her active role in 1976. At the time, she was the leader of a right-wing group, the Housewife Club. She revealed how, at the demonstration at the Equestrian Plaza against the Seni government on October 6, 1976, while she was speaking to the crowd, Chamlong had been there in disguise, managing the demonstration, and offering tips to speakers about what to say to the crowd.[24] Intended as a boast about her long political association with the popular Chamlong, the näive revelation backfired. The disclosure led to strong public reactions. Many people were shocked, given Chamlong's reputed piety. Trying to put out the fire, Chamlong denied any involvement in the massacre. Meanwhile, Chongkol, obviously still proud of her heroic role that day, was silenced by the party, no longer allowed to speak in public or give interviews.

Many people came forward both to confirm and refute Chamlong's denial. Among them were his cohorts in the Young Turk group, one of whom confirmed that Chamlong was in army intelligence and active in organizing right-wing demonstrations, including on October 6.[25] The respected scholar Chai-anan Samudavanija clarified that, based on his research, although Chamlong was actively against the students, he was not involved in the massacre.[26] Chamlong's denial, including one in front of tens of thousands people on the eve of the election, was evasive. He categorically denied being anywhere near TU that morning. However, he did admit to participating as an ordinary citizen who was upset with the students' alleged lèse majesté in the right-wing movement during that period and in the demonstration at the Equestrian Plaza, a few miles from the university, on October 6, 1976. He tried to minimize his role in the right-wing movement, saying that he was an insignificant army major (*phantri leklek*) who did not command any unit, did not have any political role, and did not know what was going on that morning. He argued that the situation during the demonstration was very confusing, that he was merely one among many who tried to make suggestions to people on stage. He denied any role with authority or special service in that gathering. "I was not good at public speaking. I never went on the stage to speak. I cannot." Last but not least, he argued that the demonstration at the Equestrian Plaza had nothing to do with the killing at TU that same morning.[27]

According to Chai-anan's interview with Chamlong several years before the controversy, Chamlong was a coordinator of the right-wing groups tasked with countering the National Student Center of Thailand's campaign for the withdrawal of US bases in Thailand in 1975 and 1976. These groups organized a major exhibition and demonstration against the NSCT in March and July 1976. Chai-anan confirmed that Chamlong was one of the organizers of the demon-stration at the Equestrian Plaza to oust the Seni government, and that he had played an active role in the larger right-wing movement as well.[28] He insisted, however, that Chamlong did not take part in the massacre.

During the controversy, several right-wing leaders who played important roles relating to the massacre, including Chatichai Choonhavan and Samak Sundaravej, were questioned by the media. All of them, like Chamlong, denied involvement, arguing that they were nowhere near TU that morning, as if complicity in the massacre required their presence at or near the site of the killings, as if the only crime could be shooting with their own hands. Like Chamlong, all of them were evasive about their roles or any relation to the right-wing movement.[29] Chatichai, for example, did not mention his role with the Village Scouts before the massacre and in the cabinet meeting that morning when he misinformed the cabinet about the incident and tried to block the declaration of emergency that could have dispersed the right-wing gathering against the elected government. All of them chorused that the allegation was a dirty election ploy. They blamed the students, who urged more disclosure and investigation about the massacre, for being political pawns of their electoral opponents. Chatichai advised that people should try to forget the past and look to the future instead.

Although the controversy cost Chamlong's party somewhat in the 1988 election, by their own admission, it had no further impact. It led to no investigation or serious interest in the massacre. The vot-ers may not have believed Chamlong's evasive excuses, but the mas-sacre was not a significant factor in their decisions. The revelations about Chamlong's involvement with the right-wing movement in 1976 did not affect his subsequent political career. He was reelected the Bangkok governor for the second term in 1990 and became a deputy prime minister in 1994. He was one of the leaders in the up-rising in 1992, though a controversial one. His political popularity faded after the mid-1990s, then revived in 2006 when he became one of the leaders of the controversial "yellow"—the People's Alliance for Democracy, the misnamed antidemocratic movement that created the pretext for the royalist-military coup in 2006.

It is likely that these right-wing political leaders of 1976 consid-ered their past actions in the right-wing movement to be justified. By 1988, however, they could no longer openly admit their past, let alone celebrate it, and they had to scramble to save their political lives but could muster only evasive and unconvincing excuses. None of them condemned the massacre. On a brighter note, the controversy in 1988 clearly marked that the discourse of the October 6 killings had shifted dramatically since 1976. The story of Chamlong's and Chongkol's roles, no matter how fuzzy, could have been a heroic tale had it been told twelve years earlier. By 1988, involvement with the right-wing's actions on that day was considered shameful. Regrettably, however, the allegation that the disclosures were dirty politics staged for short-term electoral benefit, and the suggestion that the 1976 event should be laid to rest to avoid societal rifts, were effective. The perpetrators successfully reburied the past in silence after the controversy. Their own memories of heroic actions surely persisted. But they too had to come to terms with the changing political conditions. As a result, they kept their memories mostly to themselves and went largely silent.

DISQUIETING SILENCE OF THE VICTORS

In 1994, Manas Sattayarak, a police colonel and well-known writer, wrote a short memoir about his experience on October 6, 1976.[30] He woke up that morning, he recalled, with grave concerns for students at Thammasat. He disagreed with the order of his superior to allow the police to use weapons to defend themselves. His assistant was in Thammasat throughout the night before the killing, so he knew that the demonstration was peaceful. After arriving at Thammasat, he urged his superior to order the ceasefire. His superior agreed. But Manas tried in vain to stop the police from shooting. Either those police strictly followed only their own commanders, Manas speculated, or the police there were out of control. Manas saved a man from being lynched, he wrote, by shielding him with his own body. "I definitely could not allow anybody to get killed in front of me," he wrote. In frustration, he kept trying to stop the police from shooting, almost getting shot himself. When it was over and the protesters were subdued, he urged his fellow policemen to treat the arrested students with civility until an unidentified man nearby became upset and threatened him orally. "I had to shout to make myself heard over the right-wing militants who'd ordered the arrested students to crawl on the ground," he wrote, "We could have prevented their trauma from getting worse than it already was." He then led a few busloads of students into custody at Nakhon Pathom, a prison southwest of Bangkok. On arrival, he found that one "captive" (*chaleoi*) had been shot dead for trying to escape. Despite his ambivalence, Manas decided to make an excuse for his young officer. "His [the student's] complexion is so white," he said out loud in front of the media on-lookers, "perhaps he is a Yuan [Vietnamese]," a casual whitewash of a crime by painting the victim as a Vietnamese, which was synony-mous with a communist enemy in the anticommunist discourse at the time. By evening on that dark day, he wrote, "the situation was calm. Only ruins remain, materially and spiritually." He ended his memoir with this statement: "I know that there was a rumor that I am left-leaning. I denied it because I do not like the communists. But I admit that I hate the right-wing fascists a thousand times more."

This narrative was explicitly sympathetic to the victims of the massacre. It is undoubtedly the most caring, compassionate, and hu-mane voice of any police officer in action that day. It is strikingly in contrast with the right-wing collective memory established that day partly by the officers who appeared on TV5, such as Salang Bunnak (mentioned in chapters 3 and 4). Was Manas a black sheep among his fellow officers at the time? Or was his memoir a reconstructed mem-ory by an intelligent police officer who understood the postcommu-nist political atmosphere eighteen years after the incident? Putting aside, for a moment, my cynicism and assuming that his memory was truthful and honest, one might wonder whether this courageous nar-rative could have been aired in public by a member of the police shortly after the massacre. Such a memoir was probably unthinkable then, for it would have made Manas another casualty of the right-wing hysteria. Times had changed: by the mid-1990s, triumphal nar-ratives like Salang's had faded, perhaps buried, and an apologetic and humane one like Manas's had come to light. Both Salang's and Manas's accounts may reflect simply personal memories and different views. Yet the reversal in the fortunes of their respective memories has to do with the drastic change in the political conditions—the chronopolitics of memory.

One fact was missing from Manas's memoir: on that day at TU and Sanamluang, Police Captain Manas had served in the unit under the command of Police Lieutenant Colonel Salang.[31] Manas's mem-oir gave his readers the impression that he had for the most part acted independently, under his own command. Salang and all his heroic actions did not exist in Manas's memoir. Whereas Salang boasted about the raid into TU that he had led, confirmed by a photo of him in action among several heavily armed police officers inside the university, Manas had tried to stop the police shooting, even using his own body to protect a man from being lynched. These two officers with contrasting memories of their contrasting actions never mentioned one another even though they were in the same unit that day. What Salang remembered and bragged about, and what he did not tell, perhaps fit the hysterical euphoria on that day in 1976. What Manas wrote and did not write probably reflected the memories that could and could not be expressed in public in 1994 when a more humane posture of reconciliation had taken hold. The memories that did not fit the time stayed silent.

Time changes public discourses. It changes memory and history as well. Time is not simply a passage of celestial bodies. Instead, it is filled with the changing conditions that affected the contesting memories. Guilt and shame are often felt and recalled retroactively. It is unsurprising if one feels guilt only when reflecting in the light of the present. For those involved with the killing, the October 6 incident might not have become something to be ashamed of had the fear of communism not subsided to such an extent that it seems absurd nowadays. Had the right-wing totalitarian regime remained in power, had the Cold War continued with its anticommunist dehumanization, and had the communist threat remained, the culprits and their supporters might never have had the opportunity to reflect on their thoughts and actions, and the October 1976 victims might have remained communist criminals in the public view. Being prisoners of time, the perpetrators turned into victims of their past deeds.

Chongkol's pride in her account attested to the fact that the perpetrators' original memories were still alive and well in some quarters by the late 1980s. What was disgrace for some was still heroism to others, perhaps many of them. This is evident, for example, among those who were involved in the Village Scout movement. In 1994, the same year Manas published his memoir, a scout published a memoir in the annual commemorative volume for the twenty-third anniversary of the organization. In it, the scout recalled the atmosphere at the gathering of scouts joined by the queen and the crown prince (at the time) during the October 6 incident. It is regarded as one of the most memorable moments in the history of the Village Scouts. "With the majestic miraculous power [of the monarchy], the event on October 6, 1976, was quelled. Our country returned to normal once more."[32] It is likely that in a political community distant from the main public sphere of the national media, the massacre remains not only a memorable event, but also one of their proudest accomplishments. As we see in chapter 9, most perpetrators of the October 6 massacre whom I met in the 2000s showed no remorse and the proud killers remained proud.

Monument of the Disquieting Silence

During the 1980s to early 1990s, as commemoration of the October 6 massacre declined, the commemoration of the October 14, 1973, uprising still took place every year. After seventy-two people had died in the clashes with the military, the 1973 uprising ended the long military rule in Thailand (see chapter 2). It has been celebrated as a major step toward democracy. In 1974, the cremation of the October 14 martyrs was a state-sponsored event, presided over by the king and queen, as well as a day of national mourning. Since then, the annual commemoration has been an official event attended by the head of government and the parliament (or their representatives) and other national dignitaries. That is, the positive recognition of the 1973 October uprising stands in contrast to the silence about the 1976 October massacre, despite the fact that the two incidents were related and involved the same protagonists—the student movement that turned radical. For this reason, during the period of disquieting silence, the massacre was mentioned in public only in relation to the earlier uprising. The memory of the 1976 massacre hitched a ride on the 1973 uprising, so to speak.

However, the memory of the October 1973 uprising has its own problem, which I cannot explain in full here. Suffice it to say that how one views the relatedness of the two events would shape the memory of both events accordingly. The memory of the 1973 uprising was not silenced. That event was not a wound that still hurts and not a specter that still haunts. But the heroic student movement of 1973 was largely turned into an enemy of the state by 1976. To some, the celebrated 1973 event was tarnished by the 1976 one, making the significance and glory of the former less acceptable as well. As a result, despite official recognition, the state and the conservative public have been lukewarm about the commemoration of the October 1973 uprising. This is why some people, such as the conservative student group mentioned at the end of chapter 4, tried to assert a narrative that celebrated October 1973 and blamed October 1976.

If a monument is the most conspicuous site of memory, à la Pierre Nora's *Les Lieux de mémoire,* the fate of the memorial of the October 1973 uprising during the 1980s and 1990s is evidence of the reluctant and lukewarm recognition of the uprising. At the end of the uprising in 1973, the victory was hailed by all political camps, perhaps excepting the military. Those who died were recognized as the October 14 martyrs (*Wirachon 14 tula*). A year later, in October 1974, the government agreed to partner with the NSCT to build a memorial for the uprising and the martyrs.[33] The chosen site was the former headquarters of one of the ousted dictators that burned down during the uprising. In 1975, the government agreed to buy the land, which was the property of the Crown Property Bureau (CPB). The CPB informed the government that the normal purchasing process was the sole hurdle. In October 1975, the prime minister and the supreme patriarch laid the foundation stone at the site in a widely publicized ceremony. The stone was marked by a white concrete post a few feet high. Unfortunately, during the turbulent years that followed, the government changed. The rising tide against the student movement undermined the commitment of the new government to the monument project. By October 1976, the glorious uprising of 1973 was seen in a different light. A monument for the martyrs of 1973—the rabble-rousers or the communists in the eyes of the rightists—seemed a ridiculous idea.

Early in 1978, the government confiscated the account of the NSCT, including the funds it had raised and allocated for the monument. The project was ignored, almost forgotten. Almost but not quite forgotten. During the period of the disquieting silence, the commemoration of the 1973 uprising was still held annually at the site designated for the memorial. The missing memorial was made conspicuous by the white concrete post in the middle of the empty lot. Its absence was loud in silence. The project was not officially abandoned, though it was barely alive. Behind the stalled project from 1976 to 1989 was in fact a stalemate, the result of a tug-of-war of contested memories.

Either forgetting or ignoring the promise it had made to the government in 1975, in 1978 the CPB prepared to develop the site for a new commercial project. The CPB argued that it had never given permission to lay the foundation stone in place.[34] For unknown reasons, however, the new commercial project never materialized. It was said, astonishingly, that the CPB dared not move ahead as planned for fear of political repercussions. Instead, it leased the empty lot to the Thai army, which in turn leased it to the Lottery Sellers Association. This was a slap in the face of the October 1973 martyrs and an offense to the spirit of the 1973 uprising given that one of the buildings burned down during the uprising was the headquarters of the government lottery. Nonetheless, the lottery sellers dared to set up only makeshift shelters on the rim around the site to do their business. The white concrete post that marked the location of the foundation stone was left at the center of the site under the open sky as if it were not part of the leased land.

In another twist to the bizarre affair, the lottery sellers looked after the concrete post diligently because they considered it a sacred object that could give fortunes to them. However, they were not ignorant of history. Every year on October 14, they completely stopped business in the morning for the annual commemoration. Every year, usually a group of students plus a small number of dignitaries showed up. The official wreaths from various officeholders were placed around the concrete post in the middle of the lot surrounded by the tents for lottery selling. The lottery sellers always stood nearby, participating silently, allowing the process go on as long as needed. Then, in 1985, as part of the commemoration that year, a simple clay statue was made and placed on top of the concrete post. The statue had no name, no sculptor's name, for it was not supposed to be a permanent memorial. But it was there for many years, the interim statue of the October 14 Martyrs (figure 5). No one dared to take it down.

No progress was made on the memorial project until 1989, when the call for completion of the October 1973 memorial erupted again as a result of a controversy in which an ousted dictator of 1973 demanded the return of assets confiscated by the state in 1974. The elected government at the time, ironically led by Chatichai Choonhavan, who had supported the right-wing demonstration on October 6, 1976, agreed to resume the memorial project to promote national unity.[35] More than four million baht of the NSCT fund confiscated in 1978 was returned to a special committee to oversee the project. To everyone's surprise, however, the site was not immediately available. The obstacles connected to the leases—by the CPB to the army, and by the army to the lottery sellers—remained unresolved. The project stalled again until the May 1992 uprising, which ended with another victory for the

Figure 5. The "interim" statue of the Martyrs of the October 14 uprising at the empty lot before 2000. Photo by the author.

people against military rule. The idea of a monument for the martyrs of democracy was back on the public agenda. The military, some right-wing politicians such as Samak Sundaravej, and a notorious ultra-right group, Aphirak Chakri, opposed the idea, warning that such a monument would be divisive. Despite the opposition, a new site was selected to circumvent the perennial problems at the old one. It was on the same road at the former building of the Department of Public Relations, which had been burned down in the 1992 uprising for its role in mis-informing the public in support of the military regime. This new memorial, however, would commemorate the October 1973 and May 1992 events together, though not the 1976 massacre.[36] The supreme patriarch at the time named the proposed memorial park the Peace Garden (Suan santiporn).

The new site for the memorial faced its own roadblock, however. Due to its prime location, it had been previously designated for a grand monument for the glorious historical kings. Moreover, in 1995, when the plan for the memorial was still unclear, the king proposed a plan to relieve the traffic congestion in the area, which was truly among the worst in Bangkok. Under His Majesty's proposal, the site of the planned memorial must be sacrificed to new streets and verges aimed at easing the congestion. Because this happened in Thailand, and the proposal came from the king, it generated no controversy whatsover. The plan for the Peace Garden had to be modified resulting in two separate memorials for the 1973 and 1992 events. The one for the 1992 event, eventually inaugurated in 2016, was dramatically downsized to only a monument on a small section of a side street without a garden or any of the trappings originally planned. The memorial of the October 1973 uprising returned to the old site, which was still in a legal quagmire and deemed impossible. The post that marked the foundation stone and the interim statue remained surrounded by lottery tents, as if the memory of the popular uprising was under siege. The unbuilt monument at the unresolved site under an open sky was quite a fitting memorial of the disquieting silence during this period.

I revisit the issue of this monument briefly in chapter 6 because the project was taken up again after 1996, thanks to the impact of the breakthrough of the memory of the 1976 massacre and its commemorative movement in 1996. Ironically, it would be the memory of the October massacre that would finally allow the memorial of the October uprising to be realized.

The Unforgetting

Under the general atmosphere of silence for almost two decades, the contest of memories of the two Octobers appeared in various forms and issues. Apart from the tug-of-war over the monument of the 1973 uprising, another issue that erupted from time to time involved the three ousted dictators of 1973. Although the tide had turned against the radicals, the ousted dictators were not welcome either. Government investigations into their corruption and abuse of power had uncovered their massive wealth, and in 1974 the government confiscated their assets without due process. On their return to Thailand after the 1976 massacre, they demanded the return of their assets, which did not sit well with the public, but they kept trying, sparking a series of controversies followed by public protests. Every government was reluctant to respond. For instance, the demand in June 1989 led to a protest by hunger strike until the government shelved the demand.[37] Like the monument for the October 1973 uprising, the return of assets, or any recognition of these former dictators, was caught up in the memory war.

Naming these contested events is not a simple matter either. The three bloody incidents—October 1973, October 1976, and May 1992—have names known to the public. The October 1973 uprising was called the Day of Extreme Grief (Wan maha wippayok) by the king immediately following the unrest. This name points to the violent conflict and the loss of life. That name was challenged shortly afterward by the student movement, which called it the Day of Extreme Joy (Wan maha piti). This name emphasizes the political outcome and impacts—democracy and the end of dictatorship. Trying to avoid committing to a specific political agenda, most people opted for a neutral name, calling it simply the October 14 event. The massacre in 1976 was initially known as the riot, and students as the rioters or the deceived; other names were applied as discourse about the event shifted. The CPT called the same incident the "suppression of people," and those who died the martyrs, names reflecting a counter discourse. News magazines sometimes used more sensational terms, such as the brutal killing (*kan sanghan hot*). Indirect, evasive names typically refer to something related to the incident, such as the demonstration. Eventually, the most common name came to be the October 6 event, which does not convey one way or another what happened on that date. The most evasive but imaginative name came

from a former prime minister, Anand Punyarachun, who once referred to the October 6 massacre simply as "an abrupt end" without
mentioning the date, year, or what happened, as if the void had said
it all.[38]

These kinds of evasive names and indirect references indicate
how unsettling the memories of these events still are. A noncommit-
tal, neutral name may seem devoid of any loaded meaning. But in
fact, it indicates that the contest of memories has not yet been settled.
Any name, as Michel-Rolph Trouillot reminds us, carries with it the
inarticulate voice and silence on its edges.[39] Anand's evasive reference
and other seemingly neutral names not only obscure the past, but are
also heavily loaded with silent voices and memories. The days and
months will forever cloak both sufferings and mysteries. As it turns
out, the neutral name that eschews politics sits squarely on the edge
between recognition and anonymity, between history and the silenced
past, and between memory and forgetfulness—the unforgetting.

The chronopolitics of the post–Cold War period affected the
memories of the massacre. Chongkol might still be "confused that
the October 6 incident was heroic" as Sutham commented on her
memory.[40] Manas's memory, it is fair to say, might suggest the modified memories among the authorities and the perpetrators. If we look
carefully at how the massacre was talked about in public between
1978 and 1996, we can see how memories of the massacre became
less polarized than in the immediate period after the tragedy when
the political forces behind those antagonistic memories remained
strong. For instance, the victims were said to be contributors to
changes in the country,[41] the tragedy a lesson for people of every political faction not to kill one another over ideological differences,[42]
and a turning point that brought about political compromise.[43] The
less polarized memories gained more ground in part because of the
atmosphere of reconciliation and the painful failure of both the leftist
radicals and the ultraroyalists. The growing liberal public sphere also
helped foster reconciliation, as the freer exchanges of views tended to
tone down extremes of various kinds. On the other hand, paradoxically, the post–Cold War era was a period of hyperroyalism that saw
the rise of royalist politics and culture.[44] As explained in chapter 8,
the royalist political culture and historical ideology in Thailand were
conditions that heavily affected what was and was not allowed in the
public sphere. Under the façade of reconciliation and unity, memories of October 6 were largely silenced. The massacre remained a

dangerous piece of history, although limited information about it, including photos, came out in public from time to time.[45] A report by the US government on human rights in Thailand in 1993 reads, "Among the topics subjected to censorship are police corruption, criticism of the Thai military, misconduct by members of the Buddhist clergy, and the 1976 student uprising."[46]

Chapter 6

THE COMMEMORATION IN 1996

On the morning of October 6, 1996, a symbolic cremation was held at the soccer field inside Thammasat University for those killed in the massacre twenty years earlier. At that time, their number and identities remained unclear. Details about the number of unidentified, unclaimed bodies remained unknown. The cremation was merely symbolic without a corpse. Instead, we put the name of each known victim on pieces of paper and then put the bits of paper all into an urn, placing it on the top of a platform at the same location I had spoken from that morning twenty years earlier. Around the platform were photos of a few identifiable victims, taken when they were still alive. We honored them as individuals who had names, families, and lives like everybody else, individuals whose lives had ended abruptly on October 6, 1976.

The ceremony started at sunrise with an offering of food for the Buddhist monks and was followed by merit-making for the dead. Then a Buddhist monk, a former Maoist ideologue, gave a sermon, urging the audience to abandon greed, hatred, and delusion. The gathering, he said, was not merely to make merit for the dead but also to commemorate them as individuals who deserved respect and recognition, to learn lessons from the past so as not to let such a tragedy happen ever again. "Life may come to an end . . . but dreams stay on. May all dreams become the force of wisdom and love that overcomes hatred and evils that brought an end to the lives of these loved ones."[1] After the sermon, a ritual designed for the occasion began. About fifty Buddhist monks and nuns led a silent walk

118

counterclockwise three times around the soccer field where the fallen victims had lost their lives. It was a Dharma walk, a form of meditation and merit-making for tolerance over hatred, to celebrate those lives that were dedicated to justice and a better future. In the middle of the field stood a big stone gong. Its low-pitched reverberation accompanied the walk.

> Twenty years ago, at this place, the sound of gunfire pierced our hearts. Today, the sound of the gong displaces it. The sound of peace will overcome the one of killing . . . , tolerance over hatred, and wisdom over delusion . . . and over The Evil.[2]

The ritual ceremony ended with the symbolic cremation. All participants paid their final respects to all the "bodies" in the urn by putting paper flowers for the dead underneath the urn as is normally done in an actual cremation. As we paid our respects to them one last time, the reality struck me forcibly. It had taken twenty years for us, the former radicals, to honor our friends with the dignity they deserved. In a Buddhist country where compassion and kindness are supposed to be abundant, twenty years was a cruelly . . . long time.

Twenty years later, the radicals of the 1970s had accomplished one of the most important missions of their lives (of my life, at any rate): to publicly cremate and say farewell to friends who had left us in an event that had shaped a whole generation. Unlike most of our other political activities, this one brought about peace of mind. Many of the radicals wept unrestrainedly, myself included. Shedding tears together in public for our lost friends, I think, was a sign that we would no longer weep alone, as we had done for years. Many former radicals recognized this event as a breakthrough in that it made the massacre widely known and allowed their painful past to be recognized and respected by the public. It was a cathartic moment for them, individually and collectively. Nonetheless, it was only a partial break in the silence. The limited discussion of the massacre remained a feature of public discourse. The painful and ambivalent memories were not resolved, the crime was not accounted for. The commemoration successfully established some persistent noise at the edge of remembering and unforgetting.

This chapter explores the activities at the commemoration of the October 6 massacre and explains the conditions that enabled it to successfully break through such a long period of relative silence. It examines the limits and constraints of remembering the unwanted past in Thailand. The constraints are not limited to those imposed by the state but are inherent in the contesting and retrospective memories of the subjects and objects of memory and in the cultural and intellectual norms embedded in Thai society. They appeared in several commemorating activities and in the monument to October 6 as well.

Confronting the State's Crime Twenty Years Later

I, Thongchai, initiated the 1996 commemoration. Given the unresolved silence since 1978, my uneasiness grew each year. That I had survived the massacre and had a comfortable life made my uneasiness grow stronger as time went by. The past is with me everywhere I go. It comes to mind every day. In the mid-1990s, with the growing scholarship on the memory of atrocities and the rise of commemoration in popular culture, the disquieting silence about the October 6 massacre increasingly bothered me. Then, in September 1995, while in Bangkok for research, I decided to write a letter, which I faxed to a few friends, asking them to spread the word to old friends and former activists. The letter invited them to join me at TU on October 6, 1996, one year from then, to make merit to commemorate our fallen friends.[3] Given the obscurity of the massacre in public memory at the time, I expected only a modest response. In retrospect, I did not realize how well timed my letter was, nor did I foresee the potential for such a commemoration ceremony. My letter spread among former radicals rapidly. Over the course of the year leading up to October 1996, former activists in groups and individually organized a variety of commemorative activities, turning the initial idea for a merit-making ceremony into a full-blown commemorative movement: a full year of activities and events about the massacre that would culminate in a major commemoration at TU on October 6, 1996.

The commemoration originated at the conjuncture of several conducive factors. First, by 1995, most former radicals were settled, with families, careers, and stable financial situations. Had the economic crisis in 1997 hit Thailand a year earlier, given its impact on the middle class, the commemoration might not have been so successful. Second, in the mid-1980s, quite a number of former radicals had the opportunities and resources to revive their active interests in public affairs by joining political parties, nongovernmental organizations,

or civic groups, and participating in public forums, rallies, and campaigns as active citizens. Third, their political resurgence contributed
significantly to the successful struggle against the military regime in
1992. Many sources confirmed that the active participants in the
demonstrations that year were people of the 1970s generation.[4]
Despite the relative silence surrounding the 1976 massacre, these former activists were no longer reluctant to engage in political issues,
which they had been after returning from the jungles. Fourth and
finally, since the mid-1980s Thailand had enjoyed a relatively open
political society and improved human rights situation. The 1992 uprising and victory over the military regime, in particular, had ended
decades of struggle against authoritarianism.[5] The military retreated
from politics for a decade and a half. A boom in press freedom, civic
politics, and a strong drive for political reform followed. Thanks to
the May 1992 event, we may say, the memory of the 1976 massacre
was able to break through the silence of the previous decade.

The two-day event on October 5 and 6 was not a low-key,
sparsely attended commemoration like those of previous years. This
one was huge, attended by many thousands. The planned and un-
planned programs went quite well, beyond expectations. The media's
attention was unusually high in the weeks leading up to the event,
which included an exhibit on the massacre, academic discussions,
public speeches, live music and performances, an outdoor art exhibition, publications, videos about the massacre and other major popular uprisings, and religious rituals. Despite the variety of activities,
the commemoration was able to present the facts and confront the
state's crime without evasiveness. What had happened twenty years
earlier was retold countless times, though without mentioning the
role of the palace in the massacre. Video footage of the actual event
with actual sound was shown repeatedly and several thousand copies
sold. The original video had been discovered in mid-1996 in the ar-
chive of TV5. In 1976, it had been used as propaganda to show the
state's triumph over the communists in Bangkok. In 1996, the same
footage provided vivid evidence of the police operations outside TU,
including brutal scenes with military marching songs in the background. Ironically, this army propaganda became best-selling evidence of the atrocity twenty years later.

A powerful account of the crime by the Thai state was presented
in the main exhibition hall. Hundreds of thousands of people visited
it over the two days. The exhibit was a visual chronology of the

events leading up to the massacre and an enactment of the morning including the excessive violence perpetrated on the victim of the hanging in Ulevich's photo. In one section of the exhibit hall was a life-sized photo of the hanging victim surrounded by delighted spectators. The image was pasted on a huge mirror so that visitors could see themselves in the mirror as if they were participants in the spectacle. Every visitor thus became a witness of the act, experiencing it in a way. Another section of the exhibit contrasted the radical students and the right-wing royalists—their political views and rhetoric, their heroes and enemies, their preferred books and literature, their lifestyles and dress codes. At the end, a question was posed—do these kinds of differences justify killing?[6] Undoubtedly the exhibit was the victims' narrative. After twenty years of official lies and evasions, the story from the victims' point of view was powerful and shocking to the visitors, especially the younger generation, who had heard vaguely about the incident but never known or understood what had happened, never realized how heinous it had been. It was the first time the general public had seen what happened in 1976. It took twenty years, an entire generation, for the voice of the victims to be heard loudly and clearly in public.[7]

Outside the hall was an outdoor art exhibition by many artists, most of whom were victims of the massacre. It included a live art performance to commemorate a friend, a student of painting who had been killed in the incident. An academic program also ran during the two days, offering presentations of papers on the massacre as well as on the broader and the structural violence in Thai society—from political assassinations and suppressions of civic leaders, the rape and everyday violence against women, to censorship and book banning. Inside the Grand Auditorium were political music and plays, public speeches, and other performances. A drama depicted common experiences of the twice-defeated radical activists. They had lost friends in the massacre and in the revolutionary battles. Eventually they also lost what hope they might have had for a socialist revolution.

Throughout the commemoration, some negative murmurs said that it was muddying the water instead of letting bygones be bygones. Nonetheless, these reactions were noticeably low and failed to gain any traction in public. The activities throughout the year were held without obstruction from the state or any right-wing groups, except a negligible leaflet from the Aphirak Chakri (Protecting the Chakri dynasty) group that celebrated the October 6 incident as the victory over the communists. It is perhaps not surprising that no condolences were expressed by any dignitaries, let alone the government, nor was there any regret or slightest hint of apology from anyone.

Rehumanizing the Individuals

At one corner of the soccer field where many lives were cut short were a dozen huge panels, each of which showed the face of the same person (see figure 6a). The panels could easily be seen from across the field. A closer look showed that the picture of the face on each panel was in fact made of hundreds of postcards. One side of each postcard was filled with black and white dots of different sizes (see figure 6b). Each postcard was in fact a jigsaw piece of the gigantic enlargement of a linotyped photo of the face. To put it another way, the photo of the face in black and white had been enlarged to such an extent that the matrices of dots that made up the picture were exposed. Then each face had been cut into postcards. The huge picture of the face was legible only when those postcards were put back in their right places. On the other side of each postcard was the message "We do not forget October 6" (*rao mai leum 6 tula*), and the address of the producers of these so-called Wall Posters. Thousands of postcards were widely distributed among former activists and others, who were encouraged to write anything they wanted on the postcard. Every recipient of a blank postcard was urged to return the postcards to the producers, otherwise each Wall Poster, that is, each face, could not have been reassembled. Once those thousands of postcards had been reassembled into a dozen faces, people could also read the messages in each of those postcards from the other side of the Wall Posters.[8]

The messages of this activity were in every action in the process of enlarging, disassembling, and reassembling of the face as well as in the act of writing comments by individual participants. Each small action was an expression of the making, unmaking, and remaking of an individual and its humanity. The distinctive life of each individual was large but made of unique details. But lives were dehumanized and blown into oblivion on that Wednesday morning. To rehumanize even one victim and to recognize him, in every sense of the word, required thousands of voluntary and willing participants to return every single postcard. A single missing card would have made the rehumanization of the victim incomplete. Moreover, although each

Figure 6a. Jaruphong Wall Posters at the commemoration in 1996. © Sarakhadi. Reprinted with permission.

Figure 6b. The postcard "We Won't Forget Jaruphong." Photo by the author.

postcard was part of the whole, each remained individually distinctive with messages, mostly handwritten. When one wrote on the postcard, the thought that was contemplated and put into writing was also meaningful. The Wall Posters were filled with the power of remembering and the defiance toward dehumanization. The message beside these dozen panels read, "We do not forget October 6. We do not forget Jaruphong." It was the face of Jaruphong Thongsin.

Enclosed in the envelope distributed with the blank postcard was information about Jaruphong's life and how he died in the massacre. Jaruphong's parents and the relatives of many other fallen heroes and heroines were among the dignitaries honored in the symbolic cremation. They were the first in line to lay the paper flowers under the urn before the flame was lit. In addition, on this occasion the Friends of Jaruphong Group funded the renovation of the main meeting room of the Thammasat Student Union Building. An account of the massacre, a list of names of the known dead, the biographies of four TU students who died on that day, including the one of Jaruphong, were displayed on the walls of that room. The room was named Jaruphong Thongsin. After the symbolic cremation, Jaruphong's parents and the rector of TU presided over its inauguration. The rector reminded us that it was the first room in TU and probably in any Thai university to be named after a student. He hoped it would be the last.

Meanwhile, a small ritual was independently organized by a Buddhist group to make merit for the dead at every location where people were killed: under the trees where the hanging took place, in the street and in the field where bodies were tossed, nailed, and burned, and several other places on the TU campus. In the evening, the final speeches were given in front of several thousand people on the soccer field. At the very end of the event, people paid their last respects with candles at the platform where the cremation took place in the morning.

During the year leading up to October 5–6, 1996, several reunions of former student activists were held. Attempts were made to record the oral history of the radical movement of 1973 through 1976. Some resulted in published records and narratives.[9] Quite a few groups then traveled up-country, spending a few days and nights together to recall and record their memories. For many, these gatherings were the first time after returning from the jungles that they had met old friends to revisit the past, to openly talk about it and share their grief within the community of fellow veterans. For many, this was the first time that they no longer had to keep their past strictly to themselves, could instead take pride in what they had been and done, even in the mistakes of their youth.

The commemorations of 1995 and 1996 also inspired searches for the remains of students as well as other fighters who died during the insurgency. They too faded into oblivion, mostly remembered only by a few friends. After 1996, many former radicals and ex-guerilla fighters began searching for the remains of comrades who had died in the armed struggle. This commemorative activity was, in my opinion, the most difficult and least known but most rewarding effort. Although their faces, names, and identities were remembered very well, in most cases their bodies had been buried in a rush, in battlefields on the front lines or in temporary camps. Locating burial sites was extremely difficult, given that by the mid-1990s the landscapes of the former battlegrounds had changed dramatically. The search teams had to recall and reconstruct particular battles in order to identify the locations where lost friends had been buried or left behind. Every search was painful.

These commemorative activities involved many people. In the search for each individual, the survivors had to revisit the past, recalling what happened, digging up memories of their traumatic pasts even as they dug up earth. They had to overcome the refuge of silence and the propensity to evasiveness. Through these activities, past and present could be connected in ways that people could live with, enabling them to make sense of their current lives. The reconstitution of each individual, both the fallen victims and the living ones, was significant possibly without their awareness. For the dead victims, individuality—face, voice, name, identity, and family—is what allows them to be seen as people like us, not a faceless enemy of the nation, religion, and monarchy, and not as faceless martyrs known only by the name of the incident in which they died. At the same time, it is their individual identities that remind us what has been lost in the crime—honorable people whose lives were like ours, whose pain could happen to anyone, including us. Individually—not as a collective crowd—is the proper way to honor a noble life.

For the living victims, in my view, no matter how powerful a collective commemoration may be, individual experiences of private trauma have no substitute, and their memories can never be completely merged into a collective. The activities that allow individuals to come to terms with their individual pasts in their own ways while participating in a collective commemoration were the best.

COLLECTIVELY, COMMEMORATING WHOM?

One of the most heated arguments among the former radicals revolved around how to characterize the victims and the student movement during the 1973 to 1976 period. How would we want the public to remember them? Were they communists, radicals, democracy lovers, or just young idealists? Gradually during the year of the commemoration, differences and divisions, even conflicts, emerged among the organizers and former radicals over concrete and practical issues too, such as what should the slogan of the commemoration be, what kinds of activities should be staged with what messages, whether to confront the issue of violence and brutality, the extent to which to expose the perpetrators, and so on. The debate on these issues revealed the serious contestation of memories among former radicals who had lived through the same experience. Some tried to impose censorship. Others claimed the correct memory.

On the one hand were the people who wanted to recognize the martyrs as nonradical, democratic activists who fought against military rule, whose idealism was for a better, caring, and equitable society.[10] Despite the radicalism they expressed, they were merely youthful idealists, not communists, not threatening radicals, and not enemies of the country. Some went so far as to argue that the students who died on October 6 and those who joined the Communist Party of Thailand (CPT) were not the same.[11] A commemoration in this view hoped to counter right-wing allegations by emphasizing the contributions of these young idealists for a better society. Speaking in the age of image making, some even suggested that the martyrs, and thereby the movement in the 1970s, should be presented in the romanticized image that was acceptable to the public and avoid any hint of the radical past. Some intentionally opposed mentioning the radical past in the narrative of the massacre and argued for some censorship as well. For them, the major activities leading to the big event in October included a special address on the future of Thai democracy by a former prime minister, a respected senior social critic, and other established public figures. Some people with this view wanted the commemoration not to dwell on the massacre, violence, death, state crime, or the past. The dubious past should not be the focus, they argued, so much as the future.

On the opposite end were the people who insisted that the past must be remembered as a radical, socialist movement and the massacre as an event intended to eliminate the socialist movement. To remember otherwise would be to expunge the radical movement from memory. Any avoidance of the "indisputable fact" that the student movement in the past had been radical was to deny history. "If there was even one dead victim who considered himself a socialist. . . . he should be recognized as such," one scholar noted.[12] In this view, any other interpretation distorted the facts and history, and any memory that did not recognize the socialist movement should be dismissed. They strongly censured my letter to friends that triggered the commemoration because, they argued, it propagated the distortion and the denial of radical history. Somsak Jeamteerasakul, the main propagator of this sanctimonious view, declared that it would have been better not to remember the massacre at all, had we not remembered the movement "correctly" as a socialist one.[13] This view was influential, especially among the young radicals of the 1990s generation, but not among the 1970s radicals. The radical critics of the commemoration alleged that most organizers, myself included, were deniers of history trying to cleanse their radical past.[14]

Most organizers and participants in the commemoration took neither of these polar positions but instead a mix of them, as reflected in the activities, such as the exhibits, publications, and public discussions. The polar views represented the parameters of possible memories among the former radicals. A more nuanced position is not illogical or contradictory and, in my opinion, is in fact probably more accurate. Besides, the representation of the radical past changed even during the commemorative year. The gradual declawing of the past radicalism had begun since the end of the domestic Cold War in the mid-1980s, reflected in the commercialization of revolutionary songs,[15] and the melancholic and nostalgic writings by the ex-leftists. By the mid-1990s, those nostalgic materials were no longer dangerous in the eye of the state. Yet most former radicals were still reluctant to speak out about who they once were and thus kept their thoughts to themselves. In this unclear atmosphere, many, myself included, were initially cautious about how we could represent the radical past in public that would not elicit a backlash from the authorities or the public. As the commemorative movement unfolded over the course of the year, nostalgic stories of the radical past snowballed without any sign of a backlash among the public.

The romanticized depiction was preferred in the initial phase of the commemorative movement but faded as the movement grew stronger. Advocates of the more radical view emerged later but most former radicals did not subscribe to it.

How they characterize their collective past was informed by subsequent experience and the present. Memory is always an interpretive outcome of individual and social perspectives. Most former radicals did not perceive their past the same way as radicals in 1996 do simply because they were no longer radical. The claimed "correct" history cannot and should not dictate their memories. In addition, before turning radical in the mid-1970s, they were ideologically diverse—idealist, nationalist, liberal, even conservative and royalist (as discussed in chapter 3). In the long perspective of their lives, the radical experience did not last. Looking back from the mid-1990s, they saw youthful idealists, highly politicized and engaged citizens who turned radical in response to many factors of that time. Over the years, former radicals had become a generation of engaged and often opinionated citizens subscribing to various shades of politics and ideologies. By 1996, they had diverse views of how the past is meaningful to them in (and to) the present. Their memories of the radical movement may seem akin to the first view, except that they did not deny their radical or even communist years. At the commemoration, although some were still reluctant, overly cautious, or even wanting to deny their radical past, most did not shy away from talking openly about the past and their jungle years as communist fighters. They talked about these years in public forums, wrote memoirs, and so on, apparently because most were proud of their experiences. They openly identified themselves not only by the name of the university and the activist groups they were affiliated with but also by their code names and the CPT bases at which they operated. Indeed, dozens more monuments to honor communist martyrs sprang up across the country after 1996.[16]

The hiding of their past was over. For many, individually and collectively as a community of former radicals, the commemoration was the cathartic moment when and where they could express who they were, what they had gone through, and what they thought. They no longer needed to hide for fear of rejection.[17] One personal anecdote was telling. An old friend walked with obvious joy in the middle of the gathering on the evening of the commemoration day. When he saw me, he called to me loudly from twenty meters away in a voice that dozens of people could hear loud and clear, "Hey, Thong! I want to tell everybody in my office and in the world that I was (am) a communist [pause] So what?!" In Thai, the verb to be, *pen*, is not variable by the tense. So I was not sure whether he was or still is a communist. In any case—so what?!

More important, however, the contested memories of these former radicals were not independent from the larger public memory. The media and the public reflected and informed one another in shaping the public perceptions of the radical past as well. As explained in earlier chapters, during the period of silence, the polarized views subsided and moderate views gained ground, and, as discussed in chapter 8, the public increasingly identified with the view of Puey. The commemoration took place in this milieu. During the commemorative year, the media and public on the one hand, and the former radicals on the other, informed one another. The media was influential in shaping how the public remembered the massacre and these former radicals as well. The media is, however, never a blank sheet of paper without ideology or prior intellectual disposition. It takes information and presents it through its own lenses. The media characterized the massacre, those turbulent years, and the former radicals in ways that were shaped by their own perspectives. An analysis that focuses exclusively on the debates among the former radicals gives them too much credit even as it overlooks the role of the media in shaping public perceptions and the influence of both media and public on the former radicals.

BREAKING THE SILENCE . . . BUT UNDER LIMITS

As an initiator of the commemorative movement living half a world away from Thailand at a time when email service was limited, I did not fully participate in the debate. In my opinion, breaking the silence should not be an attempt to sanitize memory, either to deny the uncomfortable past or to flaunt a sanctimoniously correct past. Memories from all perspectives should be allowed to exist and contest in the public sphere. Without control or censorship, the commemoration in 1996 opened up such a space for multiple memories. The breakthrough was possible because multiple memories found their space in the public sphere. My friend's greeting me was evidence of a joy that perhaps he had not felt in a long time. It was not the joy of triumph over an opponent. It was not a jolly mood without sadness.

It was the joy of being oneself again, to borrow Kasian's words. To me, the cathartic effects on these individuals were the most important outcome of the commemoration.[18] The stigma—the fear of being rejected—had gone. The cloud of silence was irreversibly penetrated.

The commemoration was, however, not a magic spell that could entirely dispel the ambivalence and silence about the massacre in Thai society. Many activities hit various limits of what can be spoken. The commemoration was probably the first of its kind for people who had been regarded as enemies of the nation, religion, and the monarchy. Recognition of the dead still faced many obstacles. It took place in the political environment of hyperroyalism and the post-1976 consensus. I elaborate on this condition in chapter 8. For now, it is enough to say that such conditions underpinned the regime of Democracy with the Monarchy as the Head of the State—or royal democracy.[19] In 1996, most powerful people and institutions that had been involved in the massacre remained in power. The palace was considered even more sacred and beyond criticism than in the 1970s. The participants in the 1996 commemoration, unavoidably, observed this limit and practiced self-censorship with regard to any utterances that involved the monarchy. The October 6 exhibition, for example, planned to show *Dao sayam*'s front page of October 5, 1976, with the photo that triggered the royalist hysteria. It would have been the first time since 1976 that this photo was shown in Thailand. Then, a few hours before the opening of the exhibition, the organizers and the exhibition producers had second thoughts. They were not sure whether the photo might trigger another controversy and another charge of lèse majesté from the right wing. They decided to take it down at the last minute, leaving the space blank and the description intact as if the photo were still there.

Given that the silence since 1978 was for the sake of reconciliation and national unity, such concerns were often raised against the commemorative movement. From the beginning to the end of the commemorative year, unease was palpable that the event might open old wounds and that the former radicals might seek revenge. Ironically, throughout the year, no serious discussion was held about the perpetrators. Apart from the usual targets such as the Red Gaurs, the organizers, the media, or academics made no effort to expose who should be accountable for the crimes, the propaganda, the false accusation, the Thanom conspiracy, the mobilization of hatred, the desecration of the dead bodies, and so on. In fact, former radicals, myself included, were repeatedly asked by the media to confirm that we did not seek revenge of any kind. In other words, people sympathized with the victims but were unwilling to pursue accountability in fear of ensuing turmoil. The culture of elite impunity is pervasive in Thailand, and the rich and powerful usually find ways, legal or not, to evade accountability. Retaliation against those who seek justice is a real threat. As a result, concerned citizens know to stay within certain limits and when they must keep silent. That this phenomenon was occurring with the commemorations suggests that people knew that the perpetrators of the massacre were powerful, highly placed individuals. The discourse on those perpetrators remains elusive, slippery, and off limits.

On the other hand, many journalists also asked many times if we had forgiven or were ready to forgive. In Buddhist Thailand, a victim is expected to offer forgiveness whether someone has confessed to wrongdoing or not because the aim of forgiveness is to purify one's mind. It is about individual moral well-being. Forgiveness of this kind does not require any kind of social or legal justice. Justice and the rule of law is secondary. Karma, it is believed, will do the job of justice. Many former radicals expressed their forgiveness based on the Buddhist notion of loving kindness. (I discuss the Buddhist approach to atrocity and its implications for justice in chapter 7.)

Throughout the year of commemoration, therefore, the discourse on the massacre was mainly about violence, brutality, tragedy, the intolerance toward diverse ideas and ideologies, and the toxic politics that had emerged because of these problems. Undoubtedly, these concerns were important and valuable subjects of discussion. Unfortunately, no serious probing for truth was undertaken. Justice and the rule of law were put aside. Even years later, as some critics of the commemoration point out, the discourse on the massacre remains about brutality and tears but nothing further.[20] Occasionally, calls were made for an investigation into this ugly episode of Thai history, such as the efforts of some academics in 2001 mentioned in a previous chapter, but the public did not seem to care. In this respect, it is fair to say that although the commemoration pointed to the problematic norms of the absence of justice and truth seeking, it did not put truth and justice within reach.

Despite all these limitations, an important accomplishment of the commemoration was the irreversible shift in the relative power between the perpetrator's and the victim's memories of the massacre.

Since the commemoration, the victims have become more vocal and the perpetrators have become evasive, apologetic, or even silent. However, even though earlier radicalism was no longer dangerous to talk about, these former radicals were kept within limits. The perpetrator's silence is different from that of the victims in that the perpetrators can take refuge behind the limits that the victims cannot cross. The silence protects them; they need not break it.

Monument to October 6 and Its Paradox

Today, on entering the main entrance of TU, next to the Grand Auditorium (see map), across the street from Sanamluang, we see on our right hand the October 6 Monument (figure 7). It is, as Thom Huebner describes it,

> a massive granite slab . . . approximately one meter high at its highest point, one meter deep, and six meters long. Its low contour requires one to look down at, rather than up toward the monument, as if encountering a tombstone. . . . its mass and solidity, the date 6 Tula 2519 (October 6, 2519 in the Buddhist calendar) chiseled in heavy angular letters and its color evocative of coagulated blood suggest a harsh objective reality. Its uneven horizontal surface forebodes an uncertain future . . . The bold "in your face" inscription of the date resembles graffiti, suggesting a transgressive semiotics symbolizing the monument as conceived (without government support) its emplacement (on the site of a transgressive act), and the act itself that the monument commemorates. Embedded in the crevices formed by the chiseled letters are bronze bas-relief faces of some of the students who were massacred that day.
>
> Along the vertical back and sides of the monument are engraved the names of all the known victims who died by hanging, guns and mortars that day. Around the perimeter of the base is a quote from the then Rector of the University, in both Thai and English [all in upper case]:
> "What is most regrettable is the fact that young people now have no third choice. If they cannot conform to the government, they must run away. Those interested in peaceful means to bring about freedom and democracy must restart from square one." Dr. Puey Ungphakorn, from "the violence and the coup" of 6th October 1976.[21]

A monument helps memory last, as if it stops the flow of time by planting the concrete embodiment of memory in public space. Such

Figure 7. The October 6 monument at Thammasat University. © Fa Diaw Kan.

is a positivistic and simplistic view of a monument, definitely inadequate for the October 6 Monument. In recent times around the world, a monument or monuments try to accommodate multiple memories and changing perspectives of the past rather than a fixed story and meaning. In this regard, a concrete monument usually employs paradoxical mnemonic devices to impart the unchanged and the changed, and ultimately represents the remembered and the forgotten.[22]

The monument to October 6 is the concrete embodiment of the paradoxical condition of memories of the massacre after the commemoration in 1996. On the one hand, it firmly and literally establishes the memory of the tragedy in public space, marking the changing public landscape of memories of the massacre since the mid-1990s. The memory of October 6 is now audible, not silent. It also hints at the possibility of other memories that have not yet been articulated or recognized, that have been lost and forgotten or remain in the realm of the unforgetting. Yet, the monument's design and location embody the limits, what can be said and what cannot, in subtle ways, both by presence and absence, and by selection and omission of different elements among the contesting memories. It lacks any devices that could help uncover the unforgetting. It is a testament to both the reluctance and the willingness to dig deeper into the tragedy. Even as it successfully planted that memory in public space, paradoxically it also formalized the partial silence—the huge realm of unforgetting that remains even after 1996.

The conception of this monument began during the commemoration in 1996, but the process—brainstorming for ideas, selection of artists, design, fundraising, and construction—took years to finish. It was inaugurated on October 6, 2000.[23] TU adopted the project as its own although no government money could be used for it. After struggling for several years, the funding for the monument got a boost after Puey passed away in 1999, prompting more donations from his admirers to complete the project.

Over the years, many aspects of the monument changed, including the concept and design. Having begun as a functional memorial building, it evolved into a stand-alone monument due to funding, costs, and shifting policy of the TU administration. It had to be placed inside TU because no other government agency would provide space, undoubtedly due to its sensitivity. TU insisted that the October 6 monument should be one in a series to mark the important political events in which the university has contributed to Thailand's democratization, not a single monument to the massacre. Hence the plan for the Historic Sculpture Garden of TU and Democratic Struggles, beginning with its founding in 1934 as part of the 1932 revolution and ending with the October 6, 1976, massacre, separated by six monuments to other events.[24] "The meandering stone path leading from one monument to another symbolizes a river of time. . . . From this approach, the October 6 monument . . . forms a dam blocking the flow of the symbolic river."[25]

The brainstorming session was a public event, and the entire project involved almost a hundred artists. Two of them, senior artists who were themselves involved in political activism in the mid-1970s, were chosen to lead the entire project and were responsible for the October 6 monument. A private fund supported a trip enabling the two to learn from similar projects elsewhere. They chose to go to Poland and Russia.[26] Between a realist, a semi-abstract, and a symbolic portrayal, they eventually chose the realistic one.[27] In the words of the chief artist, Suraphol Panyawachira, partly in response to criticism of the unsubtle style and the unambiguous message of the monument,

[For October 6], a symbolic [monument] is dangerous. . . . I am wor-
ried about the different interpretations that might distort history. Many
people tried to do so [for this case]. Dangerous. . . . Some other monuments [in the same series] are more symbolic. However, for this one,
instead of allowing [people] to interpret its meaning, it should be a direct punch. . . . I want it to be quite disturbing, hoping that visitors of
later generations would ask if it was really so horrifying, then question
further. This is my intention.[28]

"It must make the visitors feel shocked, unable to smile," another artist adds.[29]

Unfortunately, between 1996 and 2000, when the monument
was designed and completed, information about the victims who died
was still unclear. Many names inscribed on the back of the monument
are misspelled or incorrect. One name was, according to police records, a goon who attacked TU that morning. Finally, even though
the citation from Puey was part of the original design, the relief of
Puey was not. The addition of his image was part of an agreement for
a huge donation to the project after his death.[30]

Despite the determination of the artists to prevent interpretations of the monument other than its explicit and shocking message,
I would argue that no artist can block multiple meanings. The bulky
rock in its chosen style may shout loudly to a visitor, "October 6,
1976," in an intimidating and shocking fashion as the artists intended. Despite that, ambivalence was unavoidable, not because the
literal message—the date—is not clear enough, nor because the design and art are not immediate and loud enough, but because even
such explicit and direct messages cannot prevent multiple meanings
given the multiple and ambivalent memories of the massacre. The
date is the least controversial, most neutral name for the incident
precisely because it hides the contested memories and meanings behind it. The date is the only element that every memory of the massacre shares. Beyond that, anything goes. The shocking horror of the
event is also an element that various memories of the massacre agree
on. These elements of the memories fall within the allowable limits of
public discourse since the 1996 commemoration. The monument
therefore represents the public memory of the massacre quite well in
that it speaks as much as is allowed. The other memories, however,
remain behind the massive granite slab. The rock does not exorcise
the specter. The ambivalence may not be apparent, but it is inherent.

The monument is the embodiment or the permanent abode of the specter. Moreover, as public memory of the massacre moved closer to the moderate, such as Puey's, even the artists of the monument must have been informed and influenced by such views. The strong presence of Puey embodied in his words at the base of the monument have much to tell us about the memoryscape of the massacre since 1996.

Last but equally important, the location inside TU marks the contained public space in which the memories live on. The space outside the campus is probably too public and, as symbolically represented by Sanamluang, too connected to the Grand Palace. The noisy memories of the massacre are located literally on the fringe of the public space in which the monarchy's presence is still in command. The massacre is the noise on the edge of memory, a partial silence of the unforgetting.

After the Commemoration

It was a painfully long time before the former radicals could honor their lost friends and acknowledge the pain their families had endured quietly since that Wednesday morning. "It took twenty years to prove that those who died were not enemies of the country," a former leader remarked.[31] Clearly, the commemorative movement has expanded the limits for public discourse of the massacre considerably. If a monument is taken as a milestone of memory, then the commemorative movement in 1995 and 1996 had a huge impact on the memoryscape of the 1976 massacre and, as it turned out, on the 1973 uprising as well.

The memorial of the October 1973 uprising that had faced so many obstacles over the years finally materialized after the 1996 commemoration helped rehabilitate the 1973–1976 student movement. In 1998, a new agreement was announced. The story behind this success was the personal connection between the leader of the 1973 uprising, Thirayuth Boonmi, and the former prime minister, Anand Punyarachun, who personally negotiated with the director of the Crown Property Bureau. Nevertheless, I would argue, the success was owed in part to the 1995–1996 commemorative movement. This monument, however, was for the martyrs of October 1973 only. The events and names of the dead in the 1976 massacre could not be included. In the view of many of my friends from that generation, it was the first step toward a more formal recognition of the massacre. In my view, however, that may not be the case. The monument for October 1973 is possible, I would argue, partly because of the clear exclusion of the 1976 massacre from the 1973 memorial project.

The October 14 Martyrs was unveiled in 2001 with huge celebration and fanfare. It is a building that houses a museum of the 1973 uprising and meeting rooms for political activities. At its heart is the stupa-shaped monument, fourteen meters tall and copper colored. The front of the base is a plaque inscribed "October 14, 1973, People's Democracy" and the names of the seventy-two people who died in the uprising.[32] Maurizio Peleggi astutely observes that the monuments of the two Octobers are supposed to be related given the history of the two events. But they are in fact quite different. The monument to the uprising is prospective; that of the massacre is retrospective. The Buddhist symbolism of the former "encourage(s) reflective remembrance which is the functional discharge of painful memories and the extinction of psychic suffering," in contrast with the emotional remembrance of the 1976 monument, which implies the ongoing pain and suffering.[33] The distinction between the two Octobers is amplified. One is officially recognized by the state, the other is more dangerous and must be kept within limits.

Despite the somewhat limited recognition of the history of the October uprising, it is not without ambivalence and "its place in history still provokes uneasiness."[34] In most school textbooks, October 1973 receives only passing attention, if it is mentioned. Controversies over former dictators always revive the call to include the event in history textbooks. For example, in early 1997, the government restored the status, and thereby the pensions and benefits, of one dictator who had gone into exile in 1973. The government rescinded its decision after strong protests from the public but took no action on the textbook issue.[35] In early 1999, a different administration made a similar mistake, conferring a highly prestigious award on Thanom. It was so controversial that it almost brought down the government.[36] After this controversy, the government agreed to allow the story of the 1973 uprising in school textbooks but made it clear that the 1976 massacre and the 1992 uprising, which were still fresh at the time, were not under consideration.[37] Controversies accompanied the process from beginning to end, concerning who should be assigned to write, how the incident should be remembered, and how it would be written. To avoid offending the different sides, the finished draft omitted the necessary elements of a good narrative, including the names of key historical figures and several important but disputed details. Critical interpretations, and thus the meanings of the event, were also absent. As the author admitted, it was not a history but an almanac.[38] The draft was mired in controversy for more than a year and failed to get approval from the scholars who reviewed it. Eventually, in early 2001, the project was dropped.[39]

No effort was made to include an account of the October 6 massacre in school textbooks. If the October uprising was recognized as a major step toward democracy and a historic event that most Thai people supported, the October massacre was neither. Instead, it was a reminder that Thailand was not as peaceful or tolerant as generally believed, and that Thai people could also commit atrocities. It was a haunting history. Even after the breakthrough in 1996, the October massacre remained a more uncomfortable episode of history to many than the uprising. The question whether to commemorate the two October events together or separately, for example, was raised again and again over the years. It made allies of people with different aims. The together camp consisted of those trying to give a stronger presence to the massacre and those trying to deradicalize the past. Integrating the two Octobers in the narrative of the commemoration would achieve both purposes. In the separate camp were those radicals who did not want to erase the strong distinction between the two events, along with the nonradicals who were afraid that the massacre might "contaminate" the October uprising by making it too radical. Keeping the narratives of the two Octobers separate would achieve both purposes.

During and after the commemorative year, memoirs of former radicals abounded, especially of their jungle years, showing their growing comfort with telling the stories of their radical past openly in public. One of them, by a well-known writer, Sila Khomchai, included hilarious stories about his jungle experiences as a member of a revolutionary musical group.[40] To be able to laugh at themselves and to recall their difficult years from such an ironic and playful perspective was remarkable. This memoir is still one of a kind. It does not oppose the radical views but subverts them. Another remarkable one, published nearly twenty years later, tells the story of day-to-day living as a young revolutionary, which was full of hardship, scarcity, and the sadness of loss, but also fun, romantic love and heartbreak, and everyday irritations, such as a silly dispute over salted fish. Clearly, these former radicals did not deny or forget their radical past. It is easy to see how proud and painful they still are. But their perspective on their past was anything but radical. As one of them put it, "as time went by, those youths grew up, matured, and gained experience. Thus, they could look back on their past with understanding, and could laugh at their naiveté."[41] These memoirs are evidence that the public had provided these former radicals with the space that allowed them to be themselves and their memories to come out openly.

After the 1996 commemoration, the serious searches for fallen communist comrades in jungles began and continued for some years. Altogether, they recovered the bones of several hundred people. These former radicals at various CPT bases around the country organized commemorations and cremations for their fallen comrades, providing the honor and recognition due to them and their families. Then, at each base, a monument was erected, usually in the form of a commemorative stupa with an inscription of the names of the fallen fighters either on the stupa or a nearby plaque. At the one in Nongbua Lamphu I visited, small urns, each filled with the remains of an individual fighter, were placed in an orderly way on the shelf with names and sometimes pictures of the dead. At another memorial, a poem celebrating the revolutionary spirit and the fallen comrades was engraved on the wall, with a red-star flag and other memorabilia from the failed revolutionary wars. The stupa, which looks like a Khmer-style pagoda, is in fact modeled after an M-16 bullet. Any political significance of the design is left to the visitor's imagination. By 2016, fifteen monuments had been erected to fallen revolutionary militias. Except for the M-16 bullet stupa, all were created after the 1995–1996 commemorative movement.[42] This is more evidence that the 1996 commemoration did not try to erase the history of Thai radicalism, as some had feared, and that the former radicals did not try to deradicalize their pasts. Looking at the past from the perspective of later decades, they instead saw radicalism as a youthful idealistic part of their lives.

Since 1996, October 6 has been noisy and loud, but it stays within the limits. It is fine now to say that a massacre of students occurred on that day. It is fine now to talk about the brutality and extreme violence. Anything beyond that—who did it or why—is out of bounds and thus should remain in the realm of silence. Despite the uneasiness, the annual commemoration of the massacre has become a regular event that attracts reasonable attention from the media and the public. The unforgetting after 1996 is in an ongoing state of partial or semisilence. The noisy edge and the realm of silence are juxtaposed. This memory condition is not always opposed to remembering. Instead, it yields a peculiar kind of memory, which is the subject of the next two chapters.

Chapter 7

THE GOOD SILENCE

Thus far, we have seen that silence is not a symptom of forgetting but one of the unforgetting, the inarticulate or unvoiced memory and the liminal state at the edge of memory. This chapter takes us one step further to understand the moments when silence represents efforts against forgetting. It also contends with another problematic assumption that political silence, or silence following an atrocity, is the result of suppression, directly or indirectly, politically and socially, or psychologically. Silence is usually taken as a negative, a sign of suppression—in other words, the result of being silenced. Such an assumption may not be wrong, but it is not necessarily right, either. Indeed, voluntary silence is not uncommon.

This chapter offers two cases that illustrate purposeful silence used to cope with the painful past. In the first, a father searches for his son whose death on October 6, 1976, was unconfirmed and the whereabouts of his body unknown for more than twenty years. The father kept a detailed chronicle of his unsuccessful search for his son. The chronicle had no ending, however. It went silent while the search continued. Why? This conundrum prompted me to search for the truth about his son's death and the whereabouts of his body. The answers I found led to another heartbreaking moment that reminds us how silence can be full of memory and hope, but how fragile this silence can be. The second case is about a Buddhist approach to a past atrocity, and how a deep contemplation of its cause produces silence as a way to cope with the painful past. Silence is a virtuous act. The chapter ends with my brief reflections on the long silence of Dr. Puey Ungphakorn, the rector of Thammasat University, after the massacre.

A FATHER'S SILENCE FOR MEMORY AND HOPE

Jinda and Lim Thongsin lived in a small town in Surat Thani Province, about seven hundred kilometers south of Bangkok, which was about twelve to thirteen hours by train at the time (figure 8). Jinda was a school teacher, Lim an orchard farmer. Their eldest son, Jaruphong, had been missing since the day of the massacre, and they began the search for him immediately. Jinda wrote a memoir, a chronicle of his search. He kept it to himself for twenty years before friends of his son made it public at the commemoration of the massacre in 1996.[1]

Jinda's memoir deserves the lengthy excerpts included here for many reasons. It tells us about the experiences of an ordinary parent who traveled long distances, leaving his wife and other children at home, to search for his missing son under the difficult and confusing conditions immediately after the massacre. No one knew for certain where to find information about the victims. Even the authorities knew little. The search was frantic and chaotic. The memoir tells us about public sentiments at the time—the official who treated the arrested students and their relatives as enemies, the ordinary people who acted out of kindness and concern no matter what they thought about the radical students, the friends of the victims who shared tears and concerns, and more. The memoir tells us not only much about Jinda but also about many other parents in the same situation, whether their children lost their lives, were arrested, or simply did not return home after the massacre. The last but most important reason for me is that Jaruphong was a friend of mine who sacrificed his life trying to protect others.

"In Search for My Son: a Father's Memoir," by Jinda Thongsin

The memoir begins with background information about the family. Jinda and Lim had five children. In 1976, one was in kindergarten, three in local grade schools, and the eldest son Jaruphong. Jaruphong was the first in the family to go to college.

Figure 8. Jinda and Lim Thongsin. © Sarakhadi. Reprinted with permission.

> In that year [Jinda wrote], an unforeseeable event took place. It was a
> tragedy, incomparable to any other, that brought grief to my entire
> family. It was extremely painful, so unbearable that it can be said that
> I, the father, and Lim, the mother, of those children, have already died
> even though we are still breathing. And we will remain dead until what
> we lost is returned to us.

After learning about the tragedy on October 6, Jinda and Lim were
distraught. Jinda took a train to Bangkok as soon as he could. "On
that train, I met some fellows in a similar situation. . . . We looked at
each other, speechless, as we all were indescribably sad and concerned." Arriving in Bangkok in the early morning of October 8, he
rushed to his son's dormitory.

The atmosphere at the dorm was quite different from that during my previous visits when my son first began staying there two years before. This time, everybody just looked at each other in silence. No chitchat. Not even a noise from a radio. I sensed a calamity. I looked up at the windows of his room. They were shut. Perhaps he was still in bed. I rushed to his room but found the door securely locked from the outside. I peeked inside. He was not there, not even a trace. My heart sank, as if it had left my body. My knees trembled. As I tried to walk down the stairs, I met a young boy who lived a few doors down from my son. I told him I had come to see my son, Jaruphong. Suddenly he burst into tears, telling me that Jaruphong had not returned to the dorm since October 5, the day before the event. As his voice entered my ears, I could not hear anything else.

Jinda then met the owner of the dormitory, who tried to console him. Jinda was baffled: where should he start to search for his son? TU was shut down. "I bought every newspaper, reading every bit of news about injured students at various hospitals, praying quietly to not find Jaruphong's name. The dorm's owner told me that he had his boys going to various hospitals, but Jaruphong's name was not among the injured students." Following the advice of the owner that Jaruphong might be among those students who had been arrested and detained in various places, Jinda then rushed to the police station closest to TU to find the list of all those who had been arrested. The station was crowded with parents who looked terrified. He found the name of a nephew, Jang, who had been detained at the police school outside Bangkok. But Jaruphong's name was not among those arrested. Jinda then went back to his son's dorm, hoping that he might have left a note or some traces in his room.

> I went into the room. His used clothes were hung on a bar, but the bed was covered neatly. On the desk, books, pens and stationery were still there. . . . There was an envelope addressed to me, but nothing inside. Many documents were still in the tote bag he always carried. I delved into every piece of paper, but no trace. On a notebook nearby, he had jotted a passage without a date. I do not know when he wrote it, but it perfectly fit what had just happened. He had written, "They mercilessly sprayed bullets at us, who fought for democracy and for the country, till we fell chaotically. Our friends' blood that soaked the soil won't be wasted. Comrades, we who are still alive will take revenge for you!"

At that point, Jinda thought that Jaruphong might have returned to his place to gather his necessary belongings, then escaped without letting anyone know. Jinda kept the note to himself, then went to consult with Lim's nephew, who was a navy officer (referred to as Brother in the memoir). While listening to Brother about what happened in Thammasat, Jinda thought about Lim and recorded it in the memoir:

> She must be even more anxious and agonized than I am because Jaruphong was our first child, the one she loves most and the one whom she was so proud of for becoming a college student. When this unexpected event happened, it was as if her heart and soul were wrenched away.

Staying at Brother's house, Jinda got so drunk that he could not remember anything about that evening. The next morning, Jinda and Brother drove to visit Jang, his nephew at the detention center outside Bangkok, hoping that he knew something about Jaruphong. For several hours, Jinda stood out in the sun in the long line of parents waiting to see their children, enduring verbal abuse from several police officers. One of them said, "You parents of terrorists didn't teach your kids well. You deserve this!" Later, Jinda was told by another police officer that it would be the end of the day before it was his turn to visit Jang. He should come back another day.

Jinda left Bangkok for home that evening. When he arrived the next day, he wrote in the memoir, "my children were waiting with their mother. When I said that I had not found Jaruphong yet, all of them cried. . . . Mother told the four children not to behave like their brother." Jang's parents visited Jinda, consulting with him about how to get Jang bailed out. They put together cash and other assets as collateral. Jinda went back to Bangkok and straight to Jaruphong's dormitory, but there was no news. Then, to get Jang bailed out, he went from one police station to another, but could not get it done that day because he had to go to court. At court the next day, he learned that the land titles he had collected as collateral were not valid. Jinda then went to visit Jang again. Fortunately, this time he got the chance to talk to his nephew for five minutes.

The first thing Jinda asked Jang was about Jaruphong. Jang had encountered Jaruphong in the middle of the chaos, Jinda's memoir reported. Shortly after telling Jang to be careful, Jaruphong ran off.

Suddenly another round of fire hit several students. Although Jang did not clearly see whether Jaruphong was among them, a female student he did not know screamed, "Jaruphong got shot dead." Jang recounted all of this to Jinda. "My heart almost stopped," Jinda wrote.

The collaterals Jinda brought to bail out Jang were denied by the court again the next day. On the street outside the court, which was on the other side of Sanamluang opposite TU, Jinda saw people still gathered around the spot where bodies had been burned on October 6. Distressed and speechless, he glanced over at TU, remembering the times he had visited it when Jaruphong was there. Jinda wrote, "it is as if Thammasat was telling me that it was barely alive and could hardly stand after taking all those bullets." Without any hope and not knowing what else to do, Jinda returned home.

At home, Jinda met a district officer who told him that "my son had returned to Surat [Thani]. Military intelligence learned that five to ten students fled to the jungle [at a nearby district to join the communist guerillas] including Jaruphong Thongsin—my son." Jinda expressed doubt. The district officer backed up his words, saying that he could show evidence from military intelligence. Jinda was delighted with the exciting news, told his family, and renewed the search for his son. He went to the area mentioned by the officer. He met a former friend of Jaruphong who was a local soldier there, who told Jinda that he had seen Jaruphong a few days earlier walking in the market with some student friends. He knew for certain that it was Jaruphong, although he did not approach him because he, a soldier, might frighten Jaruphong and his friends. Jinda asked a relative who lived in that district to help find out more information. Two days later, this relative reported that it was not clear where Jaruphong was. The relative learned only that many students had joined the communists in the mountainous jungles near his hometown.

Three days later, Jinda learned that the police had stopped a mining truck at a district near his home town for transporting students from the train station into the hills. In those days, attacks by the communists on government forces had intensified and the number of casualties increased, especially in districts in Surat Thani. An additional three military posts with more weapons and cannons were set up in Jinda's hometown. The psychological units were everywhere but the communist attacks did not subside. For months afterward, whenever anyone brought news about Jaruphong, Lim would question them extensively. If anyone said that they had seen Jaruphong anywhere, no matter where it was or how dangerous the area, Jinda and Lim would go.

A few months passed. Jaruphong's siblings stopped doing well at school. They clearly missed their brother. "Whenever they mentioned him, it was like a needle pierced through my heart . . . my grief was deep inside, indescribable in words. I felt I would weep in my heart for the rest of my life," Jinda wrote. Coming to terms with the fact that Jaruphong would not return to school, that they would not see him graduate from college, Jinda went to Bangkok to collect his son's belongings and to pay the overdue rent.

> We packed up everything, including old shoes, eyeglasses, bedding. . . . We put them neatly in boxes, not because we wanted to save them for our use, but because the things he had used reminded us of him. We wanted to keep his belongings for the day we might meet him again. If it never happens, they are all we have left of him.

Jinda returned home after he finished packing up. "Everything in Bangkok hurts me," he wrote. Lim washed her son's clothes, folded them neatly, and put them in a bag. She did not let the other children use them because she believed that her son would surely return one day.

Then, one day a registered letter arrived, addressed to Jaruphong Thongsin at his home address. Inside was Jaruphong's identity card with a blood stain on it and a terse note, "Enclosed is an identity card." After crying for a time, Jinda realized that the sender's address was on the envelope and so returned to Bangkok again to track down the sender. He stopped at Brother's and they drove together to the sender's address. After looking for the place for three hours, they found it. A young mother who lived there did not know who the sender was. Jinda refused to give up. It occurred to him that he could trace registered mail through the post office. Fortunately, people there were very helpful, looking through dozens of log books until they found the name and address of the sender, Mr. Samran. Jinda and Brother tracked down Samran's place, but he wasn't there. They learned from neighbors that Samran had a son, Viroj, who was a student at TU and lived on the other side of Bangkok. Viroj must have sent the letter, Jinda concluded.

Jinda and Brother found Viroj's house. The owner, a woman, invited them in. Viroj lived there, she explained, but had left town for a few days. Jinda recounted his story, and she confirmed that Viroj had collected several cards of his friends from the police station near TU and had mailed them. Many more remained in a box that she showed to Jinda. Jinda and Brother met with the station chief, who explained that many students had thrown away their identity cards when they escaped from TU that day. Jinda saw a box full of cards on display at the station for anybody who might know the owners to pick up. The next day, Jinda and Brother visited Viroj's house again, trying to find out what he knew about Jaruphong, but again he wasn't there. Jinda returned home.

The memoir ends abruptly here, unfinished. It was kept in a box for many years, moved several times to avoid floods, until 1996 when it was published in a commemorative booklet dedicated to Jaruphong during the commemoration of the massacre.

Hope amid Confusion

From journalists' interviews with Jinda and Lim in 1996 and later, I learned more about their lives during those years as they continued the search for their son. Whenever they heard that somebody had met Jaruphong, they would follow the rumors. "The two of us, Lim and I, rode motorcycles to six jungles, but we did not find him," Jinda once said.[2] "I am so confused," Lim added. "Those who were at TU on that day said [Jaruphong] died. But people in this area said he is still alive. As long as we do not see his dead body, we have hope." About ten years after the massacre, they received a letter that contained a photo of Jaruphong being dragged along the soccer field that morning (such as figure 2). An anonymous sender wrote, "Dear Father, I was a friend of Jaruphong. I heard that you and the Mother are still searching for Jaruphong. . . . You don't have to search anymore because Jaruphong is gone. No Jaruphong anymore." Jinda told us that was when he began to believe it.[3] But even after that, they followed up on any rumors that somebody had seen Jaruphong, despite their realization that he probably would never return. They refused to give up hope as long as there was no confirmation of his death and his body was not found.

Their other children grew up under the cloud of their eldest brother's death. The sister saw the photograph while at university. She was not sure that it was her brother and dared not look too carefully. She could not bear to tell her parents what she thought because she knew they still lived with hope.[4] She believed that they also knew that Jaruphong was gone but chose to live in denial.[5] One of the brothers knew about their father's memoir long before it became public but he could not read it through.[6]

What happened to Jaruphong Thongsin did not become clear until 2000, when his body was identified. There were only a few witnesses during the chaotic moments that morning. Early on it was said that, after making sure everybody had left the TU Student Union building, Jaruphong was the last person to leave the building, at about the time that the police arrived. Word spread fast even to the prison during the first week I was there that he had been killed. Given the severe restriction of information after the massacre, however, this could not be verified. Adding to the confusion was the fact that Jaruphong's name was never among the dead or the injured or among the arrested. Moreover, because he was an executive member of the National Student Center of Thailand, his name appeared as one of the student leaders who remained at large. The photograph of his body being dragged along the soccer field with a piece of cloth around his neck was seen worldwide, but not in Thailand until many years later. A few people got it from abroad. The photograph, though, did not make it clear beyond doubt that the victim was Jaruphong.

Meanwhile, the misinformation that he had joined the communists kept his parents' hope alive. During those years, Jaruphong's friends did not reach out to Jinda and Lim. They were certain that he had died on that day, but they too were perplexed by the disappearance of his body and the absence of his name among the dead. I saw the photograph for the first time in 1978 shortly after my release from prison. I still recall the discussion among Jaruphong's close friends as to whether the victim in the photo was Jaruphong. We could not confirm it. We agreed only that the victim's clothes looked like his. If the victim was Jaruphong, we wondered whether he had been dragged or whether the abuse of his body had taken place after his death. In any case, we did not realize that his parents had not heard and had not been informed about his death. We did not know about their relentless search for their son. By the early 1980s, the former radicals had other concerns, from the crisis within the revolutionary movement, to how to survive and resume their normal lives in the society they had once despised. Jaruphong's death, although never forgotten, did not seem to be an urgent matter.

The commemoration in 1996 brought renewed attention to Jaruphong's death. As his friends planned activities to honor his sacrifice (described in chapter 6), it occurred to them that no one had visited his parents since that day. These friends of Jaruphong—including myself—were stunned to realize their negligence, which now struck them as heartless, unfathomable, irresponsible. That it was inexcusable is an understatement. With the assistance of Jaruphong's brother, a group of them made the trip to visit Jinda and Lim. After twenty years of hope and waiting for the return of their son, the truth they were afraid of was finally confirmed by their son's friends. Soon afterward, the story of Jinda and Lim appeared in the national media. Jaruphong became an icon of the victims of the October 6 massacre. His parents' unfaltering love and hope, and their anguish over twenty years, came to represent the suffering of the many parents and families of the victims.

Puzzlements

My first question after reading Jinda's memoir was why it stopped abruptly. The absence of an ending bothered me because I was anxious to know what happened after Jinda failed to find the sender of Jaruphong's ID card and how that search unfolded. Moreover, to a friend who survived the same event that took Jaruphong's life, his death and the desecration of his body were painful. The lack of closure to his parents' search, though, made that pain unbearable. I was anxious to know how the search ended, if it did, and what happened to my friend's father and mother during those years. Perhaps the absence of closure for them made the wound fresh for me as well. I could not be content with the simple assumption that Jinda had lost interest in keeping up the chronicle.

I met Jinda at the commemoration in 1996 and asked him for permission to translate his memoir, which he granted orally. In fact, he seemed indifferent to my request. Then I asked him whether he wanted to write more about how the search ended. Suddenly he was silent. He stared tensely at me but did not say a word. I realized immediately that I had just asked the most horrid and inexcusable question I had ever asked anyone. To write the ending of the memoir would have given him unbearable pain. This may be why he did not finish. My curiosity made me wonder, though, whether this was an adequate explanation, given that Jinda continued to search relentlessly for years despite the pain.

My second and related question after reading the memoir was an obvious one: where was Jaruphong's body? Its absence probably led to the misunderstanding that he was still at large and fueled the rumors of his guerilla activities. Above all, it gave Jinda and Lim the hope that their son might return. Jinda asked friends of his son to find out what happened to his son's body. How and why did it disappear, if it did? This mystery also bothered me so much because what happened to my friend and the pain of his parents were personal. I could not leave it unresolved.

In 2000, I found the materials about the October 6 trial (see chapter 2, note 94), and the autopsy reports of every corpse from TU were among them.[7] Except for a few, each report was in a standard format. The first page contained the personal information about the victim: name, address, age, place and time of death, and so on. The second page was the detailed examination of the corpse: sizes and shapes of the wounds on the body, dress, and other materials found with the body, and the examiner's remarks on the cause of death. The third page was a photo of each corpse. A few serial numbers appear on each page, such as the ones for the file, the specific case (body), and the page of each report.

Among the dead were six unidentified Thai males. From the photos, one of the six looked like Jaruphong. A piece of cloth was still around his neck, and his face was swollen and deformed. The descriptive details, however, did not match: a mustache, older than twenty-five years old. Another corpse description—body type and dress, including a TU belt—seemed closer to Jaruphong, including a piece of cloth around his neck. The photo of this body was missing, however. My assistant and I looked at the photo of the first individual more than a dozen times on separate visits to the archives. I could not be 100 percent certain, but I believed it showed Jaruphong's body. The explanation for the misleading description turned out to be simple: after careful examination over many years, we found that the pages and photos of three reports of unidentified Thai males were out of order. When we corrected the problem, the photo of Jaruphong's body and its description matched my long-lost friend. More than twenty years later, his body had been found, even if only on paper.

According to the postmortem report, Jaruphong died from a gunshot wound before his body was abused. It is highly likely that Jaruphong's body had been at the hospital from the morning of

October 6, but no one came to identify him. He had discarded his ID card before rushing out of the building. Sadly, his body was battered so badly that it was not easy to recognize his face. Thus his body became one of the six unidentified Thai males in the official reports. To find out what had happened to the unidentified unclaimed corpses, I contacted the senior police officer who had signed off on the autopsy reports. He explained that after a certain period the police had sent all the unclaimed corpses, the "corpses without relatives" (*sop mai mi yat*), for communal cremation at Wat Don, a Buddhist temple in Bangkok designated for this purpose. That is, the unidentified bodies from the October 6 incident were simply dumped together, indiscriminately, with other corpses without relatives from other accidents and crimes, and disposed of.

These findings provoked more questions. Did Jinda ever see the body or the photo at the Police Hospital, where most bodies were kept, during his search for his son? Jinda did not mention such a visit in his memoir. If not, why not? Was it because the chaos at the time or another reason? If he did go there, why did he not claim Jaruphong? Did he not recognize his son?

Silent Memory

I met both Jinda and Lim in 2001 when they came to Bangkok for the commemoration on the twenty-fifth anniversary of the massacre. I requested a private conservation with them to relate all I knew about their son's body. "I wish I could have found his remains," I said at the end of my account. We wept together. Afterward, I asked Jinda whether he had gone to the Police Hospital or seen the photo of the unidentified Thai males from the incident. Suddenly, while weeping, Lim pointed her finger at Jinda and screamed, "I told you that was Luk Kia [Jaruphong's nickname]! I told you that was Luk Kia!" Jinda sobbed. His head was down, his body slumped.

Jinda had gone to Sirirat Hospital and to many police stations but not to the Police Hospital. Jinda and Brother went to Wat Don, but after all the bodies had been cremated. They saw the pictures of five corpses. For a moment Jinda must have thought one of them looked like his son, as he still could describe the photo— the long-sleeved shirt and pants that looked familiar to him. He even recalled that one tooth was missing from that body, which made him unsure whether the body was that of his son.[8] But the bodies in the photos were bloated, very difficult to identify with certainty. Perhaps his mind refused to recognize the photo he saw. Perhaps. Perhaps.

Lim, still sobbing, murmured, "I told you that was him. I told you." Jinda probably had told Lim what he saw and what he thought, too. I said nothing more, and as both of them continued to sob, I quietly excused myself. I was shocked, realizing only then how cruel what I had just done to them was. Why did I have to know all the answers? Should I have asked them the final questions? How could I? To this day, my eyes moisten every time I recall that moment, which I will never forget. Nor would I ever forgive myself. Truth telling is cruel.

After our 2001 meeting, I believed I knew why Jinda had never finished his memoir. He probably did not want to. For Jinda and Lim, as long as Jaruphong's body was missing or unidentified, their hopes remained alive. The rumors and confusing information, together with the absence of a body, ironically, gave them hope. With that hope, Jaruphong remained alive to them, and they, too, were alive. The abrupt termination of the memoir was not an end to the story. Rather, it was a suspension of time to prolong hope and, perhaps more important, to allow a life to remain frozen in time, what we usually call memory. Closure represents finality, which in this case meant the end of hope and the end of life. For there to be any chance that Jaruphong might return, the memory and the memoir, must not be completed.

We usually take for granted that a memoir is the recording of memory. What is left unrecorded is either not remembered or something the memoirist does not want to remember. In other words, we assume that when a memoir comes to an abrupt end, forgetting or the loss of memory begins. Thus an unfinished memoir is the memory that comes to an end without the ending. But is it? For Jinda, the moment when his memoir stopped, the frozen memory began. The silence at the suspension of his memoir is full of memory. It was a good memory, one filled with hope that kept everybody alive. The memoir was suspended to prevent it from ending because it was not supposed to end.

But this good silence of memory is fragile. A grain of truth can destroy it. And with a grain of truth goes parental hope. Truth broke the silence that helped freeze time and history and helped keep Jaruphong and his parents alive. The closure that we usually yearn for was a curse to this silence. In my search for truth about Jaruphong's body and for answers about the memoir, I put an end to this good silence. Tears replaced silence; truth is unbearable.

Jinda's search for his son was over. He probably came to terms with the loss even though the scar would never go away. He spoke at every commemoration since 1996 on behalf of the families that lost daughters and sons.[9] Lim, on the other hand, continued to live with hope, or live in denial, depending on how one sees it. According to an interview in 2002, she had not yet come to terms with the truth that her son would not come home.[10] She passed away in December 2002.

Jinda did not come to the commemoration in October 2015 because he was too frail to travel. He passed away in January 2016.

THE BUDDHIST VIRTUOUS SILENCE

At the commemoration in 1996, a group of Buddhist activists reinvented a ritual to form a bridge linking the participants with the atrocity and the dead in order to come to terms with the past. The ritual did not emphasize loss but focused instead on the virtue of idealism, the spirits of those who died, and on a reexamination of ourselves in the present, what we can and should do to carry on those virtues. Refocusing on the present—the Buddhist notion of living in the moment—is a Buddhist way of confronting the past. The main messages from the commemoration are about remembering the massacre and the need for truth and tolerance for different political views. The strong message of the ritual led by the Buddhist contingent was forgiveness and letting go of the past, nonattachment, and moving on. The activists urged all victims to forgive without mentioning who should be forgiven. The emphasis on forgiveness shifts the discourse from one of legal and social justice to establish what is right and wrong for the society, to one about individual moral.

I encountered a number of former radicals who were not interested in or who refused to participate in the commemoration because they felt that revisiting the tragedy did not contribute to healing either individuals or society. Memory and truth, including the one about the perpetrators, they argued, was not necessary for closure and moving forward. Forgiveness was. To me, their discourse sounded very Buddhist. Even though I encountered only a few individuals of this persuasion, they have inspired me to learn more about the Buddhist approach to the past atrocity. In Thailand, Buddhist thinking and values are ingrained in the life and mentality of ordinary people, so it must have influenced how even former radicals made sense of and coped with the inexplicable events that had overtaken them. Some victims drew mental strength from Buddhism for their resilience.

The assumed approach to an atrocity emphasizes the need for truth, advocates remembering, and demands retributive justice to reach closure; forgiveness and moving on follow. The process is the same for individuals and for society to establish the rule of law. The Buddhist approach is different from the conventional one in many ways. I introduce a memoir written by a Buddhist activist only a few weeks after he was released from prison in 1976 and an explication by a Buddhist scholar about how to understand the massacre and deal with past atrocity. Although these activists and scholars may be stronger in their devotion, more sophisticated in their thinking, and more intense in their contemplation of Buddhist ethics than ordinary Buddhists, their discourse should help us understand the mindset of many victims and their families. I do not, however, try to evaluate the success or failure of the Buddhist approach to past atrocity, let alone judge whether it is an improvement on the conventional one that calls for truth, memory, and retributive justice. Nor am I interested in the doctrinal verification of the authenticity of the activist discourse. I only want to examine the mental and intellectual resources that are influential for many people in dealing with the traumatic past in the context of Buddhist Thailand.

Above all, the Buddhist approach to past atrocity raises many questions when contrasted with the conventional one. How does the Buddhist approach address issues of justice, accountability, punishment, impunity, and history? Does the Buddhist approach hinder the legal-secular approach? What is the significance of forgiveness for the Buddhist view and how does it work? In what way are forgetting and remembering parts of the Buddhist approach for healing? Does it encourage forgetting? What are the implications of this Buddhist approach to social memories and the historical truth?

The Massacre as the Mara

Deeply concerned by the apparent complicity of the *sangha* to Thanom's return in 1976, the Buddhist clubs from five universities visited the abbot of the Bowornniwet temple, hoping to pressure the establishment to find a peaceful solution.[11] A few days before the massacre, a number of them decided to hold a fast inside TU to put more pressure on the *sangha*. On the morning of October 6, the police arrested them along with other protesters. After their release from prison, a Buddhist activist from TU, under the pen-name Mo.tho. ko.189 (MTK189), recorded a memoir about what he went through. His memoir is strikingly different from those of the radical students. It is an introspective memoir of the battle with one's self. The references are from its 1996 publication.[12]

The memoir opens with his concern about the deteriorating political situation, which was partially caused by the *sangha*. He elaborated on his decisions to join the strike against the exam on October 4 and the fast on the next day, especially his mental deliberations about the fast, which involved serious sacrifice and high risk. The author described in detail his preparations for fasting, especially the mental one. The fasting, though, lasted only one day before the massacre. He was afraid but calmed himself down by reading. On learning that the police had shot and tortured many students, he considered how he would feel and act in such a situation. "To confront death with strength is a moral act. I tried to face the idea of death with a peaceful mind, although I must admit that my mind was not very peaceful in that situation" (58). When the armed police showed up to arrest him and his group, "I tried to concentrate on my breathing to avoid any expression of anger . . . I even turned to smile at (a friend)" (61). Like most others, he was punched and kicked along the way to the bus and the prison.

> As I was beaten up, I tried to focus on the sacrifice of Jesus. . . . Thinking of this inspired me to absorb the pain quietly without swearing or showing hatred or vengefulness. I prayed for the people . . . who committed barbaric acts today. . . . I would sacrifice myself to take the retribution they may get. . . . May [heaven] not punish them because they are ignorant and unknowing about what they have done . . . At that moment, I sincerely forgave them. I may not be able to love them. But I understood them and forgave them. These thoughts preoccupied me, much more than anger or hatred." (66–68)

Unfortunately, at that moment, a police officer kicked him very hard in the head, then the ribs. He curled his body in severe pain. It was so unbearable that he almost exploded in anger. Just almost; he put the utmost effort into suppressing his anger, hatred, and vengefulness. In his cell, he grew frightened as he thought about what might happen next. He tried to control his thoughts and feelings, concentrating only on the here and now, not the past or the future, and not TU or home (76). That night he had a pleasant dream. In fact, he had good dreams during the three nights in prison (77). He intentionally avoided talking to his cellmates about what had happened or their future because such conversation would bring despair about possibly spending miserable years in prison, and the country plunging further into violence and destruction.

> At that moment, I forced myself to get to sleep . . . to escape from reality. . . . But I still heard the noises of my cellmates. . . . I had to control my thoughts to stop thinking about my future. (82).
>
> Trying to console myself, to maintain full awareness, and to live with hope . . . I made a promise to myself. No matter what challenge I would face, even if it were the final moment of my life, I would firmly commit to non-violence and to Buddhism in order to behave with courage and integrity. . . . I made the promise because at that moment fear and the survival instinct were so strong that I feared I might relinquish my commitment to Buddhism. The power of Evil was so strong that I feared I might give in to it. (84)
>
> This promise was very important to my life. (85)

Fortunately, MTK189 did not face the ultimate challenge because he was released a few days later. In the final section of the memoir, as he looked back on his ordeal, he was surprised that despite the brutality he had experienced, he had no ill feeling toward the police. It was still incomprehensible to him how people could be hateful and cruel to one another to the extent that occurred on October 6. Then, toward the end of the memoir, his final thought:

> Both sides were victims of ignorance and delusion (104). . . . Both the victims and the perpetrators suffered. The former did so physically and mentally, some permanently. They became utterly vengeful, despairing, and depressed. The latter were consumed by their insatiable hunger for power, which would amass sins to themselves. . . . I wish to dedicate merit, to share loving-kindness and good will with both sides (119–120).

MTK189's deliberate introspection into his thinking and feeling, and his efforts to control them, remind me of the Buddhist story "Facing

Mara" (The Evil One) that is commonly illustrated on temple murals in Thailand. On the final day of the Buddha's meditation toward Enlightenment, Mara appeared in various forms—seductive temptress, scary ghost, a threatening army of beasts, and so on—to try to distract or derail the Buddha from his path to the goal. Had he been seduced or frightened by Mara, giving way to anger, hatred, or delusion, he would have failed. Mara is the ultimate challenge, testing the strength of his commitment to Buddhist awakening. "Facing Mara" is a genre, still common to the hagiography of innumerable Buddhist sages and revered monks. Their stories, too, must include the moments when they faced the test from Evil in one form or another at some point in their spiritual lives.[13]

For this Buddhist activist, the October 6 carnage was a kind of ultimate challenge by the Evil One to test his commitment to the Buddhist *ahimsa dharma* (the virtue of nonviolence). This does not mean that he turned his actual encounter with fright and possible death into a piece of fiction. Rather, the Buddhist literary and ideological convention provides him with a model for how to behave, think, and conceptualize his experience. In Buddhist mythology, the story of the Buddha's confrontation with Mara is an allegory. Mara's different forms symbolize the different mental states that are inimical to Buddhist awareness. The stories of great Buddhist sages are likewise metaphorical narratives of their mental battles. This activist memoir of October 6 was not metaphorical, however. It was a straightforward account of the author's battle with his self framed by a Buddhist story and its entailing view and ideology.

"The Evil" and "Truth with Empathy but without Wounds"

> [The] brutality [that happened in the massacre] was a manifestation of the Evil that is always ready to dress up in any ideological or religious garb in order to fulfill its wish. Ultimately speaking, the October 6 event . . . was a struggle between Evil and Virtue. The battlefield was not at . . . [the actual places where the bloodshed occurred] but was in our minds. The October 6 incident ended with the defeat of Virtue. Virtue cannot obstruct or hinder Evil. Unprecedented in Thai history, Evil exercised its power of terror over millions of people. Despite that, it was able to escape. Since that day, many have kept asking for the

perpetrators. **Who** gave the order to the officers to kill? **Who** committed the atrocious act . . .? It is true that those involved in the killing on that day should be punished according to law. Nevertheless, nobody pays attention to the "true perpetrator." As a result, it has escaped us. . . . (Paisal 1996, 125–127; emphasis in the original)

Twenty years after the massacre, a reputable scholar-monk, Phra Paisal Wisalo, delivered a sermon titled "Lesson from October 6: Evil, Death, and Victory" at the commemoration in 1996.[14] His main point throughout was that the ultimate perpetrators were not the humans—the generals, police, paramilitary gangsters, and so on—who committed the crimes, but Evil or *khwam chua rai* (wickedness, evilness, vice).

I have known Paisal since we met at a high school gathering of activists from different schools in 1972. He was an avid reader and potential scholar. In 1976, he was among the more committed Buddhist activist students at TU. He was active in several groups that advocated for non-Marxist political and social justice for the poor and the oppressed and was strongly committed to nonviolence. In early October 1976, he joined the fast and was arrested at TU. Under the Thanin government, he was among the first who dared to campaign for the release of the Bangkok 18. In 1983, he was ordained as a Buddhist monk and has remained to this day. Over the years, the avid reader became a prolific writer and translator. He has written and translated more than a hundred books on various subjects related to Buddhism. Today he is one of the most respected scholar-monks in the country, yet he remains active for social justice.

According to his sermon at the commemoration, "the Evil of the Oct 6 incident is not found in any particular side of the conflict" (128) but instead refers to the mental state—the hatred, anger and vengefulness. "Another human is not our enemy. The real enemy of ours and of every human being is the Evil . . . in our minds" (149–150). The Evil caused both sides to dehumanize one another, paving the way for inhuman acts on a perceived inhuman enemy, ironically mostly in the name of a noble cause or virtue, such as protecting the nation, religion, and monarchy, or in the pursuit of a utopian society without oppression or exploitation. Dehumanization misleads one into believing in one's superiority and enables heinous acts that a person would normally not be able to do. "Everybody [every side] is part of the problem" (151) because we have all dehumanized one another, wished malice on each other.

> Even though one side only did so verbally, and the other did so by arms and killings, all helped fuel the flames of hatred, anger and vengeance . . . All of us were partly responsible [for the October 6 incident], and cannot avoid guilt . . . one way or another. (151–152)

Evil does not reside exclusively in wicked people who should be isolated from the rest of the society. All of us have Evil hiding within us that can show up if we are not careful and mindful. An event like the 1976 massacre could happen again and again if we do not admit that Evil hides in our minds and not try to get rid of it. Overcoming Evil must start with confronting it, then building up loving kindness to drive it from our minds. The most effective way to fight Evil is with forgiveness. "If we do not forgive those who caused the violence, how can we defeat Evil, which is the root of the October 6 event?" (155).

> Evil wants us to lose our need for virtue. . . . It took away lives in the October 6 event so brutally in order to subdue the rest of us, then induce us to surrender idealism and faith in Dhamma by instigating anger, hatred and vengeance [in us]. If we lose our idealism and Virtue, it means we let [Evil] beat us. If we are full of vengeance, it means we let Evil possess us. We cannot bring back those lives that were lost. But we can turn the losses of that day into victory by empowering Virtue to defeat Evil. Don't let Evil destroy anybody anymore." (160–161)

According to this thinking, bringing "them" to justice is secondary to fighting Evil in all of us. Nonetheless, the social conditions that nurture Evil are also to blame, such as the media and social injustice. Ordinary people in normal situations cannot commit such heinous acts as those on October 6. When I met with Paisal in 2007, I asked him about the social conditions of Evil, the subject that he touched on briefly in his sermon.[15] Paisal agrees that "machines of violence" (his words) are found in politics and in everyday life that potentially can arouse and amplify Evil to a dangerous level. We must try to eradicate those social machines of violence, too. The Buddhist dharma applies as much to social norms as it does to individuals. Nevertheless, he insisted, we must learn how to control the Evil in our minds in normal situations when it is not so dangerous. Paisal made it clear that normal legal justice is necessary to maintain the social fabric. Wrongdoers should be punished. But we do not support legal punishment out of anger or vengeance. Doing so would let Evil escape again.

Even though ordinary Buddhists may not be as sophisticated as Paisal, Buddhist thinking is part of their intellectual environment. In general, people are more familiar with the concept of legal justice—a crime needs to be accounted for, the right and wrong clearly stated. The advocacy for truth and legal justice puts emphasis on the blame and punishment of someone, in which case it could become the basis for revenge—and the perpetuation of Evil. In the Buddhist approach, coming to terms with the past starts and ends in oneself. In this thinking, the primary goal of the commemoration must be reconciliation, above and ahead of justice. My conversation with Paisal, then, focused on the implications of the Buddhist approach to past atrocity. First, does the emphasis on forgiveness indirectly undermine legal justice and vice versa? Is it an alternative solution to legal justice or a complementary one? Second, if the pursuit of the perpetrators and legal justice are unimportant, is knowing the truth about the past necessary? Do truth, history, and memory matter? What is the value of remembering, individually and collectively, and for a society over the long term?

Legal justice may help contain Evil, but it may not be helpful in eradicating it. On the contrary, in Paisal's view, if the pursuit of the retributive justice originated from the desire for vengeance, such pursuit would exacerbate hatred and vengefulness, individually and socially. Legal justice, in theory at least, however, is part of the necessary mechanism to create the social conditions that prevent violence. The pursuit of justice for this purpose and without personal vengeance, in his view, is not contradictory to the Buddhist effort to eradicate Evil. He repeatedly distinguished the necessary methods and outcomes for individual and society which may not be the same but are not necessarily contradictory. According to Paisal, the perpetrators should be brought to justice according to the law. Retributive justice, nonetheless, does not tackle the root cause of Evil, and hence is not the top priority for a Buddhist monk. Only forgiveness does.

Forgiveness does not require truth or knowledge of who and what act to forgive, Paisal confirmed. He went even further, repeating from his sermon on the October 6 massacre that both sides were guilty in different ways and extents. Forgiveness was unilateral regardless of the other's guilt. If such is the case, I asked, does forgiveness blur the line between the right and wrong and ultimately undermine legal justice? Probably so, he replied, before explaining that forgiveness and justice do not serve the same purposes. Forgiveness aims at our minds. It does not help set the social precedents or moral standards that a society also needs. It may or may not lead to reconciliation either because it is not a social act.

Regarding the necessity of knowing the truth, Paisal explained how the most important truth in the Buddhist view is the realization of the Evil of certain acts or events rather than the legal or historical truth about who did what. The success in achieving one kind of truth may not lead to success in achieving the other. These different kinds of truth are not necessarily incompatible and can be complementary. The more important question, he suggested, is how we should deal with these different kinds of truth. In the Buddhist view, equanimity is necessary for legal and historical truth about the massacre. The search for historical truth should come without surrendering to anger, hatred, or vengeance. "Truth with empathy but without vengefulness," he said. Paisal himself wanted to know the truth of who did what, however. He believed that society could learn valuable lessons if people knew how to handle the truth. He argued that some former radicals might have avoided the truth-telling of the commemoration because the trauma was still fresh and painful to them (rather than concerned with the rise of the Evil in their minds). If the wound dried and became a scar, they should be able to take in the truth with equanimity. The only way to turn a fresh wound into a scar is with forgiveness. Despite their attempts to deal with their painful past in a Buddhist way, doing so may have only been a temporary measure, like a band aid, leaving them with fresh wounds even decades after the massacre. I argued that the ability to share the pain of victims is good for people and has inspired them to search for truth. Paisal understood but reiterated that he does not advocate sharing pain. We should be able to pursue the legal truth for justice and the historical truth for its lessons without feeding Evil. For an individual, he insisted, the legal and historical truth are not important because they do not help eradicate Evil. For a society, they are important because they help create a better society and reduce the social conditions that nurture Evil.

Another point, Paisal reminded me, is that the deeper the trauma, the more desirable reconciliation becomes. Legal justice is good but not a necessary condition for reconciliation and forgiveness. Nor is historical truth. In response, I argued that, in Thailand, reconciliation was often deployed in social and political discourse as a strategy to cover up past atrocity, to avoid legal justice, and to forget. Paisal agreed. In Thailand, the discourse of reconciliation usually receives strong public support because most Thais do not view justice and historical truth as preconditions for reconciliation.

Virtuous Silence?

For the former-radicals-turned-Buddhists, voicing trauma is not their way of dealing with the past. Silence is to keep either Evil at bay or their pain in check. This is a voluntary silence, not a suppressive one, for a good reason, their way of coming to terms with the past and moving on. My encounter with those who take this Buddhist approach to the traumatic past seriously at first gave me the impression that they simply wanted to avoid trouble in their lives. By the end of my inquiry, though, I truly respected their thinking. My search, however, led me to many more questions. Is the Buddhist approach good only under authoritarian conditions? Had the legal system been just and fair, if the political system worked well without suppression or persecution of those seeking justice, and if Thai people were free from their concern for the monarchy and the *sangha,* would people opt for legal justice over Buddhist silence? I can predict Paisal's answer: the two choices are not incompatible. But I am more interested in what ordinary people like those former radical activists would choose to do. The reality is that the rule of law in many countries, especially authoritarian ones, cannot be depended on for a just closure. In such conditions, will the normative approach to past atrocity—truth, legal justice, remembrance, and reconciliation—be available and effective? If not, what other options might people could turn to?

Finally, Paisal asked me whether legal justice and historical truth can really prevent future atrocities. I did not answer because I know that they cannot. The different approaches to past atrocity are various ways of moving on. If so, is it possible that the Buddhist approach is a legitimate and possibly effective path to move on under certain conditions? Is moving on without truth or justice but with good silence sufficient and satisfactory? It does not promise never again because it is not easy to beat the Evil. However, the human rights ideal of legal justice cannot make that promise either.

So far I have engaged with the arguably virtuous silence among the Buddhist activists. Let us not forget the Buddhist establishment, the national Buddhist order or the Thai *sangha*. Throughout modern history, the Thai *sangha* has been an integral component of the establishment. Unlike the Theravada *sangha* in neighboring countries, such as in Burma, that turned rebellious from time to time, the Thai *sangha* has generally been supportive of the state, the military, and the monarchy. Most of the time, they do so by their inaction to injustice and to the state's mischief, and by their indifference to people's plight, all in the name of being nonpolitical. Their silence typically signals complicity to the state.

The October 6 massacre therefore was probably a dark day for them as well. The roles of prominent monks in the pretext of the massacre were controversial, even repulsive, to some victims. The *sangha*'s absolute silence about the atrocity ever since that day, however, is surprising to no one. Its silence probably speaks volumes, though it was not clear what it says. In the decades after the massacre, even as sympathy for the victims increased, people remained very cautious and reluctant to make any serious allegation against the Buddhist establishment. Both the *sangha*'s silence and the public's silence are definitely not virtuous. This is a subject I have not been able to investigate for this book.

Mute Soliloquy

For almost a year since the day he escaped lynching by a right-wing mob, Dr. Puey Ungphakorn worked tirelessly to tell the world about the massacre by the murderous regime in Thailand (see figure 4). He traveled across the globe delivering speeches, participating in meetings, and testifying to governments and parliaments, including a US congressional committee. He wrote extensively about the massacre when others in Thailand could not. Born in 1916 to a Chinese family, he had a remarkable career as an outstanding economist, an incorruptible bureaucrat who was trusted to be the governor of the Bank of Thailand for more than a decade, a reputable scholar and educator, and a lifelong social democrat in an authoritarian land.[16] In September 1977, after a year of travel and hard work, Puey suffered a severe stroke that left him unable to speak and barely able to write. He was thus among the victims of the massacre as well. Given that his mind still functioned well, I wondered what thoughts he had in his enforced silence.

In October 1978, a month after the amnesty of the Bangkok 18, TU proposed to confer an honorary doctorate on Puey. Unexpectedly, he declined the honor. His reasons had nothing to do with TU or his feelings toward it. His son explained three reasons on his behalf. First, the October 6 massacre that had affected him directly remained murky, uninvestigated, and unresolved. Many students remained, at that time, in the jungle. Second, academic freedom within Thai universities remained limited. Third, Thailand remained undemocratic.[17] At the very least, we know that he did not at all agree with the government's attempts to silence the discourse about the massacre in the name of national reconciliation. He still demanded accountability for the incident. His second two reasons were radical rebukes at that time. Puey's silent voice of reason was loud and clear.

Was Puey's silence in the final twenty-two years of his life a testament of the continuing absence of justice for the October 6 tragedy that he had fought for up to the last day he could speak? Was Puey's life in silence a vocal testament of Thailand's darker side because people with integrity, honesty, and the courage to speak the truth have suffered consequences? To me, it was.[18] His physical silence was a mute soliloquy on the massacre, in the apt words of Pramoedya Ananta Toer.

Unfortunately, Puey has been idolized and his ideas including his views of the massacre accommodated posthumously without taking his silent protest seriously. In April 1987, Puey returned to Thailand for the first time since 1976. Thousands of his colleagues, students, and the public welcomed him warmly at every place he went during the month-long visit. He returned briefly three more times in 1993, 1995, and 1997. But he refused to stay in Thailand. We can only speculate about why he chose to stay away from the country he loved, even though the political situation, generally speaking, had improved by that time and he would definitely not have faced the same ugliness as he had before. By the 1990s, Puey was perhaps one of Thailand's most respected elders. He certainly enjoyed meeting old friends and students and visiting those places that were meaningful to his life. Perhaps he returned to mingle with people rather than to revisit the country. Perhaps the October 6 massacre had forever taken away his sense of belonging to Thailand. Physical injury is hard but the severance of belonging is harder. Puey's situation was heartbreaking. Puey passed away in England in 1999.[19] Even posthumously, he helped make the October 6 monument complete.

Jinda's silence voiced the deep love and painful hope of parents. Paisal's Buddhist silence was one of an admirable battle. These, plus Puey's silence, are the mute soliloquies that we must not overlook. Decades after the incident, for example, a common subject of conversation among the former radicals was how to tell or whether to tell their children about the past. This question has no single or simple answer. Most chose to talk to their children when they were ready. Certainly other forms of good silence exist that this chapter has not discussed.

Chapter 8

SLIDING MEMORY

In the 2000s, two controversies concerning the massacre at Thammasat University broke out involving Samak Sundaravej, a right-wing demagogue in 1976 and the minister of interior in the Thanin government. During 1976 and 1977, the government sent him around the world to spread the (false) information that the Vietnamese had instigated the bloodshed that had resulted in only a few Vietnamese dead. He has enjoyed a prominent political career since then thanks to his conservative, populist persona, which earned him a strong, loyal base. In 2000, he ran for governor of Bangkok. Ji (Giles) Ungphakorn, a professor at Chulalongkorn University and one of Puey's sons, challenged him in public to clarify his involvement in the October 6 massacre. Samak denied any role in it, let alone the actual killing, saying that he was far away from TU, as if involvement required his presence at the scene. Samak was cunningly evasive about his role in the anticommunist propaganda, in public misinformation, and in fanning hatred before and after the massacre, all of which had contributed to the tragedy. He refused to admit that he lied to the public in 1976 and 1977 about the massacre.[1] Dismissing Ji's allegation as a political ploy to damage his electoral campaign, Samak then sued Ji for defamation, forcing Ji to stop his argument about the massacre. Many former activists and public intellectuals joined the fray, mostly condemning Samak's role in fueling the massacre and his evasiveness, lack of remorse, and political and moral irresponsibility. Despite these reactions, Samak won the election by a landslide.[2] The general public was indifferent to the past atrocity.

168

In February 2008, Samak brought another controversy on himself when, as the new prime minister, he gave an interview to CNN. When questioned about his involvement in the October 6 massacre, he denied it, then added, "only one person died." The outrageous remark epitomized his denial of the massacre. Public outcries erupted from every direction, even within his party, but Samak remained as evasive as ever. He made no attempt to modify his portrayal of the massacre, let alone show any remorse. The controversy faded away by the end of the month.[3]

These controversies are emblematic of social memory of the massacre in the 2000s in many respects, but I point out two of them in particular. First, it was evident that the reactions against Samak's remarks did not affect his popularity. Polls at the time indicated that the public neither cared much about the massacre nor supported the pursuit of truth.[4] People who cared about it and hoped for an admission of guilt or remorse were only a limited segment of the political public. Second, and more troubling, was that Samak was the only target of public contempt. Despite their far more devastating actions, no efforts were made to denounce individuals within the police, military, and other paramilitary right-wing groups except the Red Gaurs. The palace was never mentioned despite its involvement in the conspiracy of Thanom's return and its role in the mobilization of the deadly Village Scout and the anticommunist hysteria that led to the massacre.

At a time when many in Thai society were trying to move on from the pains and fatigue of societal conflicts, some forgetting was understandable. Both leftist radicalism and ultraconservativism gradually lost their appeal. Meanwhile, the military's political power was in decline, and the hegemony of the monarchy was unchallenged in its ascent after the uprising against the military regime in 1992. Parliamentary democracy under the hegemony of the palace—or "royal democracy," as I call it—was in place from the mid-1990s to the mid-2000s.[5] Economically, Thailand was enjoying a period of ten to fifteen years of economic exuberance from the mid-1980s until the bubble burst in 1997. This chapter elaborates on these changing conditions of the post-1976, post-leftist generations and their effects on the memory of the two October events. In what ways was either meaningful, if at all, in a period of relative prosperity under royalist dominance?

This chapter explains the social memoryscape of the October 6 massacre in recent decades. The state's suppression and the silence of the perpetrators and victims that this book has presented thus far have had some lasting effects, certainly. This chapter, though, pays more attention to the cultural and ideological factors that have shaped the memories of the massacre over generations. After several observations on the selective memory of the massacre over generations, it turns to the importance of cultural and ideological factors in determining which truth and history are worthy of remembering. The ideological factors function like a narrative frame, on the one hand, shaping the meaning of the past, yet, on the other hand, screening out and marginalizing unwanted stories and meanings. No narrative frame in Thai cultural history, I argue, can accommodate the memory of the massacre. Instead, the normative frame renders the memory irrelevant and meaningless across generations. Hyperroyalism produces loyal citizens willing to live within the state discourse of selective memory that omits naming certain perpetrators for the sake of country. This results in a "minimalist" memory of the massacre.

These factors contribute to the memory slide or shift that takes place over generations. Memory slide is common and usually regarded only as a natural fading process in response to time. In the case of the October 6 massacre, however, the common memory slide is a false memory of the "October 16 incident" that never took place. I argue that memory of an incident that never took place is not merely a memory fade or a careless mix-up. Instead, it is a logical outcome of the dominant ideology combining with a creative literary construction of memory, resulting in a narrative suitable to the post-1976 ideological and intellectual environment. Finally, the acceptable frame that makes certain memories of the massacre more relevant to the environment of later generations than others also emerged in the form of Puey-the-icon. To move on, Thai society has opted for silence and various forms of memory slide. Public indifference to the massacre in the 2000s and unwillingness to name the perpetrators other than Samak and the Red Gaurs are among the symptoms of the memory slide.

INDIFFERENCE AND SELECTIVE MEMORY OVER GENERATIONS

Shortly after the CNN interview controversy in 2008, a group of artists presented their latest works about the October 6 massacre in the exhibit "Flashback' 76: History and Memory of the October 6 massacre." All were known for their remarkable works about the massacre since the commemoration in 1996. These new works focused on selective memory, "power-memory-erasure," and Samak was the clear target.[6] After studying every word in the brochure and every piece of art work published in it, I cannot help but wonder whether these artists recognized any other perpetrators beyond or larger than Samak. In a way, Samak was among the easier targets: easy to hate for his demagogic, egomaniac character, and his prominence since 1976 as a populist, ultraconservative politician. The Red Gaurs, too, were villains we could blame without disturbing any major political and social institutions. It seems that these artists, too, have chosen to live with selective memory.

In 2008, a historian reported on his informal survey of Thai students that asked how much they knew about the two October events and that of May 1992. First, he did a Google search by the Thai words for all three. The results for October 6, he found, were far more numerous than for the other two. He then conducted brief surveys of students at TU and Silapakorn University, breaking down the people he surveyed into undergraduate students, graduate students, and people passing through the two campuses randomly, 240 people in all. The results showed that more people in every group said that they knew about October 14, 1973, and May 1992, but not about October 6. The historian concluded from his unscientific survey that despite more discourse about the October 6 massacre on social media, people, especially the youth of that generation, knew less about it than the other two incidents.[7] A decade earlier, in 1996, I did a survey of fifty-eight undergraduate students at TU asking them to describe the two October events in brief, either the cause, the main protagonists, or the outcome. Almost all of them (fifty-five) could say something accurate about October 14, 1973. Only half (twenty-eight) could do the same about October 6, 1976. Three were confused about which October event was which.

In June 2002, Seksan Prasertkul, the most famous student leader of the 1970s (mentioned in chapter 5), who by then was teaching at TU, bemoaned that his students did not seem to care about any political or social issues. The generation that was reaping the fruits of his generation's blood and tears did not seem to understand the spirit and value of the past struggles and sacrifices. They cared for nothing but themselves. This observation was typical in intellectual circles during the 1990s to 2000s, comparing the critical and skeptical spirit of the youth in the mid-1970s with its absence in later generations.

Reactions from the younger generation are also abundant. They argued, for example, that the 1970s generation must share the blame for its inability to sustain the memory and understanding of past struggles. Even the former radicals, some younger people argue, were not willing to speak out beyond the accepted limits and failed to tell the whole truth even about themselves. Instead, they often tried to justify their past within the new political context.[8] Another questioned the focus on violence and brutality in the memories of October 6. Reproducing violence and retaliation, he argues, is the opposite of the state's anticommunist discourse but similar to it nonetheless.[9] The 1970s generation must stop blaming the later one for failing to remember the October 6 incident correctly.[10]

Perhaps the most common explanation for the younger generation's indifference and selective memory is the lack of information and knowledge. The result has been memory fade, the "short memory" of a society over generations. In the case of October 6, critics usually point to the state's control of public information about the incident for many years afterward. The haphazard public information available hardly came together in a comprehensible narrative. The state's censorship of school curricula also affected public knowledge over generations. In response to the controversy in 2000 ignited by Puey's son's challenge to Samak, a group of academics set up a fact finding commission. They interviewed sixty-two people, almost all of whom were former student activists—the victims. The testimonies were a good collection of the victim's memories, their firsthand accounts of the massacre more than twenty years later, after the memories had been absorbed and processed, and when their lives were securely normalized.[11] Its effect on public knowledge of the massacre was negligible, however, due to the lack of support by any public or private authorities. Calls to allow information about the massacre in school textbooks followed every controversy, but they always faded away without result. Silence and the unwillingness to speak out among those involved certainly contributed to the lack of public awareness. The 1996 breakthrough enabled public recognition of the massacre but did not make it adequately understood. Some scholars of the younger generation have commented that a bundle of facts, with an emphasis on the brutality of the event, may not be enough in the present context.[12]

Lack of information and knowledge is certainly a factor. But is that all that's involved in selective memory and memory fade? Is lack of information the cause of indifference and selective memory, or a symptom of something else? What are the conditions and factors that contribute to remembering or not remembering? What makes the memory of October 6 meaningful in certain ways but not others over generations?

Studying memory politics under the repressive governments of Argentina over many decades, Elizabeth Jelin argues that, even without new facts or the discovery of some unfound truth, whether a memory endures depends on the frame that makes it meaningful or not and in what ways to the present and later generations.[13] Studying the memories of Pinochet's Chile over generations, Steve Stern explains the "emblematic memory" as "a framework for collective remembrance rather than its specific content . . . that organizes meaning, selectivity, and counter-memory" of individual memory, making it meaningful in the contemporary context instead of being marginalized.[14] What we usually call the lesson from the past is the meaningfulness of memory over time and generations. It makes memory relevant, or otherwise, in the contemporary context. The meaningfulness of a memory, however, is interpretive, that is, it depends on the frame or perspective in particular political and ideological contexts and in power relations over time.

The "Thai" Truth

After the May 1992 bloodshed in Bangkok, the government launched an investigation into what happened and why. The result, however, was essentially nothing. After a long delay and much foot-dragging, the state, especially the military, obstructed the release of the report requested by relatives of the victims. In 2000, eight years after the uprising, the report was released to the public but with 60 percent of the text blacked out, including all names of military officials and key information. National security was the reason given. The report was incomprehensible. Despite that, the military warned that anyone publicizing the report would "do so at their own risk" and be subject to libel lawsuits. Samak did the same to shut up his critics when he sued Puey's son in 2000. A charge of defamation is another instrument used to prevent truth in Thailand, as David Streckfuss has meticulously documented.[15] The state and the military did not deny or forget the May 1992 bloodshed, however. They attended the official commemoration every year. Instead, they brushed aside the uncomfortable truths, recognizing only what suited them. Half-truths are an approach the Thai state and society use to deal with the uncomfortable past. Unlike May 1992, however, which has been half-heartedly accepted by the state in its narrative of progress to democracy, the October 6 massacre does not have an acceptable half-truth. No truth is another approach, no matter how noisy the demand is.

After the crackdown in 2010, the result of the conflict between the Red Shirts and Yellow Shirts, the government that ordered the killing mandated a commission to investigate it. The unwieldy name of the commission in Thai was a rendition of its official name in English, the Truth for Reconciliation Commission of Thailand (TRCT).[16] Both its name and its public rhetoric and activities, indicated that the TRCT was trying to liken itself, in concept and political mission, to the famous TRC in South Africa. It organized several meetings and seminars on the subject of transitional justice, including a state-promoted, nationally televised event with world-renowned speakers.[17] Unfortunately, especially after over two years of publicity, the commission's final report was short on both facts and truth.[18] Most important, it stops short of identifying the right and wrong of the incident. When the wrongdoings were clear on a few issues, the wrongdoers were not, except the blame on the men in black, the phantom-like protesters. No abuse of power or excessive force by the authorities was cited, even though more than two hundred thousand rounds of bullets were fired, and snipers contained the unrest, which resulted in ninety dead in the streets of Bangkok. The TRCT's recommendations sidestepped justice, suggesting mostly academic remedies and reparations. It endorsed reconciliation without truth or justice. By contrast, an independent investigation organized by a group of academics and political activists with no state support produced a thorough factual report with detailed analyses of the who, what, and when of the complex incident. Finished even before its TRCT counterpart, the 1,390-page report points to the abuse of power and excessive force for political purposes.[19] The TRCT was another whitewash of another atrocity by the state.

Why does the Thai state continue with these farcical performances and why does the Thai public allow it? Scholars of Thailand have noticed the significance of face and face-saving in Thai public culture.[20] However, the denials of these bloody events are so stark and outrageous that the whitewash would seem to damage the government's reputation even more. A clue to the conundrum may lie in Peter Jackson's suggestion, that face, looking good, or reputation in the Thai context operates differently from what we usually assume, especially the idea of face in relation to power and truth.

> The regime of images is . . . [a] form of power that exerts . . . control over actions and discourse in the private and public spheres . . . When statements or representations do not conform [to the] idealized forms, and are perceived as disrupting, the image of smooth calm . . . both formal (legal) and informal (cultural) modes of power, may be mobilized to expel the unwanted representations from the public domain. This regime of power/knowledge has epistemological implications, determining what can and cannot be articulated as public knowledge in Thailand.[21]

More simply, the conspicuous denial of what actually happened is not regarded as a denial of truth because the idealized form (image) is the higher (and more important) truth than what actually happened. Another scholar calls it "truth-above-truth" (*khwam ching nua ching*), the latter truth referring to the reality, fact, or experiential truth that we normally understand, and the former referring to Jackson's "idealized forms," which I call the "normative truth."[22] Based on the religious notion of transcendental truth, or Dharma in Buddhism, the normative truth is aspired to as the destination that one (person, institution, nation, and so on) tries to achieve. The reality is the imperfect, partial, developing stages on the path toward the normative truth. In other words, the actual reality is impermanent or transient. It does not represent the true Thailand in normative conditions.

The display of the cleansed reputation or normative image results in the kind of superficial pretension, or euphemistic and hypocritical show, which has become integral to Thai statecraft. Every military regime in Thailand has shamelessly called itself a democracy of some sort. In 2017, the junta even declared human rights part of the national agenda, despite innumerable protests from the United Nations Human Rights Commission against the junta's serious violations from the time it took power in 2014. The junta showed no concern that its declaration was an insult to the intelligence of the entire world and exposed the regime's ignorance and foolishness.

It appears that the regime's ideas of democracy, human rights, and truth are not the same as what is commonly understood. The junta probably speaks its own language about truth. The shamelessly clean image and the denial of an atrocity are not intended to fool the outside world. Rather, it represents the public image (face) in the Thai cultural grammar that the Thai state must show to the domestic public. The junta must reaffirm the normative image, not the reality, which is the lesser, partial, and unfinished truth. The latter is secondary in importance and thus should not be formalized; it is perhaps admissible in the private sphere but not in the public. The whitewash is, therefore, the confirmation of the normative truth above the transient, imperfect one that we normally call reality.

The prevalent idealized form or normative truth in Thailand has another name, *khwam pen thai,* or Thai-ness. It is a catchall ideal that Thai society yearns for even though many scholars of Thailand have exposed it as illusory and hollow. It is so deceptive and yet powerful that many Thais, for whom it is all consuming and ubiquitous, believe that non-Thai people cannot understand it. One of the most often invoked qualities of Thai-ness is harmony (*khwam samakkhi,* usually translated as unity). Harmony is a manifestation of Dharma, that is, the state of orderliness and equilibrium among life and things, human and nature, and human relations. Harmony is often described metaphorically as stories or in organic terms such as the body whose parts and organs all have their place and functions to perform.[23] Thai-ness, then, is an orderly existence with things in their proper place and functioning, otherwise, illness and disease will result for individuals as well as for society. One of the tasks of the state is to maintain such harmonious normalcy of the social order by reaffirming the normative truth repeatedly in the public sphere.

The logic of normative and transient truth also applies to politics (the power relations between the rulers and the ruled) and the social order (the orderly relations among people). That is, the normative truth of Thai-ness is the most important one. Any action, speech, or thinking that could disturb the normative Thai-ness, where harmony and unity are foremost, must be dealt with to restore normalcy. "[In] contemporary Thai political and social discourse," Streckfuss writes regarding political defamation trials, "there is in fact a difficulty in accepting, recognizing, acknowledging, or acting upon [reality]," and the ultimate criteria for guilt or innocence is not the factual truth but its effects on or danger to the normative one, namely, the nation, religion, king, Thai-ness, and the moral order.[24] Regarding the October 6 massacre, therefore, the historical truth is secondary to the normative truth. Not only does it not fit the normative narrative, it severely undermines it as well. The only normative truth pertinent to the massacre is the virtue of harmony and reconciliation, not historical truth or justice. This reminds me of Stanley Tambiah's point that the discourse on reconciliation may be even more effective in a Buddhist society in which the "cosmology of unity," or in modern incarnation—national harmony and the like—has always been an ideological premise.[25] The calls for harmony and reconciliation rather than justice and truth are always loud during and after a crisis, even after nearly a hundred were killed in 2010. Seen in this light, the absence of truth in the TRCT's report fits the Thai cultural context very well.

HISTORICAL COMPREHENSIBILITY AND OTHERWISE

History in the Thai cultural context is not necessarily the interpretive knowledge that explains what happened in the past and the changes over time.[26] It is instead primarily the story about the past that confirms the normative truth. Perhaps like the Jataka—the stories of previous births of Lord Buddha—in Theravada tradition, history is the story of previous incarnations of the present imagined community called Thailand. It is purportedly correct according to the normative truth about the state and the ideology of Thai-ness.

Modern Thai historiography is a saga of the unity of Thai people under benevolent rulers, mostly the monarchy, to confront the threats and suffering caused by foreign countries in order to survive and prosper.[27] The customary master narrative always begins with the peaceful and independent Thai kingdom facing danger from colonizing aliens. Troubles and suffering ensue. Fortunately, a heroic and benevolent warrior always emerges to protect or restore independence. Under his leadership and righteousness, the country rises in peace and prosperity. According to this master narrative, the state and the rulers were mostly benevolent and ruled by virtue. The spectacle of murder by a great king is only an allegory of his vast virtue against Evil. Mass destruction was either a justified battle against the enemy or the suppression of malicious rebels and thus not a state crime. If a ruler turned into a despot, a righteous contender would soon challenge and

depose him. A massacre by the state is therefore an alien concept, usually heard from an international news report or found in histories of
other countries. Streckfuss writes sarcastically, "[Thai kings are]
treated with laudatory odes: not depictions from real life, but edifica-
tory snippets, bloodless moments of praise so blinding that it washes
away any hint of irony or satire. Thai history will have no dictators,
no massacres, no corruption, no coups."[28] A massacre by the state, I
might add, in the reign of the most virtuous king was unthinkable, let
alone one in which the palace was implicated.

Thailand, however, is not a fantasyland that is blind to reality or
to its tragic past, even if it is considered an aberration to the normative truth. So how does Thailand deal with the reality of an atrocity
in its past? Memory is always a projection from the perspective of the
present. The latter is formed and informed to some extent by historical discourses, however. Historical knowledge provides the frame, or
the prior texts, that help determine and shape what of the past we
remember and how we remember it. Is a crime by the state a comprehensible concept? How would it fit into the narrative of Thai history?
What made the October 6 event difficult for Thais to take in is the
lack of historical precedent, the prior text, about the state's massacre
of its people.

All recent incidents of popular struggle—the October 1973 uprising, the October 1976 massacre, the May 1992 and May 2010
bloodlettings—deviated sharply from the normative Thai historical
discourse in many respects. First, in these incidents the country's independence was not at stake and no foreign threat was involved
(though some attempted to view the 1976 incident as a Vietnamese or
Chinese conspiracy). Despite this fact, in all cases the state justified its
actions as necessary measures to protect the country's security and
independence. The justification did not work; although it was accepted for the 1976 massacre for a time, eventually it failed there too.
What happened cannot be subsumed in a narrative of struggle against
an alien enemy, only in one of a state crime against its own people.
Second, these incidents were stories of mass revolts against despots
and their abuse of power in history. Some skeptical voices down-
played the legitimacy of a popular struggle, usually reducing it to
merely the pawns of a power struggle among ruling factions. Despite
that, the significance of people's power in the four incidents cannot
be discounted. Third, the four incidents show repeatedly that
Thailand is anything but peaceful. Violence and brutality on a large

scale have erupted often among Thais. Especially in October 1976, violence and brutality were committed in the name of Thai-ness.

These bloodlettings are difficult for the narrative of Thai history to accommodate. They do not fit the master narrative of the national saga of unity under a benevolent ruler for development and prosperity. They are at odds with the noble biography of the country. Yet so many people participated in these uprisings and their impacts were so significant that they are not easy to dismiss and forget. Such popular struggles will exist only on the margins of the memorable past as long as they challenge the normative national history. Over the past forty years, these events have not been forgotten but the discourses about them are limited; the truth has never been fully accounted and their places in history are unclear.

Among the four incidents, the massacres in 1976 and 2010 are probably most difficult to fathom. Because the master narrative of Thai history is also about an ever-advancing country, development and progress are always implied. The October 1973 and May 1992 incidents were major political developments toward democracy in Thailand and thus also fit the master narrative. Even though the military may view these two incidents differently, they are officially recognized by the state and widely heralded among the public. The annual commemorations of these two events are attended by state dignitaries every year. Even after the 2014 coup by one of the most repressive regimes in modern Thai history, representatives of the junta attended the annual commemorations of these two events. The October 1976 and the 2010 killings, however, were political setbacks, not political developments. The 1976 massacre was the sad end even to the radicals. It was a loss for everyone, whatever their perspective.

How the 1976 massacre should be included in the narrative of the history of democracy in Thailand is therefore an enigmatic question. In 1993, at the commemoration of the 1973 uprising, the two events were part of a seamless, linear narrative of democratization. At that time, still amid the relative silence before 1996, the October 6 massacre was worthy of mention as part of the bumpy road to democracy.[29] It survived in public memory, we might say, by taking a ride with the acceptable October 1973 uprising, by blending itself quietly into the story of political progress. At the inauguration of the October 14 Memorial in 2001, however, different views and attitudes were in force.[30] Relative to the 1973 and 1992 events, the 1976 massacre seems to exist on the edge of the comprehensible past, or has

fallen off the edge into an adjacent domain of ambivalence and silence. Mary Steedly's words about the public memory of the 1965
bloodshed in Indonesia (before the fall of Suharto in 1998) are apt
for the 1976 massacre in Thailand: "the story unspoken is no more
than an invisible inscription along history's silent edge, marking an
official limit placed upon the past by the present."[31]

Last but not least, Thais generally take pride in their history, as
much as they know it, of relatively not-so-violent political conflicts.
The massacre delegitimized their pride, destroying their belief, confidence, and trust that violent carnage could not happen in their
country. It exposed the fallacy and the limits of Thai national history.
It created a counterhistory of the nation that cannot be written out.
The question remains, what is the place of such a counterhistory
within the Thai master narrative? Currently, October 6 is considered
an unfortunate tragedy, an indescribable tarnish (*roi dang*), an aberration that should not have happened. It is a counterhistory on the
edge of the normative one. It is a thorn in history's side.

Hyperroyalism and the Minimalist Memory

Because many important and powerful institutions of the Thai state,
including the palace, were involved in the massacre, popular indifference and selective memory were partly the result of fear for possible
consequences. In a country with an authoritarian history and unreli-
able rule of law, this concern of ordinary citizens is reasonable. Such
fear could last over generations. The involvement of the palace presented a quandary. Reverence for the monarch as a semi-deity, and
especially one of King Bhumibol's stature, was irreconcilable with the
palace's involvement in the tragedy. At the very least, an allegation of
the palace's wrongdoing constitutes lèse majesté, which in Thailand
is a more serious crime than murder. Forty years later, in 2016, many
relatives of the fatal victims were still afraid to speak out because
they knew the massacre was a *la-iat-on* (sensitive) issue.[32]

The promotion of royalism and the cult of Bhumibol began in
earnest in the 1960s, thanks partly to the United States, as an ideological weapon with which to fight communism. On the one hand,
several Brahmanic rituals were revived to enhance the aura of sacred
king. On the other, thanks to television and print media, ordinary
Thais frequently saw the selfless monarch for themselves, often with
maps, pens, and a notebook in hand, a camera around his neck,

complete with beads of sweat on his face. The cult of Bhumibol promoted his semi-divinity, and hyperroyalism is the intensification of such royalism. The cult of Bhumibol and royalist fervor intensified between 1973 and 1976 when the palace and the Thai state were afraid of Thailand's becoming the next regional domino to fall to communism, and when the student movement turned radical. But even after the domestic Cold War was over in the early 1980s, hyperroyalism continued as the politico-cultural condition for the ascendency of royal democracy, which is a parliamentary system under the dominance and guidance of the monarchy.[33]

The characteristics of hyperroyalism in Thailand are as follows.[34] First, royalism permeated everyday life with increasing demands for public expressions of loyalty to the monarchy. The monarchy became omnipresent via extravagant public displays of royal symbols and platitudes. The annual celebrations for royal birthdays, which began in the 1960s, became grander, escalating at ten-year anniversaries, at every twelve-year life cycle celebration, and at other special royal occasions, sometimes involving yearlong activities nationwide.[35] Second, hyperroyalism indulges in exaggeration and exaltation, so members of the royal family are often touted by royalists and their acolytes as being the best in every field and profession, from sports, fashion, and acting, to scientific research, academics, the arts, and social service. The king and queen became the figurative parents of all Thais.[36] Hyperbole becomes normative; eulogies become truth. Every virtue in the nation must be credited to the king. Even the winning of an Olympic medal was attributed to Bhumibol's virtue.[37]

Third, the state controls public discourse about the monarchy—what can and cannot be said—by the threat of the lèse majesté law. Article 112 of the Thai criminal code reads, "Whoever defames, insults or threatens the King, Queen, the Heir-apparent or the Regent shall be punished with imprisonment of three to fifteen years." The state has been abusing the law in every aspect—procedure, enforcement, severity of punishment, interpretation—to foster and protect hyperroyalism.[38] As a result, royalism becomes akin to religion; dissention becomes blasphemy. Fourth, the manufacture, reproduction, and proliferation of hyperroyalism are not exclusively attributed to the palace and state. Civil society actively participated in the production and circulation of hyperroyalism, including the suppression of dissents. Hyperroyalism is not simply manipulation by an Orwellian state. It is a public culture.

In this environment and given the ideology that the monarchy is indispensable for the country, it is not surprising that an ordinary Thai without any particular ideological politics would not believe the palace was involved in the massacre. To them, the October 6 massacre was inexplicable. How, then, to remember and make sense of such an event? One either has to confront the truth that would likely shake one's lifelong faith in a virtuous monarchy, or keep the faith intact at the expense of the truth, history, and memory. In the environment of hyper-royalism from the late 1970s and royal democracy from the 1990s, such an enigma was resolved by silencing the truth and expunging the skepticism of the monarchy from memory in order to uphold faith in its virtue. Hence the indifference to calls for serious investigation into the atrocity and the selective memory of the perpetrators of the massacre.

These ordinary people may sympathize with the victims but would never cross the line to question the monarchy even slightly. Their faith in the monarchy makes them blind to any facts and allegation that are incongruous with it. In this environment, even some former victims are willing to forget the palace's roles in the past and to support the good causes and dedication of the monarchy instead. Moreover, many were honestly concerned that the blemish on the royal stature, let alone a criminal implication, might trigger unfathomable repercussions across the country. All of this contributed to the voluntary silence and collective amnesia about the palace and the massacre for the sake of the greater good. It is not unusual to find a former victim of the massacre and anticommunist hysteria in 1976 turned, a few decades later, to celebrate the greatest monarch on earth.[39]

Pitch Pongsawat argues that discourse about October 6 has reached its limits in the political and ideological condition that he calls the "Great Post-October 1976 Consensus." This politico-cultural condition built up throughout the 1980s and reached its full impact in the 1990s—the same chronology as hyperroyalism. Under it, permissible political discourse must fall within the following parameters: it must be beneficial to political development, supportive of royal democracy under the supremacy of the monarchy, uncritical of the monarchy, and uncritical of the conservative notion of Thai nationalism and Thai-ness.[40] When applied to the memory of the massacre, these parameters result in what Pitch Pongsawat calls the minimalist memory. This memory emphasizes the horror of the incident without naming the perpetrators to make sure that the discourse is not a threat to the political and cultural establishment or to royal democracy. Within these prescribed parameters, discourse on the radical past is not forbidden; it need not remain hidden as long as it does not cross the line and become critical or dangerous, such as by implicating the palace in the October 6 massacre.

MEMORY OF THE OCTOBER 16 INCIDENT

Pitch presciently points out that a new narrative of the October 6 massacre that fits the post-1976 condition has emerged.[41] Not only has the political environment since the 1980s expunged the memory of the perpetrators and the elements that are sensitive to the establishment, it has also produced a new narrative, but one that is not of the events that took place. Instead, it is the story of October 16, an event that never happened.

Often when people talk about the October events, they confuse the names in the Buddhist calendar (BE), namely, *14 tula 16* for the 1973 uprising on 14 October BE 2516, and *6 tula 19* for the 1976 massacre on 6 October BE 2519. The two names have a common denominator, the month *tula* (October), and the numbers that can be easily mixed up—14, 16, 6, 19. Hence, the October 16 event. But the confusion could be more than just a slip of the tongue. The two incidents shared other elements: the main actors—students and the military (although this is not precise); the actions—student protests against military rule and violent suppressions with fatalities; and the place—Thammasat University.

In the relative silence that stretched on for decades, these common denominators of the two narratives began to form a new narrative that merged the two stories into one. Memory slid. How such a slide could happen was visually explained in a performance by the young theater group known as B-Floor, in October 2013, the fortieth anniversary of the 1973 October uprising.[42] According to a report, the performance, titled "Typhoon," is about Thai political history from the 1932 revolution to the conflicts between the popular movements and the elites in 2010. It shows that

> the process by which historical facts were cut and pasted until they had become confusing, ridiculous and worthless. The search for truth was forbidden. So were questioning and curiosity. . . . This performance

takes the memory of Thai history and presents it . . . in the form of powerful physical movements. . . . The most interesting feature of this performance is not the truth or the true narrative of history in honest details, but the way [it shows] the construction of a narrative that seems to consist of the cutting of some pages [from history] and then pasting or ordering them anew. This is similar to how school textbooks are cut and pasted to make a new truth by which the younger generations can remember history.[43]

The report clarifies further that Thai history is known by the younger generations by certain keywords. In both the October 14, 1973, and the October 6, 1976, incidents, many key elements were similar, namely, the student protests, the demands for democracy, the military suppressions, and the benevolent King Bhumibol who resolved the conflicts, ended the violence, and restored peaceful society. According to the report, the performance presented how the younger generation learned history in school, as if children moved through an assembly line and emerged with prepackaged information. History is absorbed like cutting and pasting pictures. All mysteries, inglorious episodes, and loose ends are eliminated. According to the report, a student commented, "I cannot distinguish between the October 14, 1973, and the October 6, 1976, incidents." Pitch summarizes this kind of memory slide in sci-fi parlance: "In my experience of teaching students since 1995, I have found that the 'October 16 event' was a time-space compression of the two October events into the same plot, that is, the fight against military dictatorship, an uprising, but they were surrounded and killed."[44] To him, this is how the memory of the October 6 massacre survives among the younger generation and has become a public memory, regardless of inaccuracy. Pitch forgets the final act of the October 16 narrative, that is, the king intervened and brought an end to the killing.

To me, the fallacy of the October 16 memory is not upsetting. It is fascinating. The highlights of the two events (or the keywords for the report of the "Typhoon") facilitate the fusion of the two stories into one narrative (the time-space compression). It is a story of struggles and sacrifice for democracy before the king intervenes to resolve the tragic conflict. Even though the reality of the king's role in the two events was in fact quite different, in the context of hyperroyalism and the post-1976 political consensus, the king's role in promoting democracy and a peaceful resolution have become essential elements of the October 16 narrative, making a glorious ending. That the king did not end the violence on October 6 and did not resolve the conflict at the time is quietly purged from the October 16 narrative.

I found no evidence of an effort to concoct this false memory. The merged narrative seems not to be by political design. It is a public memory that was democratically created by the public for the public. As the producer of this memory, the public likes to identify itself with the heroes of democracy. Thus, no need for silencing or suppressing the victims' voices exists as long as the victims do not transgress the minimalist limits or disturb the dominant politics and ideology. In this story, the tragedy is duly recognized, together with unwavering faith in the monarchy. In one stroke of the brush of memory, the sacrifices receive recognition without disrupting the dominant historical ideology or the stability of the establishment. The October 16 narrative is a remarkable memory slide that satisfies the need of members of the public to identify themselves with democracy on the one hand and the monarchy on the other. It is an ingenious lie! Or a negotiated truth! Memory loss becomes memory gain in the new environment of the later generation. With this memory slide, Thai society can move on.

The mentioning of the October 16 event is often disturbing to those who experienced the 1976 massacre.[45] They may always perceive it as an insult. But this memory slide is indeed logical and explainable. Although its construction is perhaps akin to cut-and-paste, the narrative is neat and includes political meanings that harmonize with the familiar historical frame and are thus easier to remember. The historical ideology of Thai-ness helps organize the confusing story elements into a comprehensible and logical story according to its concepts and parameters, even though the October 16 event never took place.

ACCEPTABLE MEMORY: PUEY-THE-ICON

Previous chapters have discussed the memory of Puey Ungphakorn in two ways: as a victim whose words were chosen as the visible voice of the October 6 monument and as a silent protester for truth and justice. What is the message of the chosen statement? What is the meaning of Puey's voice that Thai society cares to hear?

Puey's words at the base of the monument read as follows: "What is most regrettable is the fact that young people now have no third choice. If they cannot conform to the government, they must run away. Those interested in peaceful ways to bring about freedom and democracy must restart from square one." The selection of this statement was part of the original design that both the artists and the public agreed upon.[46] It reflected the thinking of the artists, members of the public who participated in the brainstorming session, and probably many former radicals at the time as well. The addition of his figure into the relief and the funding from his admirers to complete the monument made his association with the memory of the massacre stronger, especially after his death in 1999. But this statement is not about a historical fact. It is a "lesson" from the massacre that, from Puey's perspective, Thai society should learn. It was how, in Puey's belief, October 6 was meaningful and relevant to Thai society at that time and long afterward. It is fair to say that the artists and the participating public also considered this lesson to be the most relevant meaning of the massacre given that the citation was inscribed in stone.

In the discourse on the massacre, this statement represents a moderate, centrist position. It reminds people of the danger of polarization and extremism. Along with the changes in the design of the monument, which made the monument to the massacre part of the broader struggle for democracy, it also reflects the strong support from political moderates and the fact that major funding for the monument came from those who saw Puey as the representative of victimhood. One of Puey's most iconic traits is his consistent and persistent advocacy for nonviolence. He coined the term *santi-prachatham* (people's Dharma of nonviolence) as the principle or philosophy for political and social relations. Although he never elaborated it into a formal treatise, it is evident in his writings over the years and in his acclaim by the public.[47] It has been an integral element of his reputation. This centrist position nudges others, including more radical ones, to the margins.

In the context and political environment since the 1990s, Puey was probably the ideal victim of the October 6 incident. An educated person of great integrity, he was denigrated, disrespected, and threatened by a mob. His efforts in the years that followed were tremendous. His writing on the massacre was probably the best known in the country. With the end of the Cold War in the mid-1980s, his courage and integrity throughout the turmoil in 1976 grew even more striking as the excesses of the anticommunist era began to appear more absurd. In his absence from Thailand, his reputation for incorruptibility and his *santi-prachatham* philosophy grew stronger. Puey has been iconized by institutions such as Thammasat University and the Bank of Thailand as well as by the public. Puey-the-icon was in the middle, under pressure from both the left and the right in 1976. A musical performance of his biography, "Mongkon salat klet: the musical" (Puey the Musical), in 2015 made this point clearly.[48] His *santi-prachatham* is integral to his moderate lesson. His philosophy and lesson harmonize perfectly with the post-1976 consensus and the hyperroyalist era. Puey-the-icon offers the wisdom that makes the memory of the massacre relevant to present generations.[49] But it is tamed. It is impossible to know whether Puey himself was comfortable with his iconization or with the way his memory has been employed to tame the danger of the October 6 memory. But neither he nor his descendants have control over Puey-the-icon in the public memory.

Although it is a counterhistory, dangerous to the historical ideology and the status quo, the memory of October 6 has been tamed in many ways that go beyond the state's attempts at suppression. The normative historical ideology of the hyperroyalist public in effect produced a minimalist memory and a false one. It also framed the relevant but harmless lesson of the massacre, none of which would disturb the status quo. The perplexing quandary of how to remember the October 6 massacre was lessened, by suppression, by silence, by the demand for reconciliation and to let bygones be bygones, and by memory slide. Even a false memory or one that is only minimally true is acceptable when truth has been swept under the rug.

Chapter 9

SILENCE OF THE WOLF

Earlier chapters explain how in a climate of reconciliation the perpetrators—the Wolf who devoured the Lamb in 1976—quieted down and in the 1980s and 1990s public perception of the incident changed, as evident in the occasional controversies about the massacre. We have seen the perpetrators' evasiveness and belittlement of the tragedy, of the number of deaths, and their denial of it. What did these behaviors tell us about the memory of the perpetrators of the 1976 massacre? Did they hide their memories behind their silence and evasiveness? In what ways and to what extent were they affected by the public and chronopolitics of memory? This chapter shows that by the first half of the 2000s, most of these right-wing perpetrators remained unrepentant, but their triumphal discourse was kept quietly among themselves. Many felt betrayed by the society for casting them as the bad people. Some seemed to forget the past, or tried to, and let go; some changed their memories in order to move on with their lives. But at least one of them hinted that he would do it again, if need be, to protect the monarchy; he claimed to speak for the Thai people.

The research for this chapter involved both documents and interviews with these former right-wing figures in the first half of the 2000s.[1] A few disclaimers are warranted. First, even though the interviews were conducted as professionally as I could manage, I cannot pretend that I was free from bias. I insist that when I did the interviews and today, I have moved beyond my anger and animosity and do not have the slightest desire for revenge. But I cannot deny that my interpretations of their words, even their body language, may contain bias. Second, I told all the interviewees that I was one of the student leaders in 1976. Only two of them failed to recognize me. I also told them about this planned English-language book. Their preparation for the encounters, their responses to my questions, even our casual chats, probably took place with the awareness that their former opponent was writing a book about the massacre. Some people, such as the two Thammasat University professors, declined my requests for interviews because they knew who I was. In addition, a senior police officer at first agreed to an interview, then changed his mind once we met in person and he realized who I was. Had the interviewer been somebody else, the encounters and the responses from these people might have been different. Nonetheless, some of them shared their thoughts and memories with me in ways that they might not have done with other interviewers. Uthan Sanidvongse, the broadcaster of Yan Kro, prepared for his encounter with me, the former radical. It was a privilege to do these unique interviews that others could not.

I admit to the limits as to how much I can understand these perpetrators of the massacre, these people who took part in the brutal killing of many people I knew. At times I did not want to understand them or care to know them better. A few times, however, I felt the opposite—a sympathy for some of them, especially the Red Gaurs.[2] I sought neither truth nor accountability for what they did or did not do on October 6, 1976. Nor did I seek reconciliation with them. In his effort to understand the ordinary Germans who took part in the Holocaust, Primo Levi once said, "Perhaps one cannot, what is more, one must not, understand what happened . . . because to understand is almost to justify." Tzevtan Todorov speculates that this dilemma led Levi to commit suicide.[3] Similarly, the dilemma for me was that to truly understand their thinking and memories comes perilously close to justifying their thoughts and actions. At that point, my intellectual curiosity shut down and refused to know them more because I did not want to do so. As a consequence, the analysis of perpetrator memories that follows may not, I admit, always probe as deeply as it could.

ENCOUNTERS WITH THE PERPETRATORS

The number of serious studies on the right-wing movement is small. Benedict Anderson writes a historical sociological analysis about the new lower-middle class who changed from the supporters of the

student uprising against the military in 1973 to defenders of the establishment under threat from radical students by 1976.[4] Prajak
Kongkirati explains the political conditions in which the movement
emerged and succeeded, thanks to the effective organization and the
fragmentation and inaction of the authorities.[5] Neither of them examines any particular group. David Morell and Chai-anan
Samudavanija as well as Paul Handley provide excellent general
backgrounds of these particular groups.[6] Katherine Bowie has written an excellent study on the Village Scouts from its history and role
in the counterinsurgency to its indoctrinating mass mobilization.[7]
Charles Keyes produced the only study of the notorious anticommunist monks.[8] Surprisingly, no study has been undertaken on the Red
Gaurs, whose name often becomes the generic one for the whole
right-wing movement.[9] Even though the Internal Security Operation
Command (ISOC), the anticommunist agency, may be the mastermind of these groups, as discussed in chapter 2, no study has yet
looked into the creation and operations of these groups.[10]

Although many of the perpetrators covered in this chapter were
public figures who were notorious for their views and actions, many
of those I interviewed and who are discussed here were ordinary people unknown to the public. My research on the memories of the right-
wing perpetrators began with an interview in 2000 with Somsak
Khwanmongkhol (Somsak K), one of the leaders of the Red Gaurs.
He repeated almost everything he had already said and published in
1996.[11] Nothing he said was new. Perhaps a public figure like him,
who had run for election a few times since the late 1990s, has to stick
with what is part of the public record. I then turned my search toward individuals who were not public figures in the 2000s, regardless
of their prominence in 1976. Based on the testimonies to police mentioned in chapter 3, I selected about thirty of those who had offered
damaging information against the students, then tracked them down
for interviews. Many could no longer be traced, and many turned
down my requests. Eventually I talked to about ten of them. None of
TU's alleged right-wing professors agreed to speak with me. One said
that she did not even know that there had been a massacre until recently—a blatant lie, probably a gesture of contempt. A few of them
were willing and eager to talk, especially the leader of the goons, who
even helped arrange a meeting with a leader of the Red Gaurs who
had not been among the police witnesses. A notorious journalist from
Dao sayam, who also had not been among the police witnesses, also

agreed to talk. I also spoke with spies of the army who had given testimonies to the police as well as with a few police officers. The most intriguing encounter I had was the meeting with the broadcaster general, who had orchestrated the deadly propaganda.

The person I wanted to meet most was Chair Guy, the dark-complexioned man who had wielded a folded chair to beat the body hanging from the tree. He also appeared to have taken part in two other heinous actions that morning, putting more papers into the flames that burned four bodies, and sitting on the body of the unconscious naked female. It was not clear whether he initiated those actions or simply joined them. Based on their testimonies to the police, I suspected one person might be him. I met that person but he was not Chair Guy. I also showed photographs of him to the leaders of the Red Gaurs and the goons and the army spies, asking whether they knew Chair Guy. None did.

By the early 2000s, these former perpetrators looked back at the massacre from various perspectives related to both their hindsight and their interests in the present. Many of them raised interesting issues regarding how the perpetrators had struggled with their memories of the massacre when their past actions were no longer seen as heroic or triumphant, but simply despicable.

The Betrayed Red Gaurs

> People think the Red Gaurs were responsible [for the killing on October 6]. They think we were bad guys. It is bitter for me.
>
> No government since then ever tried to bring the real killers and the masterminds to justice. The Red Gaurs were the easy target. We bore the burden of blame and stigma because people think we did it. [The real perpetrators] have hidden their wrongdoings by making the Red Gaurs the scapegoats.
>
> We have children. I have children. My daughter knows that I am a Red Guar. I am dejected by how she feels about me. How could I explain to my daughter when society judged that I am a bad guy?
>
> We became the victims of the society.
>
> (RG1, a former leader of the Red Gaurs group, June 21, 2006)

Most writings on the massacre in Thai or English blame the Red Gaurs for the crimes that morning to the extent that the group's name has become emblematic for all perpetrators of the massacre. All members of the Red Gaurs I met, despite the bitter relations among them today, unanimously denied any deadly actions on October 6.[12] General Sutsai Hatsadin, the "Father" of the group, had denied culpability before, but more than likely no one believed him.[13] We may dismiss their denial, but I sensed that they might be telling the truth. They admitted that they threw homemade explosives and fired shots into TU during the night to intimidate the demonstrators, hoping that doing so would scare people and deter people from joining the protest, similar to what they had done at previous demonstrations. They did not consider their actions during the night as a contribution to the eventual massacre. They insisted that they did not intend to kill because they did not get the order to kill. One of them bragged that they might have killed the protesters had they gotten an order to do so—but they did not. All those I met had been taken aback by the brutality they witnessed. Sutsai said it went way too far, was horrifying.[14] Somsak K recounted how that morning he had been roaming around outside the campus but did not do anything. A few people were angry with him for his inaction.[15] Sutsai said similarly that some Red Gaurs were at TU to help the police in small ways but did not play any important role and did not take part in the killing. He identified those who killed as those "thugs, the Bat 500 group, who are bad people."[16] According to his son, Sutsai was surprised by the violence that morning.[17] Those I met said the same; one went even further, saying that once the heavy shooting began and violence intensified, they realized that the situation had escalated beyond the order they had received (to disturb the demonstration). They then retreated to Sutsai's residence. Only a few remained and did so by their own choice.

The Red Gaurs' accounts could have been orchestrated to such an extent that they actually became their individual memories. Thus their words may not be trustworthy. Nevertheless, the substance of their accounts was corroborated by their fellow right-wing Patriotic Goons. In a meeting with the latter, they bragged about their heroic attacks at TU even as they mocked and ridiculed RG1 (one of the known leaders of the Red Gaurs in 1976) for doing nothing but retreating to Sutsai's home. Every Red Gaur I met bemoaned the fact that the name Red Gaurs, which they were proud of, had become synonymous with the killers of October 6. Sutsai's son showed strong resentment that people had accused his father and the group without knowing the truth. Those false allegations in their view had caused trouble for most of them. RG1 complained with obvious bitterness, "How could I explain to my daughter?" They felt betrayed by the public, who branded them criminals without trying to find the truth, and failed to recognize their contributions to help save the country from communism.

Of those I met, bitterness was quite strong toward Sutsai's superior, the mastermind, who assigned these dirty jobs to them but left them on their own to take the blame. According to Sutsai's son, "a very highly superior person, whom I don't want to name, whom everybody respects, asked my father to take on an important assignment for the country." This person, he said, "has blood on his hands, yet remained highly respected and venerated, untouched by trouble. Why does my father [Sutsai] have to be tarnished until the end of his life? . . . It is not fair to him. The bastards who take all the rewards are in fact all stained by blood."[18] The last sentence was repeated several times in the son's published interview. According to another Red Gaur I met, the mastermind has never been exposed to this day. Sutsai himself insisted on keeping the superior's name secret. Nevertheless, one of them agreed to name the mastermind, who he believed was also behind other right-wing groups. Many of them also named the main financiers of the Red Gaurs. None of the names was ever mentioned in relation to the massacre, let alone as sharing the blame.

They insisted that I (and readers of my book) must understand that they were merely pawns of the contesting power elite. So were radical students, they argued. We were the pawns who suffered. Somsak K and RG1 thought the brutality of the October 6 morning was excessive. Every Red Gaur I met in the early 2000s was "sympathetic" about the losses. To be precise, they were not sorry for what they did during the 1973 to 1976 period or the night before the massacre because those actions, in their view, were not part of the killings. No regret. No remorse. They still believed in their accomplishment—bringing society back on track and saving the country from communism.[19] Despite their bitterness, most were proud for what they regarded as their *Pid thong lang phra* (thankless) role. To be more precise, they saw themselves as sacrificial lambs.

The Patriotic Goons and Their Commander

The perpetrators who admitted taking part in the massacre were members of various small, lesser-known groups that earlier I called goons. Based on my conversations with them, especially their leader, I learned that they were loosely organized groups of unemployed or semi-employed hoodlums.[20] These are the people Sutsai characterized as "thugs . . . bad people." During 1975 and 1976, they took action under different group names, such as the Thai Bats (Khang khao thai), the Protector of the Thai Nation (Phu pokpong chat thai), The Thunder Bird 19 (Wihok saifa 19), and so on. These were the bold, fierce people who attacked TU in the early morning, storming into TU ahead of the police and sparking the massacre. Their leader, whom I call here the commander, was a navy captain who worked at ISOC. Three of the six whom I met, all retired military officers, were the organizers of these groups. According to them, ISOC financed the creation and operations of this deadly political machine.[21]

The commander confirmed that the Red Gaurs did not play any important role in the massacre. His people did. They boasted that they collaborated very well with the police. Mr. Samoe Oncharoon, who drove the bus that smashed the gates of TU, allowing the police and the hysterical right-wing crowd to storm in, was also a member of this group. According to his fellows, he did odd jobs on and off. But as one put it, he was "a genuine patriot who would sacrifice his life for the country."[22] He often volunteered to take action against students, such as obstructing the groups that put posters up around the city. On the afternoon of October 6, after the massacre, these people were also on the front line of the right-wing demonstrators against the Seni government. By the 2000s, these people still considered the October 6 incident their proudest accomplishment, one that had prevented the Vietnamese communists from taking over Thailand. The shift in public perception of the massacre in the 1980s and 1990s seemed to have no effect on their views and memories. Unlike the Red Gaurs, I heard no complaints from these people, who remained cheerful about their victory in 1976.

The commander, who taught courses on communism and world politics for senior military officers at ISOC, also wrote a book about the October incidents of 1973 and 1976.[23] In his view, the assassinations and violence against students in those years were the result of the conflict between the China-CPT alliance on the one hand, and the Soviet Union–Vietnam alliance on the other. The former was responsible for most cases. The killings on October 6 were exacerbated by them too, he wrote, whereas his group only tried to help the police end the demonstration. When I showed them the picture of Chair Guy and asked whether they knew who he was, the commander responded at once without looking at the photo, "he was CPT." In my opinion, his response was absurd, to put it politely. Even RG1, who was invited by the commander to join our conversation, told me afterward that he did not believe it. However, his analysis of the violence of those years was not absurd for many right-wing elements at the time. A similar line of thought was circulated among the anticommunist agencies around 1975 and 1976 and was also propagated by military propaganda. In his testimony to the police after the massacre, for example, Uthan of Yan Kro offered an assessment of the political situation that led to the massacre that was similar to the commander's view.[24] Samson Lim is perhaps right in arguing that Thais typically see the large context of history or a historical epoch in conspiratorial terms, as the course of action is instigated and controlled by somebody behind the scenes. Even the Thai state is typically paranoid that it is the victim of a mysterious hand.[25]

The commander commented that the public now blamed the right-wing groups because they were ignorant, misguided into thinking that the 1973 uprising and the 1976 massacre were part of the struggles for democracy. He believed that Thailand was currently (in 2006) under the influence of the leftists again, though the situation was not as dangerous as in the 1970s. In his opinion, the real threat to Thailand today is capitalism and the United States. Here it should be noted that during the interviews with the Red Gaurs in 2006, I asked them who or what the most dangerous threat to Thailand was nowadays. Most of them said capitalism and the United States. One of them remarked jokingly that he should have listened to the leftists and joined us in fighting US imperialism in the old days.

The Corporal-Healer

One of the active Patriotic Goons was in fact an army corporal who had been assigned to collect information about student activities during the seventies. He instead joined the actions of the goon group on many occasions.[26] He later found a more lucrative career as a traditional healer, hence I call him the corporal-healer. I met him at his huge, lavish home office. In those days, he and his cohorts looked for chances for minor attacks on student activists, such as damaging their vehicles or disrupting their activities. He claimed to know Samoe very well and told a story with a big laugh about how he and Samoe had once dumped a bucket of glue onto a student activist. To this day, he remained proud of what he had done.

The corporal-healer boasted about being in the lead group that raided TU, an account he told with joy and excitement, as if recounting an action movie. There was no regret, no empathy for the victims, even today. In his testimony to the police in 1976, he was one of the few who claimed to witness many of the ugliest actions. I eagerly sought him out because I thought that he could be Chair Guy. He was not. However, I was surprised that he did not claim to have witnessed those terrible actions at all during our interview. He only described the confusion, people's anger at students inside TU, the mob attacks on some students who tried to escape, and a few descriptions of the incident that were common public knowledge. Nothing seemed to reflect his eyewitness experience or any unique individual memories. Perhaps he had forgotten that, according to his testimony to the police, he had seen with his own eyes the hanging and other horrendous actions. Perhaps he never actually witnessed them but compiled them from what he had heard and read in the newspapers to make up a dramatic eyewitness account for the police in the wake of the massacre. After all, at the time such actions were considered heroic. His alleged personal account served his super-sized ego well. He insisted, however, that he did not kill or assault anyone—an underperformance given his bragging about how he had engaged with students so many times before that day.

Nonetheless, one story from the corporal-healer has disturbed me to this day. On that day, just outside TU, he told me that while the shooting was going on, a student appeared unexpectedly, rushing angrily at him. Luckily for him, his partner, an army sergeant with a gun in hand, was there and shot the student at point blank range. He repeated the story several times with the same precise details, as if it were a funny story. In 2006, his partner was a colonel at the military cadet school who was in charge of preparing audiovisual instruments for Princess Sirindhorn, a professor at the school. Let us call him the intelligence sergeant. I had met him. But the shooting was not at all part of his memory of the massacre. Were the events of October 6 merely an embellished war story for the corporal-healer? Or did the intelligence sergeant lie? Or had they created and lived with false memories?

The Intelligence Sergeant

On assignment to collect information, the intelligence sergeant was inside TU through the night of October 5 and outside it in the morning. According to him, he was not carrying any weapon that day. Besides, he and the corporal-healer had gone their separate ways early in the morning. He observed the situation at a distance from TU; the corporal-healer went to join the demonstration at the Equestrian Plaza. His memory contradicts not only the corporal-healer's but also both of their testimonies in 1976, given that both of them told the police that they remained at TU the entire time until the crackdown was over.

The intelligence sergeant began his military career at the bottom and rose in the ranks through education. In 1973, according to his account, while serving in the army, he was also a part-time student who supported the uprising. Between 1973 and 1976, he often attended demonstrations of radical students as part of his job as an army spy. He was also assigned to help the operations of right-wing groups. Those assignments led him to several meetings with people from other security agencies, including the Santiban (political police), the National Security Council, and the ISOC. Among the people he met at those meetings were Sutsai and the goon commander and Chamlong Srimuang. He named a few leftist leaders he came to know very well as he infiltrated their organizations. He even once joined a meeting of the leftist leaders.

The sergeant was open and politically opinioned. His views on most issues were more complex and he was more of an intellectual than other right-wing individuals I met. Indeed our conversation about Thai politics in the past and present was amicable because he was somewhat liberal in the Thai context. The intelligence sergeant learned about communism partly from the commander during those meetings in 1975 and 1976 and later at the Command and General Staff College, where the latter taught. He said he was not convinced at all by the commander's analysis of Thai politics in the mid-1970s as the contest of the two communist alliances. He giggled when he summarized the commander's analysis to me. Yet he repeated several times that he had met a Soviet agent among the leftists. Although he thought that the communist threat to Thailand was real given the communist revolutions in 1975, he did not believe that Vietnam planned to invade Thailand. He agreed with students at the time, however, that there should be no US military bases on Thai soil. He did not believe that students wanted Thailand to become communist or wanted to abolish the monarchy. Unlike most other right-wing elements at the time, he did not consider Puey to be a communist, nor did he believe that weapons were stockpiled at TU. The conflict between the left and the right in Thailand, in short, was primarily the differences of political ideas, therefore—he said unequivocally several times during the interview—assassinations and violent crackdowns, including that of October 6, were wrong. In retrospect, he said, he became more frustrated by right-wing factions because, "we did not speak the truth." He felt deceived, that he had been misled into serving a bad political purpose. At the time, he said, he started feeling conflict within himself too. But he was young and naïve, so he took for granted that senior officers knew best, and that he should follow them. By 2006, he no longer believed them.

Regarding the massacre, the intelligence sergeant said he had followed the students' protests closely since October 4. He witnessed the hanging skit, too, but from a distance. He did not believe the students intended to send any message about the crown prince. On the night of October 5, he went to TU with the corporal-healer. He recalled that he had seen the Red Gaurs gathered a block away from TU. In the morning, after the situation had worsened, he retreated to observe from the opposite side of Sanamluang from TU, where he could only hear the sound of shooting from both sides. The corporal-healer left him at this point, going to the Equestrian Plaza. The intelligence sergeant himself stayed put until the shooting was over. After that, he walked toward the campus again. He saw the hangings and the burning of people after the actions were already over. He lamented out loud to people at the hanging site, "Disgusting. How can anyone do this?" He did not care whether his outburst upset the crowd. Apparently his recollection was vivid. Throughout that morning, he just observed quietly from a distance and did not take any action, let alone a heroic one. Speaking in 2006, he believed that someone must have been behind the whole incident but he did not know who. He did not understand why such violence was needed. He did not mention the incident related by the corporal-healer.

His account to the police in 1976, however, was that he had wandered near TU the entire time and had witnessed the lynching of one student whose face looked like a Yuan (Vietnamese). When I asked him whether he had ever talked to the police or reported to his superior about what he had witnessed, he categorically denied ever talking to the police. His superior did not question him because the incident was over. If any testimony by him exists, he argued, "the police probably made it up by themselves," this despite his signature at the foot of every page of the testimony. It is hard to believe that the police would make up the testimony of a real person given that the person could be called to testify at the trial. However, as we will see, I found two other people who also denied ever giving testimony to the police in 1976.

Assuming that the intelligence sergeant gave testimony in 1976, the eyewitness accounts by both the healer and the sergeant may be entirely made up to satisfy a desire, especially on the healer's side, to play a heroic part in the victory. Or, the sergeant might have been an eyewitness in 1976, whose testimony was basically true. In 2006, however, he tried to distance himself, literally and metaphorically, from the acts he had once thought heroic, thereby denying any action, even his testimony. Instead, he talked about the right-wing goons with expressive pity, even an insulting tone at times, and recalled his verbal defiance of the heinous acts, an act of incredible courage under the circumstances. It is also possible that he lied on both occasions to better position himself in different political environments. If any of the latter two scenarios was the case, his memory had warped significantly over the decades, purging quite a bit of the old memories, adding some, and dramatically remaking it in a new frame that fits his present incarnations.[27]

The alteration of one's memory is not necessarily a deceptive and conscious process. It is quite possible that he was discomfited by his past and needed to recalibrate in order to live on in the present time with self-pride. As a result, he did not feel betrayed by Thai society; instead, he felt deceived and used by his superiors to take part in a malicious operation. Everyone modifies their memories, especially if more bearable fictions help one to live on with less haunting from the past. A society, too, needs to revisit its history from time to time, to make it "make sense" in the light of the present time. The sergeant's changed memory was probably a microcosm of the collective memory of Thai society as a whole, which has been haunted by the memory of the massacre.

If the sergeant altered his memory in order to live his life, my confronting him to find out which memory was truthful or how much he had altered it might have opened up the old wounds he had tried to move beyond. I decided not to do so. The truth about the sergeant's past and his memory would not especially enhance the value of this book. We have learned much from his case about the complexity of memories about the massacre, regardless what he actually did.

The Spy Journalist

A notorious journalist at *Dao sayam* also turned out to be an army agent tasked with collecting information via his networks and spreading certain information to the public. He revealed to me that in 1976 the army had spies in all the leading dailies, including *Thairath,* the best-selling daily in the country. Other journalists at *Dao sayam,* despite sharing his right-wing ideology, did not know that he was an army officer. As a journalist and an army intelligence officer, he had access to confidential information, which he boasted about to me. He mentioned several examples, such as a secret deal between the "most powerful person in the land" and the "three tyrants" in the October 1973 uprising that led to the latter's exiles. After he was de-commissioned from the army, the spy journalist became a full-time staff member at one of the largest Thai associations of journalists.

In 1976, he was infamous among the radicals for his ultra-right-wing column, his shameless propagandizing, and his utter lack of journalistic professionalism. But the right-wing credited him with making *Dao sayam* the media platform for the Village Scout movement, particularly at critical moments. The spy journalist said that *Dao sayam* received the photo of the controversial skit but never had the film. He categorically denied that *Dao sayam* had tampered with the photo. Instead, he argued that it took a risk in publishing the photo because in doing so the paper could have been charged with lèse majesté as well. The editorial collective decided to publish it without any order from anyone else, not even his superior in the army. He still believed that the skit was part of the communists' anti-monarchy scheme and that the students intentionally mocked the crown prince. He strongly believed that *Dao sayam* did the right thing in exposing the scheme and instigating the reaction against the communists. However, he did not anticipate or expect the massacre.

The spy journalist was quite upset that the ignorant public had in subsequent decades put the blame on the right wing. Like the Red Gaurs, he was visibly bitter that their accomplishments were not remembered or recognized. He insisted that the students were armed and fired heavily at the police and the crowd, and that the police treated the arrested students very well, even protecting them from being lynched. Speaking as a spy, he said that no order had been given to kill the students. This was the same account of the incident and the same excuse broadcast on TV5 on that day. He also defended Salang Bunnak, saying that he had not attacked Puey but in fact tried to protect him at the airport. The spy journalist refused any responsibility for the massacre, even indirectly as a media-instigated atrocity. Nor did he regret or feel sorry for the dead. However, he was also not particularly proud or feel heroic about what he did. To him, the massacre was the result of complex conspiracies, conflicts, and deals among many political groups, including factions within the military and among the communists. It was "a nightmare" that everyone should let go of. Nevertheless, by 2000 when I interviewed him, he believed that *Dao sayam*'s role against the communists had been vindicated, as was his own role for the paper and for the Village Scout movement.

The Right-Wing Professors

As described in chapter 3, the right-wing professors at TU were committed to the anticommunist narrative of the massacre. In 2001, I made contact with two who were among the most notorious before October 6, 1976. The older one was the nominal leader of the group; the younger was its most active member. Their testimonies and the materials they submitted to the police in 1976 confirmed their notoriety given that they included vicious allegations against Puey for having been the mastermind of the communists within TU and in the labor movement. These two also claimed that they recognized right away that the controversial skit was indeed mocking the crown prince. On the night of October 5, they cooperated with Salang to file charges against the students, earning Salang's praise for their eagerness to act even in the middle of the night.[28] According to Puey, these two professors also showed up at the airport when Puey was detained before leaving the country.[29]

I wanted to find out whether they still maintained their testimony to the police that Puey and their opponents in TU were communists. If the chronopolitics of memory had changed their views, how would they explain their unfounded allegations of the past? How would the fact that Puey has become idolized nationally for his integrity and incorruptibility affect their views of him and of the past? Were they still proud of their actions in the past or did they feel betrayed like the Red Gaurs and the spy journalist?

Unfortunately, both of them refused to talk. One gave me her reasons over the telephone. The country had been doing well. TU was back to being an academic institution rather than a bastion of the leftists, as in the 1970s. Talking about the past, she argued, was not helpful. We should care about the present and live for the future. The other professor complained that many people had misrepresented her as right wing. She in fact had supported the students in the 1973 uprising. She ended the conversation, also by telephone, saying that she had just learned not long ago that there had been killings at TU in 1976. Such comments signaled to me that I should not waste my time with her nonsense. I did not have the opportunity to ask either of them my questions. I can only guess that, just as the anticommunist ideology of the 1970s looks absurd nowadays, their memories and views of the past must have changed too. It is quite possible that they wished their past political actions at TU and on October 6, 1976, would fade quietly away from public view. Silence and evasiveness would have to serve instead.

Other Noteworthy Encounters

Numerous people I had managed to contact I failed to meet; numerous encounters did not produce any interesting results. Yet the missed opportunities are telling in various ways. For example, I had a telephone conversation with Salang Bunnak. Thanks to his outspoken character, Salang was a public figure who often commented on police matters and occasional national issues before and long after the massacre. He was an occasional guest on television programs and on the Yan Kro broadcast and was prominent on TV5 on the October 6 as well (see chapter 3). Over the telephone, he seemed willing to meet and talk because, in his opinion, the history of the massacre in the decades that followed had been altered and was full of lies. What he meant in particular was the accusation that he had assaulted Puey at the airport. According to him, he tried to protect Puey from the angry mob of Village Scouts by showing them that Puey had already received the harsh treatment he deserved. This excuse was exactly the same as he had given in public several times. I wanted to meet him to draw more out of him. Unfortunately, he could not find time and ultimately seemed uninterested in meeting me. In any case, such a public figure usually has a standard answer ready for all interviews, so I decided not to pursue it any further.[30]

Another police officer I met was the former deputy police inspector of the local police district where TU was located. He was heavily involved in many actions that day, including leading the local police into TU and conducting a thorough inspection of the campus after the incident. When I contacted him by telephone, even though I told him who I was in 1976 and explained the purpose of the interview, he was cordial because, as it turned out, he did not recognize me. But the moment we met face to face, he did—and suddenly turned cold. Unwilling to say anything substantive, his standard answer was that he did not know, did not see, or could not confirm or deny anything about the massacre. It was a dismissive gesture to end the conversation, similar to the elder professor's excuse. Nevertheless, I observed that he avoided eye contact throughout the brunch meeting. Did his action hint at his shame? Or was it a defensive shrug?

Another witness—let me call him Sawat—had given testimony to the police that was quite damaging to the students but insisted, when we met in 2006, that he never said a word to the police. He did not even remember going near TU that day, he said. He knew about the incident, but it did not register as an important event in his memory or personal experience. In my opinion, he seemed genuine and honest, though I doubt that the police had any reason to fake Sawat's or the intelligence sergeant's testimonies. If the testimony were true, how should we make sense of Sawat's denial or lost memory? Was this another case of altering or purging an undesirable memory, subconsciously or otherwise, to come to terms with his later career and life? Although the intelligence sergeant's memory may have been altered to a great extent, he never denied witnessing the massacre. In fact, he acted as if he still remembered the day vividly. It is hard to believe that Sawat would completely deny any experience of the incident. It is possible that the event had no relevance to his life either then or now, and therefore faded away. Of course, it is also possible that he simply lied.

Another suspicious testimony is that of a leftist defector. Among the 224 people who testified to the police, only two were leftists. One was an activist who had finished college and become a teacher at a local public school in a northeastern province of Thailand before October 1976. He later earned a law degree and was a practicing lawyer when we met in 2006. According to him, he tried to flee right after the massacre. But, lacking contacts in the CPT network, he decided to escape to Laos by himself. He was arrested by the Lao authorities as soon as he crossed the Mekong River. After an ordeal of several months in a Lao prison, he was released but sent back across the river to Thailand by himself. He did this successfully without being arrested on the Thai side. To return to his teaching job, however, he had to turn himself in to the Thai authorities in that province. He did and was interrogated heavily before being released. He insisted that he had never given testimony to the police or any authority in Bangkok. I showed him the photocopy of his 1976 statement to the police. He examined it thoroughly, as a lawyer would do. Then he pointed out several suspicious points. The statement was dated at the time he was detained in Laos. A few signs suggested that the document had not been recorded or typed by the same person, probably not even on the same occasion but pasted together afterward. He admitted to being interrogated by the authorities but not the ones whose signatures appeared on the pages I showed him. Above all, he insisted that the interrogation he had faced was about his escape to Laos after the massacre; the testimony I showed him was all about the radical movement and the leftist groups he participated in from 1973 to 1976. His argument was convincing, though I was not able to verify its details, such as whether he went to Laos. If his statement to the police was falsified, then the denials by Sawat and the intelligence sergeant may not be entirely false either, and other police statements may also be in doubt.

Patterns of Excuses and Observations

The memories and voices of the perpetrators of the October 6 massacre were discredited and silenced by the changing political conditions and public perceptions in the decades that followed. Those related in this chapter represent a range of their memories, as they reported them to me.[31] Yet most, including those who felt bitter and betrayed, insisted that their actions in the past were right and justified. Some offered explanations and excuses but no shame. None showed remorse. The commander insisted that it was a glorious day, not the dark one the public perceives it to be nowadays. Only the intelligence sergeant showed some sign of guilt and shame.

The conundrum is thus to understand how these people have dealt with their unforgetting over time. What were the reasons they gave to themselves to justify their actions? The patterns in their excuses were discernable and rational. Their language facilitated their excuses and justifications and became an integral part of the barbarization and cruelty, exactly as James Dawes observed in his interviews with war criminals.[32] It is indeed alarming that these kinds of rational excuses and language are acceptable in Thai society. What are the ideological or discursive and the social or familial environments that provide the fertile conditions for these excuses to persist?

First, many argued that their actions must be understood within the specific context of the past. No one should judge them right or wrong retrospectively according to the values or understandings of the present day. Suddenly they were historians! RG1 even explained to me a historian's approach to the past. It was a clever argument that made their actions "relatively" right or wrong, depending on context and the political values used to judge them. In other words, they argued that the normative values for crime, politics, justice, and so on, should be suspended, that we should allow the specific circumstances to override them. Such moral relativity hinges on the continuing ambiguity surrounding the massacre, the absence of a just accounting that could have established the necessary norms, legally, socially, and politically. Thai society has thus far provided the conditions that allow such ambiguity to exist.

Second, today, the main justification for their actions is the need to protect nation, religion, and king—the three ideological pillars of Thai-ness. They killed for a higher purpose, for reasons that took precedence over individual lives. For them, the enemy in 1976 was the communists, the purported Vietnamese aliens, or a subhuman class of beings. They did not see the victims as individuals like themselves. This rationale implies that they did not kill in rage or ignorance, and that the outcome justifies the brutality as long as Thais still subscribe fanatically to the ideology of Thai-ness.

Third, some of them argued that both they and the victims were too young and immature to deal with such a complex political situation. They were all pawns. I believe that they kept telling themselves this to deflect the moral censure to their patron, the mastermind, who, in their view, should be held accountable and take the blame. This argument is reasonable because it was true to some extent. In arguing this way, however, they implicitly acknowledged their guilt.

Perhaps they were trying to appease me. Yet they deflected their guilt
to others as if they had naively and absentmindedly committed an action. It is a pitiful excuse. It shifts the guilt to powerful people in high
places who, in Thailand at least, may never be identified or held
accountable.

Apart from the changed memories and patterns of excuses, a few
additional issues deserve serious examination. The first concerns the
modification of memories to minimize the haunting presence of the
past. Was the case of the intelligence sergeant an exceptional or a
typical one for individual memory change in the political and cultural
context of Thai society? Was it a microcosm of the broader social
memory of the 1976 massacre in Thailand as well, and if so, in what
ways? After all, as discussed in chapter 8, people's memories slid in
tandem with changing political conditions so that they could live
with the present and move on. But no study to date helps us understand the extent to which memories were altered in the case of the
massacre. We do not yet understand the specific political, cultural,
and ideological factors that we should being paying attention to.

A second issue concerns the culture of law and punishment in
Thailand. The hierarchical status of individuals matters very much in
regard to the extent to which a wrongdoer should be protected or
held culpable. On the one hand, the Red Gaurs, most of whom were
from the lower class and looked down on as uneducated failures,
bore the burden of blame and came to represent the violent vigilantes.
On the other hand, this was not the first time that people with high
social status, power, or wealth have gotten away with major and minor wrongdoing, even crimes.[33] As with the massacre, most of these
cases escaped scrutiny because of ambiguity, secrecy, the state's censorship and misinformation, ideological cover-ups, bad excuses, and
outright suppression. The public is not willing to pursue justice because of fear. Practically and institutionally, impunity remains an
integral element of the rule of law in Thailand.[34]

A third issue is about our knowledge of the right-wing movement in 1976, which could shed light on subsequent cases. It is understandable when the Red Gaurs complained about becoming a
convenient target of social censure. Their bitterness at the "superior"
above Sutsai is certainly justified. Even though they may appear to be
operating independently from one another, the Red Gaurs, the
Patriotic Goons, and other pressure groups (such as Nawaphon and
the Housewife Clubs) could be different branches of an orchestrated

movement. Each of them performed certain roles and took certain kinds of political actions, from vigilantism and the paramilitary provocation to the mass-based and issue-specific organizational directives. The ISOC and the "superior" seemed to have their hands in all these branches, namely, Sutsai for the Red Gaurs, The commander for the fringe paramilitary groups, Watthana for Nawaphon, and Chamlong for other right-wing civic groups.[35]

Finally, during my encounters with these right-wingers, I always talked with them about the country at the present time: what they thought were major problems or the most serious dangers Thailand was facing today. Without exception, the former perpetrators of the 1976 massacre all pointed to the United States and capitalism. In the 2000s when I talked with them, the economic crisis of 1997 was still fresh in their minds; they believed it was the result of Washington's conspiracy to undermine the rise of Asia, including Thailand. They were also concerned about American dominance in the world since the 9/11 tragedy. The idea of the US threat in leftist discourse during the Cold War was, however, different from that shared by Thais of all political shades in the post–Cold War environment. The former was based on the vision of a desirable future, for a radical change beyond capitalism. The latter is based on a nationalist dichotomy, West versus Thai (and East). For conservative Thais, Thai-ness was always under threat—from the communists during the Cold War and from the United States and the West in the post–Cold War. The anticapitalism discourse of recent decades is decidedly conservative in its desire for an unchanged future. But as it turns out, as discussed in chapter 10, many former radicals and these right-wing elements share the same ideas about today's enemies.

Encounter with the True Blue

My most intriguing encounter with the right-wing perpetrators of the massacre was one of the first (I interviewed him in 2000), but the last that I fully understood: General Uthan Sanidvongse, the army lieutenant colonel in charge of radio propaganda against the radical students from mid-1975 until after the October 6 massacre in 1976. He was probably "the" most infamous propagandist in modern Thai history. In this "psychological warfare," the phrase he used to characterize his work, apart from ideological indoctrination, he also planted false information, spread vicious rumors, threatened the dissenters, and dehumanized opponents. Hatred filled the airwaves. The ultimate message was that the radicals were proxies of the Vietnamese communists and they planned to overthrow the monarchy. His broadcast, Yan Kro, was the main culprit, perhaps even more than *Dao sayam,* because of the allegation that spread like a wildfire on the eve of the massacre, that the students had hanged the crown prince in effigy. During the night of October 5, he called on the right wing to punish the radical students resolutely. Even though he did not fire a single shot and was nowhere near TU, he was, in my opinion, one of the top people responsible for the October 6 massacre because, like the hate media in the 1994 Rwanda genocide, were it not for his broadcast, the massacre might not have happened.

After the massacre, the broadcast under his command was no longer needed. He remained active as a newspaper columnist for about six months, however. With the downfall of the ultraroyalist Thanin government, Uthan faded away from public attention.[36] He never gave interviews, wrote, or said anything in public about the massacre. No explanation, no complaint, nothing. His complete withdrawal from the public made people assume that he had already died. When I searched for him in 2000, however, I found that he was in fact alive and living in the place listed in the telephone book at the time. All I needed to do was look him up in the Yellow Pages and give him a call. Uthan recognized my name when I introduced myself over the telephone. He even asked me how I was doing in the United States. Regarding the interview, at first he refused, saying that the mission he had been assigned had been accomplished, and he did not care what people thought about him. When I persisted, he graciously accepted my request. In retrospect, he wanted to talk.

On our meeting at his residence, he established the rules for the interview: no tape recording. "Let's have a conversation," he said. As it turned out, it was neither an interview nor a conversation. It was mostly a monologue and continued for more than two hours. I began by telling him about this book project. He then set out another rule—no note-taking either. "This is just a conversation," he insisted. It can be summarized easily in that whatever questions I asked during those hours, he always responded with the same two answers. First, whenever I asked about himself—his background, his career, his ideas, or what he had done and why he had done it, including specifics about the massacre—his responses were always about how grateful he and his clan were to the Chakri kings, from

King Chulalongkorn (r. 1868–1911) to King Bhumibol. Second, no matter what I asked about Thailand—politics, the military, the situations in 1975 and 1976, his broadcast, comments on Thai society, that is, anything beyond himself—his answers were always about the significance and the indispensability of the monarchy for the country. Each question took about half a minute or less. The answers took about ten minutes each time. No matter how differently I rephrased or reframed my questions, his answers remained the same, almost verbatim every time, as if they were played from a recording. Out of frustration, toward the end, I even posed a few sarcastic questions about his behavior. His responses remained the same, expressed in the same stern voice with the same stern expression.

The encounter seemed like a school principal reprimanding a small child. In retrospect, perhaps that was how he thought of me and how he prepared for the interview. I left in frustration thinking that it had been a mistake to come and listen to his sermon about the benevolence of the monarchy for Thai society AND for him and his family in particular. The two answers were so conventional, what Thai people have heard for years, what we are taught in school, what we hear from the media, at public events, in everyday life. I learned nothing about his memory of the massacre. Yet what lingered in my mind after that day and long afterward was not frustration but puzzlement. Why did he consent to this interview? What did he mean to convey? Did he mean this for me in particular or not? What if someone else had asked him the same questions? Was there or wasn't there anything in his words to do with the October 6 massacre at all?

Was it simply the behavior of an old man? Unlikely. The conversations over the telephone and at the beginning of the meeting, when he greeted me in his home, were normal. He looked strong and younger than his age. Was it merely for the personal satisfaction of beating me up intellectually? Unlikely, because in Thai social context, he was my superior, higher than me in every respect: family background, age, wealth, recognition, and power. A superior does not need to respond to a request from a subordinate. He could have simply ignored my request as a trifle of no consequence to him. I believe the "interview" was a serious conversation he wanted to have.

After pondering this perplexing encounter for many years, I realized that Uthan might be the only perpetrator of the massacre who had spoken the whole truth, as he believed it, with the utmost honesty.[37] It is fair to assume that the "conversation" took place exactly as he intended it to happen, as signaled by the rules he set out at the beginning. It is also reasonable to assume that he had read some of my writings in Thai about the massacre. When I told him that I was writing a book about memories of it, he must have speculated about what the message of my book would be and how it would be received. Then, in response, he offered me the two sermons—one about the monarchy and his family, the other about the monarchy and Thai society. The conversation was intended as a lesson, and a warning, to me and those whose views about the massacre might be similar to my own.

Whereas everyone else offered retrospective explanations, clever and pitiful excuses, boasts about their heroism, or subdued recollections they had tried to forget, Uthan needed no excuses or apologetic explanations. He made no pretense of being a historian, or someone else's pawn, or a naïve operator who was used, then betrayed and discarded. He needed no silly or evasive deflection about where he was that morning or whether he carried a weapon. He did not need to modify his memory for the changing times or lie to himself in order to move on with his current life. He was so confident in what he did and why he did it that he had no self-doubt, let alone regret or remorse. The massacre was the culmination of his career and life. For him, time had probably stopped since that day in 1976. As a cavalry officer, he must think of himself as the king's knight. He had no reason to be evasive about what was right and wrong regarding the massacre. Anyone who disagrees with him is simply wrong.

The two sermons appeared unrelated to the massacre but in fact were all about it. Uthan wanted to battle with me head-on, without wasting time or making unnecessary excuses. Unlike most royalists, who denied the palace's involvement, he did not. The two sermons implicitly acknowledged the unspeakable truth about the monarchy and the massacre. He and I may agree on this fact. We simply draw completely opposite conclusions from it. I take it to incriminate the monarchy; he takes it as confirmation that the massacre was what the radicals deserved.

Uthan wanted the monologue to send a message to me that the students (including me) were wrong that day in October 1976. He wanted to confront me, like a powerful elder reprimanding a stubborn young troublemaker, to reaffirm that he was right; he had done the right thing for the country and for the monarchy. Decades later, I was still wrong and he was still right. He must have wanted to remind me that his view was easy to understand, and that most Thais do understand it. Only people like me are too stubborn to understand, and that is our error.

Last but not least, Uthan's sermon suggests that I keep in mind that he is not alone in his beliefs. Many more people are on his side than on mine.

Chapter 10

PRAXIS OF MEMORY

The Octobrists

At the 1996 commemoration of the Thammasat University massacre (discussed in chapter 6), the final item on the program was the speeches by well-known figures among the former activists of the 1973–1976 era. Special attention went to Seksan Prasertkul, a charismatic leader of the radical period who, as we may recall from earlier chapters, returned from the jungle as a "historical ruin." By 1996, he was both a prominent writer who later received one of Thailand's most prestigious honors for writers and a scholar with a PhD from Cornell University (a student of Benedict Anderson) and a teaching position at TU. His reputation as a scholar, thinker, and social rebel, combined with his literary and oratory prowess and his leadership charisma, have earned him the highest respect even from his opponents and the state. Furthermore, Seksan's public appearances were infrequent and always commanded special attention.[1] His speech at the commemoration was memorable because it declared the name *khon duan tula* as the collective identity of former activists who had gone through either or both of the two October events in 1973 and 1976, many of whom went through the jungle years as well.[2] Literally, the name means "people of the October month," or the October people. Kasian Tejapira rendered it the Octobrists.[3]

Seksan urged the Octobrists to get over their wounds, politically and emotionally, to restore honor and pride, to regain confidence and strength, and to reengage with the political and social issues of the time. He called on them to be active again: "For two decades . . . [we've been] licking our wounds . . . but now we've grown up, we've learned some lessons. It would be regrettable if we don't rise up again."[4] Seksan did not, however, make a concrete suggestion—be it the establishment of any organization or movement or any kind or agenda. Instead, it was a general declaration to the public on behalf of his fellow former activists that the Octobrists were back. At the end of that historic and cathartic commemoration in 1996, the Octobrists were born.

This chapter argues that Octobrist is a political identity shaped by the diverse memories of the past among the former activists of the two October events, not by their politics or ideologies in the present. In other words, the Octobrist identity was a praxis of their collective memory. The Octobrist identity was accompanied by high expectations, thanks to the romanticized perception of the former radicals by the public after the rehabilitation in 1996, especially by the younger generation and political activists. Unfortunately, it was not suited to the political conditions of the 2000s, thus the Octobrists eventually failed again. This time no one defeated them; they defeated one another. Such identity and praxis of memory belonged to the 1970s, not the 2000s.

Octobrists in the Eyes of Younger Radicals

My argument engages with a recent book by Kanokrat Lertchoosakul that chronicles the rise and fall of the Octobrists.[5] She understands the Octobrists as a social movement of a group of people with common characteristics thanks to their common political past. The book is rich in information about who is who among them, offering brief accounts of their political experiences in the student movement and in the jungles, then their subsequent rise in every important sector of society—business, media, intellectual, nongovernmental organizations, and politics. The book explains the success of these people despite, and because of, their radical past. They are smart in framing and deradicalizing, in her words, their new identities after the revolutionary years in such ways that made them not only acceptable to society but also recognized as heroes of democracy; she shows not only how they found a space for themselves but also benefited from their new identities. Eventually, some of them went even further, "reconciling" with the monarchy and the military and supporting their antidemocratic politics. Titled *The Rise of the Octobrists*, the book explains their fall as well. As they distanced themselves from their radical past, they turned to various politics—liberal, democratic, nationalist, and even conservative and royalist. In the polarizing Thai politics since the mid-2000s, the fierce antagonisms among the Octobrists led to public disdain, hence their fall.

In a nutshell, the book argues that their successes were due to their ability to alter their radical pasts, both in life and career, as well as in memory. Doing so, however, diminished the history of the Thai radical movement in social memory. The book is fascinatingly informative, yet its arguments are problematic because of its questionable approach to its subject. It takes the radical phase of the long lives of these people as the pivot that defined who they essentially were. The narrative of the deradicalization of these people, then, reads like their degeneration, which denigrates not only their individual pasts but also the place of radicalism in Thai history. The book is a narrative of disenchantment with the Octobrists who prospered at the expense of the history of radicalism.

I offer a different reading. In a nutshell, my narrative is about the Octobrists' short-lived political identity around the turn of the millennium. Rather than taking radicalism as the pivotal essence of these people, we can take it as a brief phase in their lives, though a very important one with lasting impact. In fact, most Octobrists embraced the radical past in their memories, recognizing its impact in shaping their lives ever since. But their radical past was one part of life that included the pre- and postradical years. Their perspectives of Thai radicalism also depended on their longer perspectives. Rather than crafty and effective actors with an extraordinary intellectual and political ability to manipulate their identity minus their radical past to achieve success (that is, the marvel who degenerated), the Octobrists are simply ordinary historical actors who have tried to cope with life in the postrevolutionary years. They struggle with life choices and other conditions like ordinary people. Unlike most others, however, they could not escape from their past or deny it, but had to come to terms with it and move on. From time to time, however, the curse of the past calls on them to take action again; they often respond exactly because they did not, and could not, deny their past as active politicized citizens. Thus, in the late 1990s, they became active again in the name of the Octobrists.

The Octobrist, in my view, was not some radical essence of these people, but primarily a collective political identity of the former radicals of the 1970s who returned to political activism in the late 1990s to the 2000s. The rest of the chapter is my alternative story of the Octobrists relative to Kanokrat's.

WHO WERE THE OCTOBRISTS?

Most people, including Kanokrat, understand the term as the meaning provided in the first paragraph of this chapter—real people in actual history. But I propose here to understand Octobrist differently (though not in contradiction to the first meaning), namely, to take it as it is, as a collective political label or identity. It was constructed by the memory of the October events, by the political past as understood and remembered in retrospect by the activists of those events, most—though not all—of whom were former radicals. The first notion is essentialist; the second is discursive. In fact, the first depends on the views and perspectives of various interpretations of history. As a result, the definition of the first meaning is very close, if not identical, to the second—the discursively defined individuals and collectivity. Memory gave birth to this identity, not the other way round. In this light, it was not at all coincident that the name Octobrist emerged and was recognized at the historic commemoration of the October massacre.

Did the name include every activist involved in those October events or only the former radicals? Who were and were not the Octobrists? People understood it variably, depending on their views of the two Octobers, regardless of the inclusive nature this identity intended.[6] In analyzing the Octobrists, Kanokrat faced the problem of who should be considered in or out throughout her book. By taking the radical experience as the defining characteristic of who the Octobrists are, she does not resolve the problem but compounds it. First, factually speaking, many individuals she identifies as Octobrists in fact never turned radical, and thereby had no need to deradicalize their past. They were active as Octobrists in the late 1990s as well. The more complicated question is what it meant to be a radical in 1970s Thailand. Kanokrat takes it as self-evident given that these former radicals were part of the radical student movement under the heavy influence of the Communist Party of Thailand (CPT) and later joined the CPT's armed struggle. The answer was anything but self-evident, however.

Collectively, by 1976 the student movement was undeniably a radical one, ideologically and politically, in rhetoric and in actions.

Kanokrat's argument assumes that the collectivity and the individuals mirror one another. A collective identity, however, is not the sum of individuals, nor do the individuals necessarily mirror the collective whole. Individually, I would argue, the radicals in the Thai student movement of the 1970s were predominantly college youths. Their immersion in the radical ideology was probably like that of most twenty-year-olds. The terms "radical" or "leftist" cannot not tell us anything about their intellectual maturity, cannot distinguish between a committed and a novice radical. It conceals how much and in what ways their pre-radical thinking remained in their radical-ness. As Prajak shows in his study of the student movement during the October 1973 uprising, not only were the activists of the time from diverse backgrounds, including conservative and royalist; the uprising itself was also an outburst of eclectic ideologies, from liberalism to conservativism, from royalism to the New Left.[7]

Also, as I argue elsewhere, the 1973 uprising was the turning point for the ascendency of two parallel forces in Thai politics: popular democracy and the monarchy.[8] Although many turned radical during the three years afterward, many have remained royalist to this day, and many are neither. Furthermore, the CPT's radicalism was an umbrella for many kinds of discontents at the time. It was the dominant alternative discourse. People were attracted to radical discourse for various reasons: opposition to military rule, capitalism and neo-imperialism, the invasion of Western culture and modernity, or the decline of Thai culture and Buddhism. Some were brought up in the radical environment under Chinese schools with radical teachers.[9] These discontents converged to fight military rule, which they blamed for these social problems. They converged under the CPT's umbrella whether they believed in communism or not because it provided the most systematic and rigorous explanation of what ailed Thai society in their limited knowledge. In this light, the deradicalization could be seen as a return to their diverse nonradical origins, instead of a departure from some radical essence.

The second notion of the Octobrist as an identity does not resolve the problem of who is or is not an Octobrist, but the problem becomes irrelevant for two reasons. First, the narrative of the Octobrists is about people who claimed to be, and who were understood by others to be, Octobrists, regardless of whether they were radicals or the degree to which they were radical. Second and more important, in this notion, the deradicalization narrative falls apart.

Kanokrat's plot begins with the assumption of radical essence as the original point from which these Octobrists have departed or, in her words, been transformed and reframed.[10] To many Octobrists, their radical past was only a slice of their lives, though a remarkable one with lasting impacts. Their deradicalization can be understood simply as part of the normal process of growing up and maturing, the life struggles of the ordinary people whose lives were turned upside down by radicalism and its failure. This is not to deny the radical history of the movement in the past or the deradicalization of their memories. Yet the deradicalization of these individuals was ordinary, not a crafty manipulative act by people trying to deny their pasts to benefit in the present. They simply changed, probably heavily informed and shaped by their predisposition before the radical experience and by the context of their life after the revolution years. This approach does not deny that these former radicals have deradicalized. Instead, the deradicalization was not degenerative, not negative, just the ordinary changes of ordinary human things. It was not an attempt to deny the radical past but to come to terms with the past in a postradical phase of life.

THE PRAXIS OF MEMORY

In fact, many activists of the 1970s had actually been back before the Octobrist identity was born in 1996. They had not taken a long break after their disillusionment with radicalism. As Kanokrat superbly tells their stories, from the 1980s through the 1990s, they had been active and risen to high levels in social movements for development, education, human rights, and various other social causes.[11] They were successful in the arts, music, and cultural domains. Some emerged notably in the business world and in parliamentary politics. Kanokrat attributes their successes to their extraordinary skills and experiences with past activism, which became useful assets in their careers. Apart from those skills was their general disposition as engaged citizens, regardless of their left, right, radical, or conservative politics. As their lives and careers grew more stable, they responded to calls for citizens to engage, such as in the uprising of May 1992 and the movement for political reform afterward.[12] On those occasions, many of these former activists were present in various roles—as leaders, organizers, and rank-and-file operators—although they did not assume, and were not recognized by, any collective identity relating to their past. The Octobrists were active before they were recognized as such. Their collective disposition to be politicized and engaged citizens is the legacy from their past. It was a blessing sometimes and a curse eventually.

The cathartic moment at the 1996 commemoration gave rise to enormous enthusiasm and energy among the former radicals. Seksan's announcement of their return to active political engagement under the new identity was a positive opportunity. It raised their profiles, individually and collectively. The collective identity, however, did not help formulate a particular collective agenda, let alone a coordinated movement. Their past activism in itself was not necessarily relevant to the contemporary politics of the 1990s. To the contrary. "Octobrist" was a broad collective identity mediated by the past, like a school alumni identity, rather than a social movement. As it turned out, these energetic citizens drove the various civic groups, advocacies, and political organizations of diverse politics and ideologies. It was common to find the former radicals taking up with other nonradical and even conservative friends for diverse causes, not just radical ones. Furthermore, not all of them were successful, despite their extraordinary skills and qualities or the lack thereof.

A few illustrations of political action groups associated with the Octobrist identity should suffice. But, first, consider the general context at the turn of the millennium. The two most pressing situations in the country in the mid-1990s were political reform and the economic crisis. The former was a consequence of the May 1992 uprising that prompted the nonmilitary elites and the public alike to demand more stable, effective, and sustainable democracy. The tension reached its breaking point in mid-1995. Fortunately it was resolved and eventually resulted in political reform under the constitution of 1997. The latter was the global financial crisis, which started with the bursting of the bubble economy in Thailand in 1997 that triggered global economic turmoil.[13] The domestic consequence of the latter situation was enormous and lasted more than a decade, especially for Thailand's middle class.

The first political action group I consider is the official organization of, by, and for the Octobrists. After the 1996 commemoration, a group of organizers continued to act as coordinator among the Octobrists. In 1997, they formally formed the October Network (Khrua khai duan tula) to maintain the network of the October people and to organize collective activities from time to time. At first, the group organized public forums related to past October events and the annual commemorations. It did not take long before it turned its attention to political action. Many commemorative events addressed the political issues at the time such as the perils of globalization and neoliberalism, and the necessity for political reform. The newsletter of the network, *Suebsan* (Carry on), featured articles and news about the history of the two October events, the commemorations, and also current political issues, domestically and internationally.[14] Often during those years, the group's name appeared in political campaigns of the day as well, especially the protests against the government.

Like many activist groups of the time that were supposed to represent its members but did not necessarily do so, lending the name to a protest was mostly a decision made by a small group of leaders. The Octobrists never showed their force as a collective beyond the commemorations of the October events. Above all, it is fair to say that the network did not have and could not find any unique agenda. Despite meetings with the fellow Octobrists in every region around the country since 1999, the leading essay for a newsletter in 2001 asked in its title "The Octobrists: what are we supposed to do?" The essay rambled on about how individuals could do this or that without any particular suggestion for a collective agenda for the Octobrists.[15] When Thai politics became polarized in the mid-2000s, the actions by the network in support of one faction against another led to internal fractures within the group. The network quietly dissolved.

Another group, the Prachachon phua prachathipptai (People for Democracy), was an Octobrist group that tried to carry on the agenda and spirit of the popular democracy of the 1970s in the context of the 2000s. Known by its acronym PxP (*por khun por*), this group was definitely Octobrist, led by Seksan himself. With the revival of their energy and passion for politics, a group of Seksan's friends had convinced him to lead a civic group whose key members were former activists who by then were in various professions but were mostly entrepreneurs and businessmen.[16] From the discussion group in 1999 to the action group of 2000, the PxP group was formed in response to the economic crisis in the era of political reform.

Dismayed by elected politicians, viewed as being hand in glove with transnational capitalism and neoliberalism, the group was determined to build up and strengthen people's power, especially among the lower classes and in communities, as a counter to the state.[17] Its activities consisted mostly of holding public forums, especially among leaders of various sectors outside Bangkok, and producing a news-letter. The group saw its role as mentoring local people, enabling them to analyze a problem and find the solution by themselves. As reported in its monthly newsletter, the issues the group was interested in ranged from the general political situation, the constitution, political reform, people's organizations and movements, multinational corporations, transnational capitalism, and consumerism, to various local disputes related to those issues, and so on.[18] The newsletter featured those subjects plus articles about labor disputes and the labor movement, the crisis in Thailand's agrarian sector, the history of the 1932 revolution, the agrarian situation in Latin America, the Zapatista movement in Mexico, the people's movement in Bolivia, and more. As an illustrative case of community rights, the group launched a campaign in 2001 to legalize local liquor, pitting it against the monopoly of the liquor industry in Thailand by a few powerful families.[19]

The diffuse agenda and interests—antiglobalization, people's power and civic movements, and democratization—were common at the time, similar to those of the October Network and other groups. PxP was unable to find its political footing or distinguish itself, however. Neither its agenda nor its advocacy for local liquor production galvanized the public. By 2002, it was gradually fading from public view. Its newsletter became irregular and quietly disappeared. The group fizzled and was formally dissolved in 2004.

THE EXTRAORDINARY OCTOBRISTS

Despite these less than stellar cases, the many successful Octobrists, well documented by Kanokrat, gave rise to the image of the Octobrists as a potent political force.[20] Most widely known is their role in the most successful political party in Thai history, the Thai Rak Thai (TRT) party of Thaksin Shinwatara, which won every election between 2000 and 2006 by a landslide before it was ousted in 2006 by a military putsch. TRT's unprecedented success—from its ideas, policy crafting, and strategic planning, to its political operation and tactics, and its election machines—was partly attributed to a number of Octobrists in key positions within it.[21] This was the beginning of the hero narrative for the Octobrists, a narrative that focuses on their success and extraordinary abilities, making the TRT-Octobrists unduly representative of the group as a whole.

The hero narrative that emphasizes the extraordinary ability and success of the Octobrists is problematic. It cannot account for the many Octobrists who were ordinary or for those groups that failed. Moreover, it implies that failures—such as the PxP and the October Network—and those involved—such as Seksan and others—were not smart or skillful enough. A better approach is to look beyond personal attributes, to try to understand the political, social, institutional, or contextual conditions that contributed to their success and failure. To do so would require a careful examination beyond what I am prepared to do here. Nonetheless, I would like to make one observation, which is related to my suggested approach that takes the Octobrist as a political identity and a praxis of memory.

The Octobrist identity contributed to the creation, the raison d'être, and the political character of both the October Network and the PxP. They were activist groups on the fringe of the political mainstream. In the view of social movement theories, these fringe groups had limited political opportunities and other resources. Even the extraordinary personal attributes of Seksan and his high caliber team could not make the PxP successful. On the other hand, the successful Octobrists, such as those in TRT, were in established social institutions, like political parties, or professions like media and law. They were able to grow and spread their wings within the established framework of mainstream institutions, where resources could be mobilized and opportunities were abundant. The Octobrist identity contributed nothing to their organizations' raison d'être or their operations, but it did not encumber them.

It is true that most of the successful Octobrists deradicalized their past. As Kanokrat describes, this was done by emphasizing 1973 October as a major moment in the progress for democratization, and by glossing over the radical period and the October 6 massacre as an unfortunate bump in the road to democracy.[22] It was the same for everyone, though, so the new framing of their past did not determine success or failure. The Octobrist identity was an asset when it enhanced personal attributes that served an established institution or profession. But it could become an insurmountable burden if it became the rationale or essential purpose of a group.

The narrative of extraordinary success is problematic for another reason, that it is either a hagiographic narrative as described, or its opposite, one of disenchantment. Both require a certain sensationalism: glorifying the great men or women or using their extraordinary attributes as a pretext for eventual disappointment. To put it another way, the disappointment or disenchantment with the false hero demands a retrospective explanation. The answer is usually to be found in how the hero has degenerated, misused his extraordinary attributes, or made a serious mistake. The hero narrative turns into an antihero one by taking stock of how low the hero has fallen from his original point. This is the case for the story of the Octobrists who were seen eventually as fallen heroes.

By the mid-2000s, talk about the Octobrists drew mockery and disdain. Disappointment in them arose in many people, especially activists of later generations and young radicals. Central to the disappointment and contempt were the extraordinary TRT-Octobrists. From 2001 to 2006, when it was in power and even after, the Thaksin administration became an increasingly polarizing element in Thai politics. On the one hand, its effective style of governing and many of its policies earned overwhelming support from the public across constituencies. Many became fanatical supporters. On the other hand, the government and Thaksin himself were increasingly scorned by critics and opponents for various reasons—his government's controversial policies and actions that disregarded human rights, its abuses of power, and especially Thaksin's alleged corruption and conflicts of interests. His demagoguery often made things worse.[23] The Octobrists who had been credited with Thaksin's unprecedented success remained key to the government, thus becoming collaborators who bore the brunt of growing dissatisfaction. At the October anniversary in 2003, for example, the Octobrist identity was likened to a fraudulent political brand because the Octobrists had lost their souls to the point that "the majority of Thais loathed them."[24] The more loyal to Thaksin the TRT-Octobrists were, and they often came out in defense of their boss and his mistakes, the more quickly they became villains. Many fellow Octobrists, including the October Network, urged them to distance themselves from Thaksin, to no avail.[25] What had been a heroic discourse for the Octobrists in the late 1990s had turned into one of disenchantment in less than a decade.

THE OCTOBRISTS DIVIDED

But Thailand's political crisis since the mid-2000s was more complex than simple dissatisfaction with the government. As many scholars and analysts have pointed out, the crisis reflected structural changes in the country's socioeconomy and demography. Thaksin the billionaire could represent the poor, the lower class, and rural society because electoral democracy was a political system in which these disenfranchised populations could make their voices heard and their demands met, effectively bypassing a self-serving, highly centralized bureaucracy that primarily served the elites. The majority of Thais can exercise their power via politicians, regardless of the latter's corruption. Thaksin and his party were smarter about responding to these disenfranchised people than other parties and the old establishment, hence their landslide electoral victories. However, the palace, the bureaucracy, the military, and those elites who had enjoyed royalist democracy for decades struck back, with support from the majority of the Bangkok middle class, who disdained Thaksin and his rural and provincial supporters.[26]

It is fair to say that the majority of the Octobrists were against Thaksin and supported the anti-Thaksin movement, the Yellow Shirts. Not understanding the conflict beyond the frame of bad government versus good protest that they were familiar with and had been for decades, they saw the Thaksin government as a "parliamentary dictatorship" that was a proxy for threatening capitalism. Some of them became prominent leaders of the anti-Thaksin movement.[27] Amid the conflict between these Yellow Octobrists and the TRT ones, quite a number remained cautious—cynical toward both Thaksin and the Yellow Shirt movement. The fractures among the Octobrists mirrored the increasing polarization of Thai politics. The October Network, for example, fractured seriously in early 2004 when it suspended any political engagement other than the October commemorations.[28] During the Yellow Shirt protests that began in early 2006, however, the movement called for the military and the palace to intervene, asking for a "royal government" to replace the elected one, even illegally. Thanks to their distrust of both the military and the palace, many Octobrists left the Yellow Shirt movement. The majority remained, however. As the Yellow Shirt movement turned even more royalist and antidemocratic as the protest went on, the Octobrists became royalist and antidemocratic as well.

The first round of conflict resulted in the royalist coup in 2006, ending electoral democracy and bringing back military rule for the first time since 1992. The coup was the last straw for many Octobrists, the ultimate price after so much sacrifice and lost friends. Although the majority of Octobrists continued to oppose Thaksin, the number who were anticoup and antimilitary rule—the Red Shirts—regardless of their stance toward Thaksin, grew rapidly and became quite large. The fragmentation of the Octobrists was public, and all shades and colors vehemently disparaged one another (myself included). One accused the other of selling out to the oppressive capitalist (Thaksin). In return, they were pilloried for betraying their October ideals and lost friends by supporting the military and the monarchy against democracy.

The commemoration of the thirtieth anniversary of the October massacre in 2006, one month after the coup, was obviously tense. It was planned to commemorate the two Octobers together. However, according to the event brochure, the program featured Yellow and Red views of the past, but separately, in different forums and different time slots. The split was visible not only in the politics of the 2000s but in their memories as well. A young scholar smartly pointed out comparable features of the coup in 2006 and the one in 1976: the ideological contentions in both cases (unlike most other coups in Thailand, which were the result of factional rather than ideological politics), the threat to the monarchy as the pretext of both, and the right-wing mass mobilization leading to both coups. The major difference, he noted, was that in 2006 the majority of the Octobrists abdicated their political principles against military dictatorship.[29] In 1976, the Octobrists were the target of the right wing, but in 2006 were part of the right wing.

The crisis intensified after the 2006 coup, leading to several clashes and tumultuous incidents, including the one between the Yellow Shirts and the police on October 7, 2008, that resulted in one dead, and the massacre of the Red Shirt protesters in May 2010 that resulted in ninety-two dead, the highest political fatality in Thai history. The former incident was a clash of antidemocracy protesters against the elected government. For a few years, supporters of the Yellow movement, which included a large number of the Octobrists, likened their clash with the police to the October 6 massacre only because it was a violent clash with the police. Such comparisons disappeared after a few years. Perhaps they realized that it was a bizarre comparison given the contrasting political contexts of the two events: one a pro-democracy protest crushed by the military and the palace, the other an antidemocracy rally supported by the military and the palace. Or perhaps they realized that if they reminded the public of the October 6 massacre, the public might find the 2010 crackdown on the protesters against the government more apt: the pro-democracy politics of the victims, the use of excessive force against the besieged protesters, and the false pretext accusing the protesters of being antimonarchy—these were similar to the massacre in 1976.[30] Above all, as in 1976, the 2010 massacre appears to have been backed by the political establishment, namely, the military and the palace.

After the 2010 massacre, some Yellow Octobrists expressed delight and provided justifications for the brutal suppression. This shameless behavior was not lost on the rest of Octobrists. Whatever side one may take, to support the killing of political opponents crossed the line for these former victims of political killings. The October commemoration in the year 2010 was unforgiving to the Yellow Octobrists, and they were strongly condemned by old friends. Given the pretext, the actions, the politics, the scale of violence, and the fatalities, all comparable to 1976, a prominent journalist who was an Octobrist himself castigated his old friends in disgust for betrayal. It was unthinkable, he wrote, for victims of the previous massacre to condone 2010, let alone to support it. "Doing this, you no longer possess even a tiny bit of the October spirit."[31] At the commemoration that year, the parallels between the two massacres were mentioned repeatedly, especially the tacit reference to the alleged role of the palace. Meanwhile, the Yellow Octobrists were conspicuously silent about the commemoration. A year later in 2011, shortly before October, a few Yellow Octobrists on the organizing committee of the commemoration of October 6 announced their withdrawal from the committee. The reason given was that the commemoration of the past massacre was becoming too aligned with that of the Red Shirts. They wanted the commemoration to be strictly about the past and have nothing to do with the present. This phenomenon is telling. The Red tragedy had found its precedent in that of October 6. The memory of October 6 was gradually preempted by the pro-Red Octobrists, who have been in charge of every October 6 commemoration since then. The Yellow Octobrists had become alienated from their past.

The Reds were not alone in calling up the October 6 memory to serve their politics. The arts exhibit, "Flashback' 76," which targeted Samak after his controversial remark to CNN in 2008 (mentioned in chapter 8), was a good example. All the artists involved were supporters of the Yellow movement. This exhibit displayed a selective memory of October 6 with its absence of even the slightest allusion to perpetrators other than Samak, who at the time was a proxy of

Thaksin. This was possibly not a memory slide but political intent. The artists appear to have chosen to live with selective memory, ironically, the same criticism they made against Samak. In 2010, during the Red protest against the military-backed government, a counter-demonstration was held against the Reds. A placard called the Reds *nak phaendin* (scum of the earth), the same name the right-wing agitators had called the leftists in 1976 to dehumanize them. Under a tree at the demonstration site, a red, long-sleeved shirt was hung from one of its branches as if a body had been hanged. The sign on the red shirt read *"pho sa thi"* (enough!). This disturbing allusion to the 1976 massacre suggested that those at this counterprotest did not lack the knowledge of that event, had not forgotten October 6. The meaning of the past massacre, for them, was clear too.

In 2014, another antidemocracy mass protest took place under the leadership of the People's Democratic Reform Committee (PDRC).[32] The PDRC's demands were clear, though bizarre: no more electoral democracy and no more elections because they always resulted in the dictatorship of the majority. Instead, they called for royalist military rule, calling it Thai-style democracy. In their several demonstrations, a hundred former CPT revolutionary soldiers showed up in the uniform of the revolutionary army. They signed a petition to the king asking for a royal government to replace the elected one they opposed. An Octobrist writer exclaimed, "[This is going] too far!"[33] Meanwhile, the PDRC adopted as its anthem the famous song "Su mai thoi" (Unretreating struggles), which was the anthem of the October 14 uprising.[34] Composed in 1973 by Seksan during the democratic uprising against military rule, the song was sung in 2014 by thousands of the PDRC demonstrators against democracy and for the military rule. The PDRC protests eventually led to another military coup in May 2014. Not only did this coup sweep the country's deep, structural conflicts under the rug, it also brought to power the most authoritarian regime since the end of the Thanin government in 1977.

DEATH OF THE OCTOBRISTS

During the decade-long crisis, the rivals often expressed their wonder at why and how their old comrades had changed so much. On the one hand, why did some Octobrists take a right turn and support the military and the monarchy? On the other, how could Octobrists support an authoritarian demagogue who was a proxy of predatory global capitalism? Many scholars, too, have tried to explain the same phenomena.[35] Explanations are abundant, but each seems inadequate. Perhaps they are all correct to some extent in one way or another. As the animosity among the Octobrists grew larger, Seksan tried in vain in his successive public lectures in September and October 2013 to remind everyone of the October ideals that all of them were supposed to share.[36] The criticism and disappointment with the Octobrists went far beyond the Octobrists themselves to the public, which had once had high expectations of them for their contributions to democracy. From every side in the polarized politics, people derided their missteps, mistakes, and failure, and probably concluded that the Octobrists had betrayed October politics and spirit in one way or another. Young activists and radicals, probably including Kanokrat, who had once looked up to the Octobrists with admiration as their predecessors, were disenchanted.

Where do those high expectations and the admiration come from? They arise in the illusion that the Octobrists were not merely ordinary political operators. They were supposed to advocate democracy, justice, dedication, and sacrifice, unlike corrupt politicians and military junta. The illusion also stemmed from the perceptions of the historical October movements, that is, from memories of the Octobrists' past. To put it differently, the Octobrists were believed to be real people. In fact, they were a constructed political identity, thanks to the noisy memories on the edge of the silence surrounding twenty years. That constructed political being was loaded with high expectation and informed by heroic discourse. The higher the expectation and the more unrealistic the illusion, the further it could fall. And it did fall.

The Octobrist collective was a praxis of memory. Their common property was the shared experience in the past, not their views of the past in later decades and certainly not their present politics. The Octobrist identity can be meaningful or relevant today only by invoking the past. It may be inspiring or intimidating, boast-worthy or contemptible; it may be a valuable asset for some, such as those TRT-Octobrists, or a liability to others. As a praxis of memory, it does not determine or foretell the politics of those individuals in the present. As a collective, Octobrists may take action together in the present only if it is about their past, a nostalgic action such as a commemoration. As a praxis of memory, such as a school alumni association, it does not inform an ideological or political community or a collective action or a social movement in the present. To keep the memory of October 6 belonging to all Octobrists, its praxis must avoid present politics.

Nonetheless, the memory of October 6 had inspired some to believe unrealistically that as a collective, the Octobrists could make a difference in the 2000s. The fate of the October Network and the PxP were telling. The discourse of the Octobrist identity has also created romantic expectations of them so that disappointment was inevitable. Even the mild political actions of the October Network and the PxP went beyond its limitations. When the Octobrists tried to take on certain roles in the 2000s, it became clear that their political identity was inoperable because its meaningfulness was irrelevant to the present. In the polarized politics of the present, the identity split and the memories divided because they were not suited to the present. The same memories that had created the romanticized Octobrist identity set them up for failure because the relevance of the memories and their praxis to the present had limits. This is perhaps a fundamental logic of the praxis of memory.

In October 2010, Prajak Kongkirati, an expert on the history of the 1973 uprising, advised that it was time for the Octobrists "to go to bed."[37] His advice was polite compared with an earlier comment from the disenchanted Octobrist journalist who, in 2007, published a book of essays that contrasted seven pairs of opposing Octobrists (myself included). In my opinion, the book is awful and poorly written. The essays are full of inaccuracies, the prose crude and rude, the tone sanctimonious. It offers no thoughtful argument, not even a slight analysis of the split. Despite these flaws, its title, *Khon tula tailaew* (The Octobrists are dead), turns out to be prophetic.[38] Of course the author knew that the Octobrists as real people are mostly not dead yet. But the Octobrist as an identity and a praxis of memory probably is. It died not because it has split but perhaps because the October 6 memories have been overworked in Thailand's polarized politics to the extent that the noise of the memory became too coarse to make any sense or to inform any meaningful politics.

The stingiest verdict on the Octobrists belongs to one of the Octobrists. In 2018, after years under one of the harshest dictatorial regimes in Thai history, which came to power partly with the help of the Octobrists, he wrote this on social media (Facebook):

People of different generations usually have distinctive identities, for they have left good and not-so-good legacies to society and to later generations. . . . There was the Octobrists of 1973–1976, a generation whose legacies can still be felt today. It was a generation of absolute, ultimate failure. They were defeated in the past and in the present. And now 90 percent of them serve and worship the dictatorship. All recent political crises, from [the antidemocratic coup] in 2006 to the coup and military rule since 2014, have been the accomplishment of this generation.[39]

In response to Prajak's call for the Octobrists to "go to bed," even Seksan, who had years earlier given the group its identity, declared that it "had gone . . . a very long time ago."[40]

Epilogue
Haunting

To this day, more than four decades after the tragedy, the victim in Ulevich's Pulitzer Prize–winning photo remains unknown (see figure 3). The same is true of the Chair Guy. The silence surrounding these two men is hard to believe given the notoriety of the photo, which has been in the public sphere for more than twenty years. In other countries, would they still be unknown after forty years? Perhaps the deeper silence in Thailand is because of, not despite, the wide publicity. This photo and the silence surrounding its two main protagonists epitomize the entire story of the unforgetting of the October 6 massacre.

Forty years after the massacre, in 2016, a famous writer in exile after the 2014 coup, wrote a short story about the memory of the 1976 massacre. Its title is simple: "Pak" (Mouth). The first person narrator of the story laments that he has unusual eyes, for they can still see many things that other people cannot, such as events in the past, including the one forty years ago. But the eyes of most Thais are blind. Even many of his friends, he bemoans, cannot see the past any longer. He sees so much that he has to go into exile. Most people have mouths that cannot speak either, "particularly about the October 6 incident. Even though there is a commemoration every year, the hanging and the victim beaten with a folding chair . . . they're mentioned every year, but that is it! That is how much they can talk about. Nobody can say anything more." One day, he is asked by a young inquirer to reveal who the perpetrators of the massacre were, and suddenly, his mouth cannot say a word. His mouth disappears! Gone![1]

History is cruel. That past incident was cruel. The account of it is cruel. The absence of any explanation for the desecrations of the dead is cruel. The politics of the past is cruel. The memory of it is also difficult. It is not merely the mental act of remembering what happened. Rather, that it has taken place through suppressions, physical

231

and ideological, through silence, voluntary and not, and through the painful chronopolitics of memory. It is cruel that the political, ideological, and literary conditions have allowed only limited fragments of memories to survive. The diverse, tampered, limited memories are still struggling to find their free and full expression. Until then, the cruel unforgetting lives on, like a mouth that cannot speak.

Largely silenced until 1996, the unforgetting is a little noisier now. The memory of the October 6 massacre has been a very inconvenient truth that the Thai state and society has dealt with uncomfortably. The most common approach is to put aside the undesirable memory by a typical method, namely, silence. If a controversy breaks out, dismiss it, or trivialize it, then urge all parties to move on. If necessary, invoke the higher purpose for silence, such as national reconciliation, harmony, unity, the future, or the monarchy. The evasiveness implies that memory is the opposite of these higher purposes. If blame is warranted, put it on a phantom culprit, such as the "third hand," the unidentifiable wrongdoer often cited in Thai politics.[2] Or blame transcendental Evil like a good Buddhist should do.

Silence is quite telling about Thai society. The various moments of silence about the massacre in 1976 occurred in different ways for different reasons to different people—the victims, the perpetrators, the sympathizers, the bystanders, supporters and friends, state officials, goons, and professors. Those moments of silence speak quite loudly about Thai historical ideology, the normative truth, and the process toward forgetting, but also about the opposite—the censorship of truth, historical lies, and the dark side of Thai-ness. Above all, silence tells us about the persistent condition of ambivalence and the inarticulate memories—the unforgetting.

Those moments of silence also speak loudly about another absence—impunity, the absence of accountability. In Thailand, impunity is common for the powerful, the rich, and those people in high places. It is a privilege that ordinary Thais never enjoy though it is so familiar to them that it is predictable, even anticipated, when an abuse of power happens to people who are low in the social hierarchy. Those moments of silence in the October 6 memory also hint at impunity.

Justice is rarely mentioned either by the state or the public as a desirable avenue for closure, not because the judiciary is considered untrustworthy, but because retributive justice implies the perpetuation of conflict, which, in the Thai normative truth, is undesirable. Sometimes, the justice process can cause disruption to order, or disorder. Reconciliation without justice is more desirable because it can bring harmony and normalcy. Finally, justice requires fact-based truth. Yet every method and approach typical in Thailand tramples on truth. Instead, all of them demand various degrees of silence and the suppression or restriction of memory.

Moving On . . .

For a society and individual to move on after an atrocity, the past must be put to rest. In most places under the rule of law, this means to find out the truth of the past and to hold the wrongdoer accountable. Justice is the proper closure of a painful past. Truth and justice are therefore the most important requisites for reconciliation, enabling a society with a painful past to move on, collectively and individually. But this normativity does not apply to Thailand, nor, in fact, to many countries. If the truth might be harmful to political stability and the social fabric, doubt may arise: is it needed? Too often, instead of truth and justice, we get partial or relative truths, or convincing but false memories. Nevertheless, I have wondered at times while writing this book, if a society survives for hundreds of years with a partial and not quite truthful knowledge of the past, why does it need truthful history now? Is it more prudent to move on with the same lies and silence it has always had?

In *In Praise of Forgetting,* David Reiff challenges today's conventional wisdom as represented by George Santayana's dictum, "those who cannot remember the past are condemned to repeat it" (2016). Reiff questions the moral imperative of this "false injunction." Does remembering really lead to a better outcome? Given that forgetting is an unavoidable human condition, biologically and socially, are we deceiving ourselves in believing that a society can remember something—even a mass atrocity or a genocide—forever? Even if we can partially do so, no guarantee is in place that the retrospective remembering would be better, morally, than forgetting the painful past. Besides, in many cases, neither a society nor its individual members can afford the high cost of remembering (perpetuating violence, for example) because "memory has been and continues to be toxic in many parts of the world." Forgetting and not clinging to the past, on the other hand, also have benefits.[3]

We usually take forgetting as the opposite of remembering. Reiff's argument reminds us that multiple paths move forward from the painful past and onward. In a world filled with atrocities, people can move and have moved on in different ways—victims, perpetrators, observers, bystanders. Moving on is not naturally coupled with either remembering or forgetting. Most people move on without getting what they hope for. Some hope for memory and justice but do not get it. Some would rather overcome pain by forgetting, but do not get that either. By taking memory as the opposite of forgetting, most studies of social memory deal with certain questions and issues that may not be fruitful to reality. As a social phenomenon, more often than not, remembering is the antithesis to moving on. Unforgetting while moving on could probably be an actual norm in real life. If this common phenomenon were taken seriously, it could produce different questions and issues, such as the limits of remembering as a social practice, the consequences of unforgetting rather than forgetting, and so on.

In Thailand too, remembering is the antithesis to moving on. Reiff's systematic argumentation, with citations from one sage after another, could have been written by a thinker of the Thai establishment. Reiff may not realize that his proposition has been the conventional wisdom in Thailand and many other authoritarian societies for decades while Santayana's dictum is unheard of. They never need to praise or preach forgetting; they have practiced it as a norm for a long time. No treatise is needed either, for they already have the playbook, the manuals, and the rich experience for how to prescribe forgetting and unforgetting, and how not to mention justice.

Despite all of this, I argue that memory has not been erased. Forgetting has not prevailed, at least not yet. Moving on does not require the eradication of all memory of the massacre. It allows the unforgetting. Every method of handling the October 6 memory contributes to the unforgetting, the silent, the unarticulated voices of memory that linger on at the edge between memory and forgetting. The unforgetting breaks out in a freaky noise piercing the normative Thai-ness from time to time. The October 6 memory continues to haunt. It cannot rest in peace because it has no resting place yet in public memory.

. . . With the Haunting Unforgetting

The unforgetting of October 6 appears here and there as part of Thai culture today. Yet its appearance is often illusive, partial, and implicit: indirect instead of straightforward. The hanging in particular has become emblematic of the massacre. Superficially, it signifies the horror, brutality, dehumanization, and evil of that day. But it also implies an unsolved mystery because key participants and elements in the scene remain unknown—the victim, Chair Guy, the cheerful boy. Even the location where it took place is not clear because the tree cannot be identified. Perhaps it has been removed. That one scene with so many unknowns is a microcosm of the entire incident and remains clouded with mysteries and the knowable but unspeakable truth. The massacre was therefore reduced to a few signifiers—the chair, the shirt, the tree, the noose and so on. The final reason that makes the hanging scene the ultimate representation of the October 6 massacre is that the scene is haunting. The October 6 massacre was *a-dit lon*, the haunting past, as the Thai title of the art exhibit in 2008 referred to the massacre.[4] The unforgetting is haunting.

It is haunting because the meaning of the death and the entire tragedy remains ambiguous. Should we recognize those who died as martyrs? Of what? Can we commemorate and praise them as a sacrifice for the noble cause? What noble cause? Can we praise them as socialist idealists, whether we ourselves agree with socialism? These questions have no answer yet and perhaps will have no answer for a long time to come. As long as Thai society cannot find meaningful closure for those who died, it will remain haunted by the massacre. But how can we get close to closure when we are not even allowed to talk freely about the tragedy, let alone justice? Until then, the unforgetting lives on.

The haunting appears in various ways to different people. The hanging of a red shirt without a body under a tree at the counterprotest in 2010, mentioned in chapter 10, was a disgusting intimidation of a political opponent. It was disgusting not because it was a dirty political act, but because it knowingly exploited a heinous crime whose wounds remain fresh to many people. Whoever did this must have been aware that the symbolism was still frightening. To me, it was nauseating rather than threatening. It is sad that someone could come up with such a sickening idea.

A popular series of political cartoons began to emerge on Facebook in June 2013, titled "Mani mi chae" (Mani has a chair).[5] Mani, a young girl, is a primary character in the elementary school textbooks that many generations of Thai children are familiar with. In the cartoons as in the original textbook, she is an innocent-looking girl who always dresses in the simple style of a rural village girl, with short hair and often with bare feet. Each episode is created in the form of one-page lesson from a dated textbook, sometimes with one act per page, but often with multiple acts, like a cartoon strip. In each episode, Mani encounters political stupidity, callousness, demagoguery, and even wrongdoing that is presented by a human-like (walking, speaking, thinking) dog, Chao To. The cartoon is full of sharp wit and deadly sarcasm about current issues. In the early episodes, when the cartoon was becoming popular, most of the time the final act ends with Mani beating Chao To with a folding chair, as seen in Ulevich's photo of the hanging in 1976.[6] Although the cartoon is sophisticated and hilarious, I have never understood why it uses the device of the folding chair of October 6. Does the chair represent the madness or insanity that the toxic politics deserve? Is this an eye-for-an-eye revenge in the form of a-chair-for-a-chair satire? Is the picture of Chao To, the dog, beaten up by a chair in the final act too brutal to laugh at? Perhaps its creator anticipates the laughs from the readers and wants to discomfit them by not allowing them to laugh freely. Hence the symbol reminds readers of that Wednesday morning in 1976. A very funny satire that discourages a laugh is probably the twist we choke on every time we reach the end of an episode. The chair haunts us.

In recent decades, the ghost of October 6 is best illustrated in film. Not all Thai films have taken the massacre seriously. A popular film in 2009, for example, used the massacre and its revolutionary aftermath as the background of a romantic comedy, "Fasai Jaichunban" (Blue sky of love).

> The creation of this romantic comedy was inspired by the true story of those with idealism who struggled for the people. Amid the atmosphere of ideological conflicts . . . , not many people noticed the humorous operations [*patibatkan khwam ha*], . . . and the indescribably deep intimacy going on among those comrades . . . The "for the people" ideology [*udomkan*] confronts the excess [*udomkoen*] of love. The revolutionary path was shaken by the comedic path. Inumerable relentless and frightening battles led to thrillingly narrow escapes via humor . . . (the film's promotional poster)

Is it an ironic comedy—the foreground of humor and romantic comedy to remind people of the overlooked historic tragedy in the background? Or the opposite, that is, a straightforward mockery of the tragedy, making nonsensical fun of those who suffered the state's

บทที่ ๑๔

โต ขุด ดิน
เจอ ของเล่น ใหม่

มานี บอก
ให้ เอา ไปเก็บ
โต ไม่ ฟัง

ทุก คน เลย
เล่น กับ โต

มานี มีแซร์

Figure 9. Cartoon "Mani has a chair." © Mani mi chae. Reprinted with permission.

crime? Given that the dictum "History can be hilarious" appears on its poster, the latter seems to be the case.

Apart from those few, most took the massacre seriously. Observing that the year 1996 marked a turning point in "art for October," Sudarat Musikawong argues that before that year some visual artists produced works that expressed the victim's voice, an aesthetic of grief or trauma to remember the silenced histories. After 1996, artworks, including some films, used the shock of the massacre to speak out loud as a critique of forgetting and silence.[7] Matthew Hunt examines how Thai films, mostly the noncommercial ones, deal with the October 6 massacre.[8] Most of them, however, mentioned October 6 indirectly or in passing, through metaphoric acts, words, and symbols such as the killing of students, the hanging, a folding chair, the Red Bull energy drink, and even by the name of an actor. The massacre was not an important element of those stories. Talking openly about the massacre remains uncomfortable and risky. A few films, however, referred to or engaged with the massacre in substantial ways. In 2012, the film *Checksapia tong tai* (Shakespeare must die) was banned because it bluntly captures the horror of the October 6 massacre, including the emblematic scene of a hanged man repeatedly beaten by a folding chair. In 2017, the court upheld the censorship on the grounds that the film could cause division in Thai society.[9]

A few films may be less direct but are probably even more provocative. For example, a sequence in the 2011 film *Phukokanrai* (The terrorist), shows a masturbating naked man as captions about the October 6 massacre appear; it then cuts to the footage of the desecrated corpses on that day while playing a romantic song. "Outwardly, the man's orgasm and the military and massacre have nothing in common," Matthew Hunt writes, but for the filmmaker, "one is a metaphor for the other."[10] In another film, from 2006, *Dek hen phi* (Colic), a general from 1976 is reborn as a baby who is tormented by spirits. This horror story suggests that even though a crime is beyond legal justice, karma may still be effective. Another *Ya lum chan* (Don't forget me), from 2003, left me stunned, not sure whether to laugh or to cry after watching it. As Hunt describes it,

> [The film] is a multilayered documentary featuring archive footage of [the October 6 massacre] and scathing political captions, accompanied by the plaintive title song and a narration appropriated from an

ethnographic documentary on the nomadic Mlabri tribe. The voiceover describes the tribe's ceremonies and rituals, its tone and content providing an intentionally ironic counterpoint to the massacre footage.[11]

The juxtaposed footage, songs, and captions are ridiculously at odds with one another. The film is bizarre. That, however, is how the unforgetting of the October 6 massacre materializes in contemporary Thai life. It is present but not recognized. It is mentioned but not understood, apparent but not meaningful, and unforgettable but not remembered.

THE PHANTASMAGORIC OCTOBER 6 . . .

In October 2018, amid the brewing discontent with the junta that has ruled the country since 2014, a music video of a rap song, "Prathet ku mi" (My country has got these), was released on YouTube. The rap is quite a long list of the negatives about the ruling junta. The music video (MV) caused an uproar, reaching almost a million views in the first few days. The police threatened to block it and to charge the group, Rap Against Dictatorship (RAD), who produced the song and the MV. The threat backfired: people rushed to watch it until the number reached ten million in less than a week. The police and the junta backed off. What was special about the MV? Apart from the satirical rap, the video was shocking—the reenactment of the hanging of the October 6. At first, as the rappers sing in front of the cheering crowd, the camera moves around and around in a circle, showing the spectators cheering and clapping with satisfaction. As the rappers and the camera move closer to the center point, a tree appears with a body (an effigy) hanging from it. Then a man holding a folding chair smashes it on the hanging body and the crowd cheers even more.

The millions of people who watched this MV likely recognized this horrific scene although the song does not mention October 6. To the rappers, the MV is the crystallization of what happened in Thailand. One explains:

> It is like a loop of the repeated [events] . . . of killings, killing, and killing again. . . . with no way out. . . . There was never an investigation. Nor a lesson. Only try to forget them. . . . October 6, those smiles, that chair, the victim who remains unknown even to this day. . . . We don't know when it will be our turn [to get killed].

Given their months of hard work on the MV, he even reminds people to watch it carefully, noting that "Everybody in the crowd is male."[12] The massacre and the all-male spectacle still haunt us.

In a recent film by Anocha Suwichakornpong, *Dao Khanong* (By the time it gets dark), the October 6 memory is phantasmagoric. Released in 2016 after six years in the making, to coincide with the fortieth anniversary of the October 6 incident, the film was inspired in part by the fragmentation of the memory of the massacre.[13] By 2017, the film had been shown in more than a dozen countries worldwide and won a number of international awards, but in Thailand only half a dozen theaters showed it, and only for a week or less in mid-December 2016. This Indy film has no coherent story to tell. Instead, it invites the audience on a journey into a few scenes from an ongoing life, none of which has a narrative, or a true sequence of happenings, or a beginning and end, either.

The first episode is about a young female filmmaker who wants to produce a film about the life of a female writer who survived the massacre. The tragedy is shown through a bizarre reenactment that is not even realistic, let alone close to the past reality. The incongruity probably speaks of the generally crude understanding of the facts, due to the haphazard truth about the massacre, and because it is hardly imaginable especially to people of later generations like the fictional director in the film and the real one of *Dao Khanong*. The conversation between the fictional filmmaker and the writer barely touches on the massacre. At one point, the writer refuses to be called a living history. She insists instead that she is merely a survivor of the killing. Making the film seems to be a way to probe into the writer's life journey as much as that of the filmmaker or filmmakers.

The second episode involves the hectic lives of an actor and actress, performed by the real actor and actress using their real names. In other words, they act as themselves and their fictional selves in the film. Their roles include as the actors in their real (fictional) lives and as their fictional characters in a film within a film. Given that those actors play themselves, the real actors who perform the actors in the fictional *Dao Khanong* have to perform both the fictional reality and the fictional fiction. It is not clear which is their real life in the film and which is a fictional role in the fictional film. The lines between reality, fiction, and fantasy disappear. After all, in their real lives, they are actors. Acting is their everyday life.

The two episodes begin at similar locations. They begin with exactly the same conversations among people of the same names played by two different sets of actresses. This parallel hints at a logical relationship between the two sets, whether it is compatible, recurring, overlapping, or merely coincident or serendipitous. The two episodes are loosely connected by another young female who appears doing various jobs at different moments during the parallel scenes: a food-stall attendant, cleaning lady, a waitress on a cruise ship, an ordinary fun-loving girl, and a nun. She (or they?) appears to be cleaning various things. Her (their?) ordinary life (lives) crisscrosses with those of the female director and writer, the actor and the actress, serendipitously, with a few conversations but mostly in silence. The ordinary life of this woman (in plural forms) weaves through and over those of others in the two episodes at random moments without creating logical relationships of any kind, without a coherent whole or a unifying story, and without a purpose, so to speak. Serendipity.

Because the truth of the massacre is frustratingly limited and fragmented, the film does not try to provide a comprehensible account of it. More precisely, the film probably tries not to offer one. Rather, it exposes this condition of memory visually. Approached forty years later, from a director's lens, literally and metaphorically, the past tragedy was, perhaps, like a pastiche of an old clipping, imaginable anachronistically like a crude reenactment. After all, not even the victim of the incident can claim to possess some slight truth of history because the writer insists that she is merely a survivor, something left over from the incident. She is a memory; she is a personification of the unforgetting. The theme song of *Dao Khanong,* titled "Lie," sung by the actor of the second vignette, begs, "Please, don't lie to me. Please don't fool me anymore. . . . even though I may not be ready for the truth, please don't lie anymore . . . Even if you don't tell me, one day the wind will." Given the predominance of the normative truth in Thai society, truth and fantasy or fiction are inseparable. The past is (not was) abundantly full of lies.

What is left to the present is the normative Thai life in which fact, fiction, fantasy, reality, role play, and real life are fused. It is the life of actors and actresses who act out the reality in the glorified normative environs of Thai-ness. Living normatively with lies, a Thai life today flows mindlessly with the current like a Nile Tilapia, or Pla Nin in Thai, as performed by the fictional actor in the second episode. The Nile Tilapia breeds rapidly and is popular in Thailand even though it is considered harmful to native species in other parts of the world, according to the short animation on Pla Nin that supplements *Dao Khanong*. However, an ordinary life is in touch with history all the time, serendipitously and otherwise. The past and present, the leftovers from the past and the true living history of the present cross paths all the time without any purpose or grand narrative. But the past, like the October 6 massacre, still touches ordinary lives today, affecting them in ways that they do not recognize.

. . . Fantastic Haunting

A film critic suggests that *Dao Khanong* reminds him of a section of my speech at the commemoration of the massacre on its fortieth anniversary in October 2016 at Thammasat. The speech was delivered, coincidentally, only an hour before the first preview of *Dao Khanong* at a small theater a few miles away in Bangkok.[14]

> For forty years, [those who sacrificed] never left us, never left any of you, even those who are only in your twenties. Because every life that had gone has become part of each of us. Not only are they in our memories, but we are who we are today because they sacrificed themselves to make today for us. They gave me the opportunity to live on. . . . We are who we are today, thanks to their sacrifices that morning, and thanks to many others who . . . took actions with hope and faith for a better Thai society. Those people ask us . . . if we are willing . . . to confront suffering, difficulty, and to stand tall in face of any challenges.[15]

Dao Khanong, which is also a placename, is a road sign along that temporal journey. By the time it gets dark during this life journey, with and without purpose, people have carried with them some part of that Wednesday morning in October 1976.

As cruel as it may be, history is still with us, it is part of all of us today. By the time it reaches the present, even a fragmented and phantasmagoric memory of the masscre is not merely in a book, a film, or at a commemorative event. It is within us.

Notes

This prologue is drawn from my memoir, originally published in Thai in 1996 (Thongchai 1996).

1. Pichian Amnatworaprasert, the president of Thammasat University Student Union.

CHAPTER 1: THE UNFORGETTING OF OCTOBER 6

1. About this law and its unjust procedure, see Streckfuss 2011.

2. Lawrence Langer differentiates five types of memory of the Holocaust. First is the deep memory, the buried self of those who tried to forget by locking up the painful memory inside. Second is the anguished memory, the divided self of those who were ambivalent, wanting to forget yet wanting to remember. Third is the humiliated memory, the besieged self of those who tried but were unable to forget. Fourth is the tainted memory, the impromptu self of those who perpetuated the guilty feeling. Last is the unheroic memory, the diminished self of those who survived and lived on without good feeling or pride, and unable to do anything much beyond barely living (1991).

3. *How Societies Remember* is the title of a study by Paul Connerton (1989).

4. Crane 1997, 1374.

5. Halbwachs 1980, 78–79.

6. There are many more explanations and debates on the distinction between memory and history (for elaboration and extensive references, see Crane 1997). A major contribution is Pierre Nora's essay "Between History and Memory," the introduction to his magnum opus, *Les Lieux de Memoire* (1989, 7–24). However, I find Nora's proposition too rigid and misleading unless we adopt his thinking and the entire set of terminology and logics. I agree with most of Stern's criticism of Nora (2004, xxvii–xxviii). Walter Benjamin's views of history and memory is the opposite of Nora's. He relishes the spontaneous memory of individuals as the authentic, unalienated, and unmediated recollections of the past, unlike the mediated, ideological, and class-based historical construction. However, his notion of memory seems restricted only to the narrow sense of

243

personal memory and includes no social dimension or any relations to the collective one. I do not find his ideas especially relevant to this book.

7. Reiff 2016, 73–74.

8. Lisa Yoneyama studies the multilayered memories of the atomic bomb at Hiroshima and the complex dilemma of the issue (1999).

9. Halbwachs 1980, 43–44.

10. Crane 1997, 1376.

11. Jelin 2003, 11.

12. Stern 2004, 105–112. Stern also explains how individual memories are brought into the emblematic ones (113–119). Like Langer's types of memory, this classification helps me understand and conceptualize the various collective frames relevant to the memory of the massacre. Nevertheless, the actual ones are nuanced and usually a mix of several types. This book does not try to sort them out for the sake of verifying the classification, though I am indebted to Stern tremendously.

13. Halbwachs 1992, 173.

14. Jelin 2003, 52–54.

15. Igarashi 2000.

16. Gluck 2007, 61.

17. Jelin 2003, 20–21.

18. Weinrich 2004.

19. Ernst Renan's classical essay "What Is a Nation?" was published in 1882.

20. Stern 2004, xxvii.

21. Stern 2004, 149–151; Jelin 2003, 100; Gates-Madsen 2016, 4–6 (and throughout the book).

22. Trouillot 1995, chapter 3.

23. Stern 2004, xxviii–xxix.

24. Joshua Oppenheimer, dir., *The Look of Silence* (Drafthouse Films, Participant Media, 2015), http://thelookofsilence.com, accessed July 12, 2019.

25. Gates-Madsen 2016, 120.

26. The terms "right wing," "left wing," "leftists," "radicals," and the like in this book are based on political and ideological divisions of the 1970s to early 1980s Thailand of the Cold War. Members of the right wing were anticommunist in their politics and ideology. In the Thai context of the time, they were identical to royalists because in their view communism meant antimonarchist and anti-Buddhist sentiments rather than adherence to a political-economic ideology and program. I use the term "right wing" to include people who took action against the radicals, regardless of whether they accepted that identity, they were directly involved with the massacre, and their ideologies and politics in the decades afterward.

27. Jelin 2003, 17.

28. Trouillot 1995, 146–147.

29. Frielander 1992.

30. LaCapra 2000.

31. Daniel 1996, 1–7, 105–107.

32. Nguyen 2016, 19 (emphasis in the original).

Chapter 2: The Massacre and Unanswered Questions

1. Viroj Mutitanond, aka "Viroj M-16" of *Thairath,* in *Sarakhadi* 1996, 153. In regard to the allegation that the demonstrators fired heavy weapons from inside the campus, he explained that the police firing from different sides of the campus were mistaken for the ones from inside.

2. Penn 2003. Because of this, his colleague from UPI was shot in the neck, even though he was not among the protesters.

3. Orissa in *Sarakhadi* 1996, 162; testimony of Pairatchote Chankhachorn (2519.net, "History testimony," http://www.2519.net, accessed May 12, 2017). The police initially reported that they found only a few personal handguns inside the campus. After the massacre, however, the coup regime put on an exhibit showing the weapons found from Thammasat, which included several AK automatic rifles and grenades (NARC 1976, photo; Samokao 1977, 39–48). Some of these heavy arms were cited in the indictment in the October 6 trial (Thawatchai 1978, 76–80).

4. Kong 2016. Ulevich said similarly in my interview with him on September 1, 2016.

5. The number of the hanging and tortured victims outside TU here differs from my earlier articles about this incident (Thongchai 2002), thanks to subsequent research of the Documentation of the October 6 (Doct6) project. To this day, the number remains inconclusive.

6. The chronology of that night until the end of the shooting in the morning as described here is from my memory, which may be different from other sources (especially Puey 1977, 1993).

7. Maurizio Peleggi remarks, "This procedure . . . amounted to the figurative divestment of students of their citizenship" (2017, 155).

8. The recording of Radio Thailand and Seni's press conference at 2 p.m. of October 6, 1976, is available at the Doct6 website (https://doct6.com).

9. Observers and historians of Thailand agree that the military faction that plotted the massacre was not the one that staged the coup in the evening (see Morell and Chai-anan 1981, 275–276; Ji and Suthachai 2001, 159). After the coup, several top military officers allegedly associating with the massacre faction were removed from their positions of power. This does not mean that those who staged the coup had nothing to do or did not agree with the massacre.

10. The classification into two groups appears in the autopsy reports by the police. See AAGO, "The October 6 Case," Box 70, Bangkok. It is available at Doct6. Many people believe that more than a hundred were killed, but no concrete evidence supports this belief.

11. For the trial, see chapter 4. For the efforts by academic and activists, see chapter 8. For publications, apart from my own, Somsak Jeamthirasakul is a notable contribution, especially the chapter on who was who in the massacre (Somsak 2001; Thongchai 2016b).

12. Ferrara 2015; Thongchai 2008.

13. Nattapoll Chaiching explains the history of the revival of power of the monachists after the end of absolute monarchy in 1932 until the 1960s (2013).

14. Thongchai 2008, 20–21.

15. Probably the best account in English about these turbulent three years is that of David Morell and Chai-anan Samudavanija (1981).

16. Ibid., 251.

17. Prajak 2006.

18. Morell and Chai-anan 1981, 161–176, 235–252, 276. About half of them were leaders of the Farmer's Federation of Thailand (for the list, see Haberkorn 2011, appendix).

19. Most newspapers reported with photos on October 5, 1976, that five policemen were arrested for the murder of these two activists. After the massacre took place the following day, no further news about the arrest was released. In 2016, Patporn Phoothong, a researcher for the Doct6 project, found that since then no investigation whatsoever had been undertaken into the murder. The five policemen were released without any consequences for their alleged actions.

20. The government later announced at 2 p.m. on October 6 that these students were arrested from TU at 8 a.m. Seni said the same during his press conference that afternoon. It was not clear whether Seni knew that the students went to his residence.

21. For a lengthy argument against these allegations, see Ji and Suthachai 2001, 179–203.

22. Handley 2006, 219; Anderson 1977, 24.

23. Keyes 1978, 153. For his exact words, see the interview of this monk in *Chatturat,* June 29, 1976, 29, 32.

24. See the lyric of this song in Philips 1987, 331–332.

25. "Document 425, Telegram 28513 from the Embassy in Thailand to the Department of State, October 14, 1976, 1117Z," in *Foreign Relations of the United States, 1969–1976, Volume E–12,* Documents on East and Southeast Asia, 1973–1976, para. 3, https://history.state.gov/historicaldocuments/frus1969 –76ve12/d425 (accessed March 24, 2017).

26. "British ambassador David Cole to Foreign Minister Anthony Crosland," confidential British cable on the October 1976 Thammasat massacre and coup, October 13, 1976, 5, https://web.facebook.com/notes/andrew-macgregor-marshall /confidential-british-cable-on-the-october-1976-thammasat-massacre-and -coup/568611373158206?_rdc=1&_rdr (accessed June 1, 2019).

27. Bunchana 1982, 185–187.

28. "Document 425, Telegram 28513," para. 3.

29. "British ambassador David Cole to Foreign Minister Anthony Crosland," 7–8.

30. Morell and Chai-anan 1981, 277.

31. Nations 1976.

32. The absence was so conspicuous that it requires an excuse. Nakharin Mektrairat explains that the king faced limitations, unable to intervene to solve the conflict as he did in 1973 (2006, 256). He does not explain what limitations.

33. "British ambassador David Cole to Head of Chancery," titled "Situation in Thailand," *Political Prisoner in Thailand* (blog), November 5, 1976, para. 2.ii, 2.iv.

34. Handley 2006, 214–237. This is a subject of discussion among scholars of Thailand outside the country (see, for example, Morell and Chai-anan 1981, 271; Mallet 1978, 89–91; Girling 1981, 213–215; for a brief summary, Bowie 1977, 128). Inside the country, it remains a forbidden subject.

35. Handley 2006; Thongchai 2008, 2014.

36. Nattapoll 2011.

37. Bowie 1997, 82–86, 97–99, 108; Morell and Chai-anan 1981, 242–244.

38. Bowie 1997, 81.

39. "British ambassador David Cole to Foreign Minister Anthony Crosland," 8.

40. Thongchai 2016a.

41. Somsak 2001, 115–148.

42. In 2006, thirty years after the massacre, the Village Scouts have officially denied that the organization took part in the October 6 siege of TU. See "Announcement from the Village Scout Operation Center, Region 3" (Thalaengkan sunpatibatkan luksua chaoban phak 3), May 27, 2006, attached to a letter to the daily newspaper *Matichon*, dated June 3, 2006. Both the announcement and the letter are available on Doct6.

43. *Sayamrath,* September 24, 1976, photo news.

44. *Daily News,* September 24, 1976.

45. Hyun 2017.

46. Information provided by a BPP officer in court (see Thawatchai 1979, 345–346).

47. Paul Handley mentions the BPP's training of Village Scouts in mock attacks on students and mock beating and hanging of students before the actual incident (2006, 237).

48. *Daily News,* October 9, 1976. The photo news does not specify the time of their visit to both places.

49. *Dao sayam,* October 9, 1976; *Daily News,* October 9, 1976.

50. *Daily News,* October 22, 1976. Kobkua Suwannathat-Pian mentions that the queen and princesses visited TU after the massacre, and offered food to

the Village Scouts who were camping there (2003, 174). I find no evidence of this visit. Furthermore, after the massacre, TU was shut down for a few months for safety concerns. No Village Scouts camped there.

51. *Sayamrath,* September 9, 1977.

52. Surin Matsadit, a cabinet minister in Seni government, wrote these letters in October 1977, one year after the massacre. See copies of the original documents in TUA, the CPT documents, B.4/11 to B.4/16, later published as Surin 1979.

53. A year later, *Dao sayam* put the blame on Seni's cabinet ministers for their failure to declare an emergency on October 6, 1976. Chuan Leekphai, one of the ministers, sued *Dao sayam* for defamation. *Dao sayam* pled guilty before the trial began, prompting Chuan to comment that he wished there had been a trial so that truth would have been revealed as to who had toppled democracy in Thailand. See *Sayamrath,* September 30, 1977; *Sayamrath Weekly,* October 9, 1977, 24.

54. For a study of the police force on that day, see Somsak 2001, 182–189.

55. Radio Thailand, 2 p.m. news, October 6, 1976, interview with Police General Chumphon Lohachala, from the tape recording of the news on that day, see chapter 3.

56. Based on interviews they conducted with many witnesses, on the published testimonies of witnesses in the October 6 trial, and on the radio broadcast in the afternoon of that day, Ji and Suthachai identify three branches of the police forces, the second to the fourth (2001, 169). They fail to mention the most obvious one, the local police. There were also some individual policemen from other branches, such as the Special Branch (Santiban)—the political police.

57. First Puey and then Ji and Suthachai call them the "informal" *(nok rabob)* or "fringe" right wings (Puey 1993, 76; Ji and Suthachai 2001, 174).

58. Ji and Suthachai 2001, 138.

59. Sondhi 1975; Mallet 1978, 84–85; Puey 1993, 75; Morell and Chaianan 1981, 238–240; Sarakhadi 1996, 95; Ji and Suthachai 2001, 137–139; Prajak 2006, 16–20; Handley 2006, 224–238; Suthachai in Netiwit 2016, 18–20; Bowie 1997, 105; Phutthapol 2003.

60. Handley 2006, 225; Morell and Chai-anan 1981, 239. Prajak Kongkirati said the financial and material support to the group was from the state agencies, especially ISOC, although it was kept secret from the public at the time (2006, 4, 18–19).

61. Handley 2006, 225, 226; Bowie 1997, 105; Phutthapol 2003, 87. Tyrell Haberkorn mentions the fear among leaders of the farmer organizations of Nawaphon's assassins (2011, 126). I also recall the rumors at the time about Nawaphon's assassins. In retrospect, it was not clear whether the rumor was based on any facts.

62. Morell and Chai-anan 1981, 239–240.

63. Handley 2006, 225.

64. Such as the call to mobilize on October 6 (cited in Bowie 1997, 26).

65. Ford 2017, 259–260.

66. For ISOC's mass operation for antidemocracy in the post-Cold War era, see Puangthong 2017. It is reasonable to think of the similar operation during the Cold War period. Prajak suggests that Nawaphon's organized cells imitated the leftist ones (2006, 4, 17–18). To me, they looked like ISOC's grassroots organizations more than the leftist ones.

67. The radical movement also created a phantom organization, the Anti-Dictatorship National Front (Naewruam totan phadetkan haeng chat). It claimed a vast base of individuals and groups, including some famous ones. In fact, no separate organization, members, or mass base existed—only the outspoken leader.

68. Handley 2006, 135–179; Hyun 2014.

69. "Document 425, Telegram 28513," para. 4.

70. Zimmerman 1976, 66–67. The British ambassador raised the possibility of both, see "British ambassador David Cole to Foreign Minister Anthony Crosland," 7.

71. *Tulakan* 1996, 34–36.

72. Morell and Chai-anan also raise similar possibilities that the skit was a design by the students to poke fun at the monarchy, a conspiracy by the right-wing movement, and a conspiracy by the CPT, but they too agree that nothing supports these theories (1981, 274, 281–282).

73. For example, Puey 1993, 38. For a list of authors who believe that the photo was doctored, see Ji and Suthachai 2001, 26.

74. See *Matichon,* February 16, 1979, February 22, 1979, and March 3, 1979. Seni was specific that it was not a film doctoring but a photo make-up, then retaken (Thawatchai 1979, 429).

75. *Bangkok Post,* "The Truth about that Photograph," October 7, 1988, 6.

76. Vira Prateepchaikul, "Oct 6, 1976: Setting the Record Straight," *Bangkok Post,* October 7, 1996. Vira was a senior editor who was also with the *Post* in 1976.

77. Interviews at the *Bangkok Post* office, October 11, 2000.

78. In 2000, I interviewed a columnist of *Dao sayam* who was part of the decision to publish the photo in 1976. He firmly denied that *Dao sayam* retouched the film or the photo. Interview, 12 October 12, 2000 (see chapter 9).

79. The US ambassador hinted at this possibility while denying the conspiracy theory (see "Document 425, Telegram 28513 (from the US Embassy)," para. 5). The view was shared by his UK counterpart ("British Ambassador David Cole to Head of Chancery," para. iv).

80. For conclusive argumentation with evidence, see Somsak 2001, 149–154; Ji and Suthachai 2001, 182–188.

81. Ji and Suthachai 2001, 182–188.

82. *Post* sued *The Nation* for defamation and false allegations (*Bangkok Post,* October 7, 2000).

83. Somsak asked the same question and reached the same conclusion (2001, 155–160). A number of former student leaders shared the same wonder (Dr. B, interview, June 26, 2006).

84. The NSCT leader, Sutham Sangprathum, offered the same reason (1979, 28–29).

85. Here I disagree with Dr. B, who puts blame for the massacre on his fellow student leaders because, in his view, the massacre could have been foreseen (interview, June 26, 2006; memoir circulated among former activists from Mahidol University in 1996, provided by Dr. B).

86. Thikan 2009, 61.

87. See, for example, Rudee 1996, 324.

88. Morell and Chai-anan 1981, 282.

89. Sutham denies the allegation that some student leaders tried to block him from ending the demonstration (1979, 42–43).

90. *Su-anakhot,* July 20–26, 1988, 4. A well-known NGO activist and later leader of the antidemocracy movement has made this attack on me in public several times. The latest one was reported on *Prachatai,* April 19, 2010.

91. The last meeting of student leadership I attended was on the night of October 4. The responsibility with the crowd control prevented me from participating after that. In any case, the decision to end the demonstration must have been a collective one. I could not make it by myself. Dr. B wrote an unpublished memoir circulated among his friends describing my political inclination at the time regarding the demonstration. It was contrary to the allegation.

92. Given this possibility, in 2016, the Doct6 project was launched. With a shoestring budget and volunteers, the project creates the digital archives of the massacre—documents, testimonies, audio and visual recordings, newspapers, and more. The purpose is straightforward: help the digital archives be the source for more investigations by the later generations, thus help the world remember the massacre as long as it can. One of its most urgent tasks is to collect as much information as possible about the deaths and the families. A third of the victims' families agreed to give interviews, which are now available on Doct6. A third declined our requests for fear of the repercussions to them even today. The remaining third is still untraceable.

93. For example, Puey 1981b, 70; 1993, 57; Nicholas Bennett's letter to *Bangkok Post,* February 14, 2008. No source was given. This information is often attributed to people working for the Chinese charitable associations who collected the bodies that day. However, we have no evidence who these people were or where they said it. In 2016, a researcher for the Doct6 project interviewed two of them. They did not mention the number.

94. Thanks to Thanapol Eawsakul, my research assistant at the time, who found these materials that the police generated and gathered for the October 6

trial, then transferred to the public prosecutor after the trial was over. At the time (in 2000), the archives were part of the Library of the Attorney General Office, in a room adjacent to the library. Officially, the room and the archives were open to the public. In fact, they were practically closed most of the time, and air conditioning turned off, due to a lack of budget and scarcity of users. By the time I went to examine the materials, the librarian was delighted that a scholar was interested in the treasure under her care. The seventy-three boxes, altogether more than thirty thousand pages of materials about the October 6 trial were unorganized, uncatalogued, and covered with think dust. More than half of the thirty thousand pages were records of those three thousand students arrested at TU (personal information, bails, releases papers, formal letters among the officials, and so on). More than ten boxes are substantive documents waiting for further examination, such as the police forensic reports of TU after the incident with maps, photos of damages, bullets and weapons found there, the testimonies of the police witnesses, and the autopsy reports. Over the years since then, the museum was created, maintained well, and open to the public. The archives, which include all the lèse majesté cases and many well-known political trials since the 1950s, have been organized, catalogued, and impressively tended.

95. My earlier article on the massacre was wrong on this point (see Thongchai 2002, 243).

96. There is a misunderstanding that the victim in this photo was Wichitchai Amornkul, a Chulalongkorn University student (for example, in Peleggi 2017. 156). Wichitchai was another hanging victim whom we have identified, but not the one in this photo.

97. Puangthong and Thongchai 2018.

98. According to many studies, the desecration of the bodies in public lynchings is a ritualistic act and part of one of the following two types of public performances: first, the racist kangaroo courts against black people that took place in the US South between the 1870s and 1930s to confirm white supremacy at a time when that racist social order was beginning to crumble (Brundage 2013; Garland 2005), or second, the communitarian act of people who are neglected by the authorities and deprived of the formal justice process (Goldstein 2004; Godoy 2006). What happened on October 6 was akin to the former, even though the social order under threat from the radicals was not a racist one.

99. Ing et al. 2008, 5.

CHAPTER 3: THE BEGINNING OF MEMORIES

1. The recording of several hours of Yan Kro that morning is available on the Doct6 website (https://doct6.com). In 1982, while studying in Sydney, I obtained a cassette tape recording of the audio of TV5 during those hours. The recording began probably around 10 or 11 a.m. that day, given that the commentators mentioned the transportation of the arrested students to prisons. Then it recorded the live interviews of the right-wing demonstrators at the

Government House before 2 in the afternoon. The recording then switched to Radio Thailand news and the press conference of Seni Pramoj at about 2 p.m. The final section of the recording included the announcements and orders of the coup group, as broadcast on every radio starting at 6 p.m. In 1996, an hour-long video recording of TV5 from the morning of October 6, 1976, was found in the archives of TV5 and went public. Some live sounds of shootings and chaotic crowd noise with the background military songs are audible. The filming was entirely from the perspective of behind the police line. Both the video and audio recordings of TV5 are available at Doct6.

2. *Sarakhadi* 1996, 152.

3. See Thikan 2009, 30. This is an incomplete list because many well-known ones are not included such as *Thairath, Prachathippppatai, Prchachat, Chaturat,* and *Athipat.*

4. *Matichon,* June 16, 1979.

5. Ulevich, interview, September 1, 2016. Ulevich's photo of the hanging won the Pulitzer Prize for 1997 (figure 3). In Thailand, the news that the prize was awarded to a photo of the massacre was reported only in *Bangkok Post,* and without reprinting the photo.

6. NARC 1976 is the booklet. It also shows a few photos of the exhibit. The documentary film (26 minute in black and white) of the same title as the booklet is also available at Doct6. Samokao catalogues an extensive report of the exhibit (1977).

7. The quote is from the booklet produced by the NARC (1976, 7).

8. See for example in TUA, the CPT documents, section B.4/10.

9. *Sayamrath,* January 8 and 14, 1977.

10. *Sayamrath,* January 10 and 11, 1977.

11. AAGO, the October 6 Trial, box nos. 17–18.

12. For unknown reasons, not one of the most notorious paramilitary right-wing group, the Red Gaurs, testified to the police or were due to appear in court.

13. For example, the testimonies of witnesses nos. 15, 136, 137, 187, 219, and 220. No. 187 in particular mentioned a student leader who is a Vietnamese.

14. Witness no. 23.

15. Witness no.141.

16. Witness no. 131; however, he later asked the interrogator to correct this testimony.

17. Witnesses nos. 147, 156, 157, 161, 165; none of them reported to the police or the media, however. Many other witnesses from TU across the ideologies, however, testified that they did not think the skit is a mocking of the crown prince, see nos. 143 (who said the actor looks like a dead person), 144, 146, 149, 150, 153, 163, and 164.

18. Witnesses nos. 155, 156, 157, 161–168, 172, 175, 179, 187. Witness no. 154, a TU security guard also named the left-leaning guards. Two high school

teachers, nos. 173 and 177, told the police the names of leftist high school students.

19. Witnesses nos. 161 and 162.

20. Witnesses nos. 161, 162, and 165, but also 164. The quote is from no. 161, p. 11.

21. Witness no.167.

22. The person identified by witnesses nos. 141 and 142 as the one who hid weapons and threatened them was a military spy, according to witness no. 224 who took him out from prison without any charge.

23. That police officer was witness no. 43 who later gave testimony of the same event to the court as well.

24. Wat 2016, 9.

25. *Sarakhadi* 1996, 141, 163.

26. TU was closed until November 21 the same year for repairs (*Sayamrath*, November 6, 1976).

27. Cited in Bowie 1977, 30.

28. Sanphasiri 2001, 212–239.

29. For an example, see *Sarakhadi* 1996, 163.

30. The sentiment as described in this sentence can be found in almost every memoir of the former radicals (see, for example, Kanthima 2013, 79–85).

31. In a nutshell, the right wing believed that the movement led by the NSCT was in fact a proxy of the CPT. The CPT and some radicals claimed similarly, though from the opposite point of view to claim the historic accomplishments of the leftist radicals. Many other retrospective assessments lie between these two poles, however. The differences are in substance and in semantics, in the words used to characterize the radical movement at the time, in the narratives of the 1973–1976 period, and in the interpretations of critical events during those years.

32. Thikan 2009, 34.

33. See examples in *JCA* 6, no. 4 (1976): 515–516; De Beer 1978, 153–154.

34. In Thai, see TUA, The CPT's documents, sections A.1.6.1/3, /5, and /6. For their background and context, see also Thikan 2009, 98–102. In English, see, *JCA* 7, no. 2 (1977): 263–267.

35. *JCA* 7, no. 2 (1977): 263–264.

36. The entire document was translated and published in *JCA* 7, no. 3 (1977): 430–434.

37. Kasian 1996a, 16 (first published in 1983).

38. The lyrics of the song were written by a novelist and singer, Wat Wanlayangkul (see his memoir about this song in Wat 2001, 9–10). The title captures the sense of journey from the urban political activism to the CPT's armed struggle. Lanpho is a historic place at TU where many protests, including the popular uprisings in 1973, began. Phuphan is the name of a mountain range

in northeastern Thailand where a famous CPT base was located. The CPT's anthem was also titled "Phuphan patiwat" (The Revolutionary Phuphan).

39. Thikan 2009, 61; for details and names, see 56–68. Many are prominent leaders in their professions today.

40. Thikan 2009, 32.

41. An example is Krisadang Nutcharas, the first president of the TU Student Union in the post-massacre period (for an interview, see 2519.net, "October Thai Political and History Records," September 22, 2000).

42. This is an explanation why these radicals deradicalized quickly, as some radicals have nostalgically bemoaned in recent years, after the disillusionment with the CPT in the early 1980s (see Kanokrat 2016; Thikan 2009). I contend that their radicalism was not as strong as it might seem and that therefore their departure from radicalism should not be surprising. The radicalization is a detour in their lives, so to speak. I also contend that the diversity was a fundamental factor that resulted in the conflict between these students and the older CPT cadres that resulted in the former's disillusionment and the latter's collapse. This issue is, however, beyond the scope of this book.

43. Prajak 2005. More discussion on this point is in chapter 10.

44. Cho-chongkho 1996, 108, 111, 113, and 113.

45. For example, Swearer 1991.

46. In the 1980s, when the CPT and leftist movement collapsed, the radical Buddhist one did not. Instead, it thrived during the decline and absence of the leftist influence. The NGO movement that blossomed in the 1980s and 1990s can be partly attributed to the influence of these Buddhist radicals in the civic movement.

47. See Puey 1993, 40, 80–82. Salang denied Puey's allegation. He explained that he merely tried to show to the right-wing mob that the police was taking a proper action in order to prevent them from doing more harm to Puey (*Matichon,* August 7, 1999). According to Salang's testimony in the October 6 trial, he went as far as to say that he saved Puey's life (see Thawatchai 1979, 332–333). For more on this issue, see Somsak 2001, 186–188, 208–210.

48. He began the campaign in London only one week after leaving the country (see *JCA* 6, no. 4 [1976]: 497–500), and carried on throughout the world—to the United States, Canada, Australia, New Zealand, and more for almost a year (see, for example, TUA B.4/17–19).

49. See TUA, CPT's documents, B.4/6; it was first published in 1981 (Puey 1981a; translated in 1981b).

50. Puey 1993. The testimony took place on June 30, 1977.

51. Ibid., 13, 58–69, 77–78, 90.

52. Ibid., 15.

53. Puey 2000. Written in English for an academic meeting in June 1973, the Thai translation by Puey himself appeared on October 10, 1973, four days before the uprising, titled "Khunnahap chiwit patithin haeng khwamwang chak

khanmanda thung choengtakon." The English essay was first published in *Bangkok Post* on October 18, 1973, four days after the uprising, under the title "The Quality of Life of a South East Asian: A Chronicle of Hope from Womb to Tomb." The Thai version has been reprinted frequently.

54. *Sayamrath* daily and weekly, starting in 1950 and 1952, respectively, are journalistic institutions in Thailand for they have survived every political and financial crisis over the decades to the present day, thanks probably to the influence and stature of their original founder, Kukrit Pramoj (1911–1995), a minor royal who was a renowned conservative scholar, journalist, politician, banker, and once a prime minister (1975–1976). Readership of *Sayamrath* has been consistently average among Thai newspapers.

55. Atsiri 1981, 135–140. It was awarded the Southeast Asian Writers in 1981.

56. Information about these extended victims is mainly from two sources: first, the published interviews and stories of them, especially in 1996 and after; and, second, the search for families of the deaths by the Doct6 project. By mid-2017, more than a dozen families had been contacted and interviewed. The short films about these families and interviews of them are available at Doct6.

57. Some families suspected that their children were killed after arrest (see the cases of Manu Witthayaporn, Phoranee Jullakharin, and Manas Siansing in *Tulakan* 1996, 337, 348, and 356, respectively) or were shot again after dead (see the case of Suphon Phan, interview with his brother in 2017, at Doct6).

58. See *Tulakan* 1996, 336, 376; *Sarakhadi* 1996, 142, 144, and the interview of Suphon Phan's brother at Doct6.

59. Examples in *Sarakhadi* 1996, 134–144. One of them mentioned being assaulted (163). See also the interview of parents of Aphisit Thainiyom at Doct6.

60. Interview with Suphon's brother, at Doct6.

61. A mother made merit to her son every day for more than ten years after 1976 until she was too sick to do it (*Tulakan* 1996, 349).

62. Somtat, interview, 2017, at Doct6.

63. *Tulakan* 1996, 331–340. Lek was a subject of the short film "Silenced Memory" (2014) by Patporn Phoothong. The interviews of Lek were all made in 1996 and after. It is not clear when Lek was politicized before or because of her son's death, or after her regular attendance at the October 6 trial that became a political activity (see chapter 4).

CHAPTER 4: THE TRIAL AND THE BEGINNING OF SILENCE

1. See, for example, Sila 1996, 94–96. All personal records (finger prints, addresses, and so on) of the arrested, what lies they told the police, the paper trails of their bails and releases, and more, are more than half of the seventy-three boxes of the documents about the October 6 trial at Archives of the Attorney General's Office.

2. *Sayamrath,* February 11, 1977, August 14, 1977.

3. *Sayamrath,* August 25, 1977.

4. For all the details of the names of these alleged ringleaders, periods of their detention, the indictment and relevant laws, and the chronology of case before the trial, see Thawatchai 1978, 47–97, 329–338. While in prison, I was responsible for keeping all materials relevant to the case and trial. After the TU Archives was established in 1990, I gave the materials to the archives, see TUA, CPT documents, Section B.5.

5. *Telling the Truth* is a memoir of life in prison immediately after the arrest from TU (Sila 1996). His experience from the bus to the "animal cage," as he calls it, was almost the same as mine, except that he witnessed some people from his cell who were called out and beaten up (see 93–99).

6. The well-known book of essays and interviews of the Bangkok 18+1, *Rao khu phu borisut* (We are innocent [of the charges]), first published in 1977 after our releases and reprinted several times, was in fact prepared while we were still in prison.

7. Mallet 1978, 93.

8. Thawatchai 1978, 338–339.

9. Ibid., 302–305.

10. *Sayamrath,* September 6, 1977.

11. Thawatchai 1978, 101, 123–126. At first, we, the defendants, suspected that it was to discourage people from attending the trial since at that time the new location was inconvenient—far from Bangkok with poor transportation services. As it turned out, it was not a problem at all. People traveled there throughout the trial in 1978.

12. See this letter in Thawatchai 1978, 310–311. For a partial list, compiled from several Thai newspapers, of these thousands of people detained under this reason, see TUA, CPT documents, A.1.3/196.

13. Among them were academics from TU and Chulalongkorn University (November 22), the Coordination of Religions for Society Group (November 25), relatives of the Bangkok 18 (November 28), Thai citizens in France including the statesman Pridi Phanomyong (December 7), more than a hundred lawyers (December 8), and more. See *Sayamrath,* November 24, 26, 29, and December 8, 9, 1977.

14. Haberkorn 2015, 59n65.

15. For the full text of the formal charge, see Thawatchai 1978, 67–97. Apart from personal pistols, the ammunitions prohibitive to ordinary citizens included three AK machine guns, seven grenades, and a large number of bullets.

16. They orally denied the charge in court on September 5, 1977, but elaborated in writing on March 9, 1978.

17. Thawatchai 1978, 139, 141.

18. For the list, see Thawatchai 1978, 113–116. I did not recognize the remaining five of them, and they had not appeared in court by the time the trial was over.

19. All testimonies in court at this trial were published (see Thawatchai 1978, 1979). A few more court hearings were held without the testimonies of witnesses, mostly before January 23, 1978, dealing with various matters of the trial such as the procedures, threats to lawyers, and so on. The last was on September 16, for the judges to declare the end of the trial after the amnesty law passed the day before.

20. *Matichon,* July 7, August 18, 1978.

21. Two major political parties announced that they would bring justice to the defendants if they had power (*Matichon,* August 25, 1978).

22. Haberkorn 2015, 60.

23. *Sayamrath,* February 16, 1978, cited and translated by Haberkorn 2015, 61.

24. See *Matichon* and *Thairath,* September 13–16, 1978. The amnesty first appeared as a "surprise" news, as *Matichon*'s headline put it, on September 13.

25. *Matichon,* September 14, 1978; *Thairath,* September 16, 1978. His revelation of the king's involvement contradicted his warning a day earlier not to involve the king (*Matichon,* September 14, 1978).

26. Surachat 2017.

27. Handley 2006, 268.

28. Somsak, letter posted on Facebook, September 16, 2017.

29. *Thairath,* September 16, 1978; Haberkorn 2015, 63. The total number of the appointed legislative body was 360, of whom two hundred were military officers. The vote for the bill was 180 to 1, with fifty abstentions. The rest were not present to vote. Technically speaking, the bill was approved only by half, not the majority, of the legislative appointees.

30. *Matichon,* September 27, 1978. However, I cannot find the report of any demonstration.

31. Thawatchai 1979, 415–416.

32. Haberkorn 2015, 63, 60.

33. Ibid., 47.

34. Scott 1992.

35. Haberkorn 2015, 49–59.

36. Haberkorn seems to overlook the rightist demonstration, as if the massacre was the only event that morning or as if the two formed a single event. In my opinion, the drafters and the members of the legislative assembly distinguished the two events but were concerned more about the antigovernment demonstration than the massacre because, in their views, the former contributed directly to the fall of the Seni government and could be considered the wrongdoing.

37. Haberkorn 2015, 52.

38. Ibid., 49.

39. Chai-anan, Kusuma, and Suchit 1990.

40. Morell and Chai-anan 1981, 169–172, 213–228.

41. Ettinger, cited in Bergin 2016, 30.

42. Rousset 2009.

43. For example, Kriangsak himself, General Prem Tinsulanond, General Chavalit Yongjaiyuth, and the Thai "Young Turk" group.

44. TUA, CPT documents, A.11.3/1, February 10, 1978. The order was repeated several times, see *Sayamrath*, March 1, 1978; *Matichon*, September 19, 1978.

45. *Matichon* and *Thairath*, September 18, 1978. The CD version of the film recording of this event was distributed with the cremation volume for Kriangsak's funeral in 2004. The original is kept at the National Film Archives.

46. Sutham's remark becomes the title of a well known book about the Bangkok 18, *Rao khu phu borisut* (1978).

47. See *Matichon and Thairath*, September 19, 20, 1978.

48. *Matichon*, September 22, 1978.

49. Streckfuss 2011, 267.

50. *Matichon*, June 16, 1979.

51. Ibid., September 22, 1979.

52. *Sayammai*, October 16, 1982, 21.

53. *Matichon*, October 7, 1983.

CHAPTER 5: DISQUIETING SILENCE AFTER 1978

1. Suchit 1987, 49–76, 90–104.

2. Bergin 2016, 25.

3. Chaiwat 1986.

4. Wanit 1988.

5. As an example, see Suthachai 2015.

6. Gawin 1990, 27–33.

7. Ibid., 37–41.

8. Ibid., 43–64, 70–76.

9. *Matichon*, October 6, 1980.

10. Cited in Patcharapha 2013, 96, which quoted from the script of the film *Moon Hunter* (2001), which was based on Seksan's biography. The script was approved by Seksan.

11. The comment by Kasian Tejapira, who later becomes a professor of political science at TU.

12. For a former leader who mentions his guilt repeatedly, see Kanthima 2013, 83, 139, 301.

13. The first memoir was first published in 1983 by the TU Student Union in the booklet to welcome the incoming students of that year (Kasian 1996b). The second was first published in 1984 by the Committee of the Graduates of Thammasat University in the book to honor the graduates of that year, including Kasian himself (Kasian 1996c). The two memoirs were reprinted several times including in 1996.

14. Kasian 1996b, 50.

15. Ibid., 53.

16. Ibid., 54.

17. Kasian 1996c, 72.

18. Ibid., 75–76.

19. Chai-anan 1984; Anek 1992.

20. Thongchai 2008, 17.

21. See the entire episode from *Matichon*, March 23, 24, 27, 1981.

22. Chai-anan 1982, 22–29.

23. For a political biography of Chamlong, see McCargo 1997.

24. *Lak Thai*, June 30, 1988, 26–28.

25. *Khaophiset-Athit*, July 27–August 2, 1988, 16–17.

26. Chai-anan 1982, 32–33.

27. For the full text of Chamlong's speech, see *Matichon*, July 18, 1988; *Khaophiset-Athit*, July 27–August 2, 1988, 18.

28. Chai-anan 1982, chapter 5. Chamlong was mentioned by a rightist I interviewed in the early 2000s as a participant in the meetings of the coordinators of the right-wing groups (see chapter 9).

29. *Khaophiset*, July 27–August 2, 1988, 16–17.

30. Manas 1994.

31. Thawatchai 1979, 282.

32. See in *23 pi luksua chaoban nai phraborom rachanukroh* (Twenty-three years of the Village Scout under the royal patronage), 88. A similar memoir also appears in the 2011 volume on page 279.

33. Unless stated otherwise, the information below regarding this memorial project is gathered from three sources: *Bangkok Post*, April 6, 1997; *The Nation*, October 13, 1998; and *Saithan duan tula* 1990.

34. *Athit*, October 11, 1978, 27.

35. *Sayamrath Weekly*, October 29–November 4, 1989.

36. *Matichon*, May 11, 12, 1993.

37. *Matichon*, June 25, 26, 27, 1989.

38. Anand 1996. Thanks to Kasian Tejapira who informed me about Anand's keynote address. For his comment on Anand, see Kasian 1996a.

39. Trouillot 1995, 114–115.

40. *Sayamrath Weekly*, September 18–24, 1988, 18.

41. A remark by the rector of Thammasat University at the small commemoration in 1983, *Matichon*, October 7, 1983.

42. Comment by Sutham in *Matuphum*, October 7, 1983.

43. Comment by Sutham in *Sayamrath Weekly*, September 18–24, 1988, 18.

44. For this condition of royalist liberalism, see Connors 2007.

45. Wattanachai 1988.

46. US Department of State 1994.

CHAPTER 6: THE COMMEMORATION IN 1996

1. *Sarakhadi* 1996, 177.

2. *Phithikam 20 pi 6 tula* (The ritual for the twentieth anniversary of the October 6), the booklet for the ritual at the TU soccer field, October 6, 1996, 22.

3. The letter went public, published in *Maitchon,* on October 6, 1995.

4. Anek 1993, 87–88, 127.

5. Thongchai 2008, 17.

6. All the displays in this exhibit were published as a small booklet (*Nithatsakan 6 tula,* 1996), which was available at the event.

7. Due to public demand, the exhibition was extended long after the commemoration, altogether for fifty-seven days (*Suebsan,* no. 4, January–March 1997, 6), and went on the road to various campuses around the country for some months afterward.

8. The creator of the Wall Posters is Mr. Prcha Suveeranond, a survivor of the massacre and one of Thailand's reputed graphic designers today.

9. Among the most serious efforts was the oral history project for former activists of Mahidol University, which was compiled and published subsequently in three volumes (see Sa-nguan 2003–2005).

10. For an example of this view, see *Pratimanuson* 2000, 17–19, 24–27.

11. *Pratimanuson* 2000, 25.

12. Sirote 2013, 383.

13. He expressed his view at a few public forums during the commemoration.

14. Kanokrat 2016, 104–108.

15. "Senthang phleng phua chiwit" (history of the songs for life) in *Anuson sathan* 1998, 12.

16. In my opinion, Kanokrat Lertchoosakul takes the dichotomy too rigidly and statically, then tries to put people in the two boxes, and takes those advocates of the first view as the representatives of the majority of former radicals (2016).

17. My argument here is contrary to Kanokrat, who argues that the former radicals purposefully reframed their past, denying their radical past and the history of radicalism (2016). In a nutshell, she argues that the hiding and erasure of the past took place over time, especially after the 1996 commemoration. I argue here that the cathartic moment in 1996 released them from fear and the uncomfortable feeling to speak out about their past.

18. This sense was captured very well by the newsletter of the October Network, *Suebsan,* no. 4, that published several responses from the participants.

19. Thongchai 2008, 2019.

20. Sirote 2013, 383.

21. Huebner 2017, 113–114. The quotation in the last paragraph is from Puey (1981a). See Puey 1993, 90 (in Thai) or Puey 1981b, 92 (in English).

22. Nelson and Olin 2003, 7; Gillis 1994, 7–19.

23. For information on the entire process, see *Pratimanuson,* 2000, 53–57. Details are from this source unless noted. The 1980s–1990s was a period of proliferation of memorials and other mnemonic sites around the world, including the Vietnam War memorial in Washington, DC (dedicated in 1982). In South Korea, the 1979 Gwangju student uprising and massacre has been recognized since 1993, and several memorials have been erected throughout the city. This case was known among the Thai former radicals for its resonance with the October 6 massacre.

24. *Pratimanuson* 2000, 53. The entire project took much longer than 2000 to finish.

25. Huebner 2017, 114.

26. *Pratimanuson* 2000, 54.

27. To Mauizio Peleggi, the October 6 monument is "strongly reminiscent of socialist realist monument" (2017, 151).

28. *Pratimanuson* 2000, 61–62.

29. Ibid., 57, a comment by the coordinator of the artists.

30. Ibid., 56, 59–60.

31. Kanthima 2013, 301.

32. For these details and more, see *Anuson sathan* 1998, 8–11.

33. Peleggi 2017, 154.

34. Wong 2006, 135.

35. *Matichon,* March 31–April 10, 1997.

36. *Matichon,* March and April 1999.

37. *Bangkok Post,* April 20, 1999.

38. *Bangkok Post,* August 5, 2000.

39. *Bangkok Post,* January 29, 2001; see the letter from Ministry of Education to the author, and the front matter of Naowarat 2001, which is the draft published by the author.

40. Sila 1997.

41. Suthachai 2015, 6.

42. The fifteen monuments are: the Pha Chi Memorial of the Martyrs of District 7 at Phayao (Province); the Chong Chang Memorial in Surat Thani (Province); the Mong Khua Memorial of the People's War, Tak; the Phu Sang Memorial, in Nongbua Lamphu; the Tanaosri Martyrs Memorial in Phetchabubri; the Phatthalung, Trang, Satun Memorial, in Nakhon Sithammarat; the Memorial of the Ao Srimuang District in Nakhon Sithammarat; the Phu Phan Peace Memorial, in Kalasin; the Memorial for the Revolutionary Martyrs at the Three Province District in Phitsanulok; the People's Memorial of Southern Isaan, in Buriram; the Memorial for the District 196 Martyrs in Chaiyaphum; the Phu Phayak Memorial in Nan; the Memorial of the Dong Mun People's Army in Kalasin; the Thang Daeng Memorial, in Phatthalung; and the Phudanyao Memorial in Mukdahan.

CHAPTER 7: THE GOOD SILENCE

1. Jinda Thongsin's memoir was first published in 1996 (Kulvadee and Suthachai 1996, 48–72).

2. For a list of the jungles and the Border Patrol Police camps they visited, see *Tulakan* 1996, 406.

3. Wandee 1996, 139.

4. *Tulakan* 1996, 405; Wandee 1996, 139–140.

5. *Tulakan* 1996, 408.

6. Wandee 1996, 140.

7. AAGO, Documents of the October 6 Trial, Box 70.

8. The information about his visit of Wat Don is from two sources (*Tulakan* 1996, 403–404; unpublished interview by Ponthai Sirisathitkit, September 28, 2002, Doct6).

9. *Tulakan* 1996, 407.

10. Unpublished interview by Ponthai Sirisathitkit, available at Doct6.

11. Paisal, Sulak, and Mo.tho.ko 1996, 39–42.

12. The author completed the memoir on October 21, 1976, but kept it for twenty years before publishing it (see Paisal, Sulak, and Mo.tho.ko 1996, 17–122).

13. Confronting a spiritual test is also common in the well-known Buddhist folk stories in Thailand and elsewhere in the region, such as the story of Prince Vessantara (see Jory 2017; Bowie 2017).

14. It was also published on the same occasion (see Paisal, Sulak, and Mo.tho.ko 1996, 123–162).

15. Interview, April 6, 2007.

16. Thammasat University 1999.

17. *Matichon*, October 19, 1978.

18. Thongchai 1999, 107–109.

19. *Sarakhadi* 1999, 168–169.

CHAPTER 8: SLIDING MEMORY

1. *Matichon*, June 15, 2000.

2. Ji's challenge began on April 12, 2000. The controversy heated up in June. Samak filed a defamation suit on June 15. The election took place on July 23. Most newspapers closely reported, and took part in, the controversy especially during June to July.

3. See details of this controversy in any daily newspaper in Thailand, starting February 20, 2008, for a month.

4. See *The Nation*, June 24, 2000; *Bangkok Post*, June 27, 2000; *Krungthep Thurakit*, February 21, 2008.

5. For a full account of the ascendency of the palace, see Thongchai 2008; for the royal hegemony, Thongchai 2016a; for how this political system operates, Thongchai 2019.

6. See Ing et al. 2008.

7. Thamrongsak 2008.

8. Kanokrat's reaction cited in Charnvit and Thamrongsak 2013, 375, 377–378.

9. Yukti 1996.

10. Kanokrat cited in Charnvit and Thamrongsak 2013, 376.

11. Titled "The 6th October 1976 Fact-Finding and Witness Interviewing Committee (Khana kammakan rap khomun lae sueb phayan hetkan 6 tula 2519), the commission's summarizing report was published a year later (Ji and Suthachai 2001). Despite serious efforts and dedications, the committee made no claim that its work was adequate. Instead, it called for a true Truth Commission (Ji and Suthachai 2001, 16, 223–225). The interview materials are currently kept at the Thammasat University Archives.

12. Comments by Kanokrat Lertchoosakul and Sirote Khlamphaiboon in Charnvit and Thamrongsak 2013, 373–375, 382–383.

13. Jelin 2003, 52–54.

14. Stern 2004, 105, 107.

15. Streckfuss 2011, 278.

16. The name in Thai is *Khana kammakan issara truatsop lae khonha khwamching phua kanprongdong haeng chat*. Note the word "for" rather than "and" in the English name.

17. The event took place on September 23, 2011. For the list of all activities in the commission's report, see Truth for Reconciliation Commission of Thailand 2012, 23–24, http://www.innnews.co.th/images/assets/report.pdf (accessed June 4, 2019).

18. For the facts, see TRCT 2012, 90–196, for the analysis, 197–218. The rest of the report was the bureaucratic report of the commission's activities including lists of seminars and meetings organized by the commission and the names and dates of meetings with world dignitaries.

19. Sun khomun prachachon 2012.

20. Mulder 1997.

21. Jackson 2004, abstract.

22. Nidhi 2006, 249–253. Streckfuss argues that in the West the religious notion of truth also remained predominant in the practice regarding the defamation laws until the eighteenth century, after which the "secular truth" prevailed (2011, 73–74, 139–140).

23. David Chandler also explains the Cambodian perceptions of order via stories (2008).

24. Streckfuss 2011, 266.

25. Tambiah 1992, 105–109.

26. Many passages in this section are revised and edited from an earlier publication (Thongchai 2002, 263–265).

27. Thongchai 1994, 159–161.

28. Streckfuss 2011, 277.

29. Kanokrat 2016, 98–99.

30. See chapter 6.

31. Steedly 1993, 238.

32. Information confirmed by Patporn Phoothong who made contacts with these relatives for the Doct6 project.

33. Thongchai 2016a, 2–7; 2008; 2019.

34. See Thongchai 2016a, 7–11.

35. For a list of the special royal ceremonies since 1976, see Thongchai 2016a, 7.

36. In 1960, the Sarit government changed Thailand's national day from June 24, the day of the revolution in 1932, to King Bhumibol's birthday on December 5. Queen Sirikit's birthday celebration was declared the annual Mother's Day in 1976 and King Bhumibol's as Father's Day in 1980.

37. In 1996, when the first Olympic gold medalist from Thailand, Somluck Khmasing, knew that he had won the boxing bout, he raised a photo of the king high above his head in the middle of the boxing ring. He later told a story about why he attributed his victory to the king's benevolence. On his return, he had an audience with King Bhumibol and offered his gold medal to the king. Since then, most Thai athletes raise the photo of King Bhumibol when they win.

38. Streckfuss 2011.

39. Permit me to indulge in a personal anecdote here. In the early 2000s, the Wisconsin Alumni Association of Thailand (WAAT) offered a Royal Thai Pavilion (*sala thai*) as a gift to the alma mater to celebrate something of the Thai king. I declined the university's request to sit on the committee for this project because I did not want to be involved with any promotion of royalism. But I never tried to undermine it either. Despite that, rumors went otherwise in Thailand. The head of the WAAT at the time and I had known each other since 1976, when he was the editor of a liberal newspaper accused of supporting the communists, thus was shut down on October 6. By the 2000s, his new daily became one of the most successful in the country and he was among the most highly respected journalists. At one of his visits to Madison in mid-2000s, he lambasted me at a public reception for him, accusing me of trying to sabotage the project. I denied it. He then preached to me of the virtue of the king. "You are stuck in the past, unable to see the greatness of His Majesty," he said. He pitied me for not being able to move beyond the past. "The past" definitely meant the October 6 massacre. His allusion to the incident suggested that he, too, was aware of the dubious involvement of the palace in the incident.

40. Pitch 2016, 209–211.

41. Ibid., 207, 214–215.

42. The group goes by this English name and has no Thai name. The performance was by students from the Theater Department at Thammasat University and members of the B-Floor Group, directed by Thirawat Munwilai.

43. Report of this performance in *Prachatai,* October 15, 2013.

44. Pitch 2016, 207.

45. For example, see Sila 1996, 5.

46. This information is from Sinsawat Yodbangpoey, the coordinator for the construction of the monument, as I asked him on July 16, 2017. He did not recall any remarkable discussion, let alone disagreement, why this passage was chosen because it was "common feelings at the time" (*khwamrusuk ruamruam kan*) among the artists and people who participated in the public discussion about the design.

47. See Janjira 2016; Wanrak 1996, 175–187; for Puey's writings in English, see Puey 1981b.

48. See "Ruang yo lakhon wethi mangkon salat klet de miewsical" (Preview of Puey the musical) *Manager Online,* April 23, 2013, http://www.manager .co.th/Drama/ViewNews.aspx?NewsID=9580000046384 (accessed November 3, 2017).

49. Pitch Pongsawat makes a similar argument on this point (2016, 224–225).

Chapter 9: Silence of the Wolf

A Thai and longer version of this chapter was first published in Chaiwat Sathaanan, ed., *Khwamrunraeng son/ha sangkhomthai* (Violence: hidden and found in Thai society) (Bangkok: Matichon Publishing, 2010), 407–512; later reprinted as Thongchai 2016b, chapter 3.

1. I mention the real names of those who appear on public documents or whose words are available in public. For the others I interviewed privately, I create noms de guerre for each of them.

2. The development of sympathy for and understanding of the "Evil Men" he interviewed is also a crisis for James Dawes (2013). See also Dawes' interview with Gal Beckerman, *Globe Correspondent,* April 29, 2013.

3. Todorov 1996, 260–271; Levi cited by Todorov (269).

4. Anderson 1977.

5. Prajak 2006.

6. Morell and Chai-anan 1981; Handley 2006.

7. Bowie 1997.

8. Keyes 1978. A few articles in Phutthapol sought to advance our knowledge about the right wings but without much success (2003).

9. Tho. Krating is the only publication about the Red Gaurs in Thai (1975). However, it is not a study of the group but publicity for it, explaining the background and reason for its creation.

10. Norman Peagam's original news report on the Red Gaurs and Nawaphon emphasizes the role of ISOC (*Far Eastern Economic Review,* July 25, 1975, 13–14). Every writing by Puey about the massacre also mentions ISOC. Subsequently, it was mentioned quite often. Despite that, no serious study of it had been been undertaken until Puangthong (2017).

11. *Sarakhadi* 1996, 159–160.

12. I met RG1 twice, in June 2006, once at the interview of the Patriotic Goons on June 12, when RG1 was called to join them, and the other time on June 21 for separate interviews of him with two other former Red Gaurs.

13. *Sarakhadi* 1996, 167. This was repeated by his son Amnuaysat Hatsadin, who was also a member of the Red Gaurs (2001).

14. *Sarakhadi* 1996, 167.

15. Somsak's interview in *Sarakhadi* (1996, 160), repeated in his interview with me.

16. Sutsai's interview in *Sarakhadi* (1996, 167). He meant the Thai Bat group. The word "500" (*ha roi*) here is an idiomatic suffix in Thai usually added to the name of a group of bad people. It suggests that Sutsai did not think the Red Gaurs were such bad people.

17. Amnuaysat 2001.

18. Ibid. Other former Red Gaurs whom I had met and interviewed also shared this view.

19. Somsak K's and Sutsai's interviews in *Sarakhadi* 1996, 161, 169; interviews with other former Red Gaurs.

20. The people whom I met in 2006 offered this characterization of their people in 1976. According to them, other people in these groups later became teachers, bureaucrats, and small business owners.

21. In the early 1980s, according to them, some years after the massacre, Mr. Pavas Bunnag, the royal secretary at the time, supported these people to form a single group. He allowed them to use an office of the Royal Household inside the palace compound as the group's office. He also gave the name of the new group, the Apirak Chakri (Protecting the Chakri Dynasty). The group was known in the 1980s and 1990s. The association with the royal secretary was short lived, however, though the group kept the name. The last time I heard of it was from its leaflets against the 1996 commemoration of the massacre.

22. His royal cremation was presided over by Princess Sirindhorn and Chulaphorn, a special honor for a person of his background as if, as the princesses praised him, he were a soldier who died on the battlefield. Thanks to the cremation, the public understood that he was a Village Scout. His political actions were part of the Patriotic Goons, however, not of the Scout movement. Some said he was a Nawaphon who was an army officer, but offered no evidence of this (Ji and Suthachai 2001, 168, 175).

23. Amorn n.d.

24. AAGO, Documents on the October 6, 1976 trial, box no. 17, witness no. 3. Sudarat Musikawong, who did her PhD on arts and films about the October 6 massacre, informed me that a famous novelist who was notorious in the right-wing movement at the time, Thommayanti, also shared this view in her analysis of the political situation between 1973 and 1976.

25. Lim 2016, 131–142.

26. Among the 224 witnesses who testified to the police, twenty were soldiers. Most were weapon experts and other technicians and did not witness the massacre. Only this corporal and his partner, who were assigned to collect information about the situation, were the soldiers who witnessed the massacre.

27. Certainly, the intelligence sergeant did not modify his memory to satisfy me. Of all the interviewees, he and the corporal-healer were the only ones who did not know who he was talking to. I informed every interviewee who I was in 1976. But the person who helped arrange the meeting with the sergeant did not tell him who I was. I realized this mistake during the lunch after the interview when he advised me to find more information about the student movement from Thongchai Winichakul. Clearly he knew me only by name.

28. For Salang's testimony in court that mentioned these professors, see Thawatchai 1979, 268, 284, 296–297, 305. Salang also told a slightly different story of how he met these professors on the Yan Kro Broadcast on October 6.

29. Puey 1993, 82–83.

30. Salang was also controversial in some other incidents, usually concerning the abuse of power but unrelated to the massacre. He committed suicide in March 2018.

31. Astonishingly, the range was similar to the ones of the perpetrators in Argentina and Chile (see Payne 2008).

32. Dawes 2013.

33. An account of the incidents and people who enjoy the impunity in recent political history would need several volumes. For a pioneering one, see Haberkorn 2018.

34. Kaberkorn 2018.

35. Chamlong admits in public that he was involved in the countermovement against the NSCT, although he insisted his role was merely as an ordinary citizen. The intelligence sergeant said that Chamlong was an organizer of those groups. When asked whether Chamlong was involved in the October 6 massacre in some way, the Red Gaurs said, "certainly." The intelligence sergeant and the corporal-healer also said that Chamlong's role in the demonstration at the Equestrian Plaza was greater than the public realized. I cannot verify this assertion.

36. He spent the rest of his career in a nonpolitical role. He died in 2014. In the cremation volume for him (Uthan 2014), his family chose to publish his writings as the scripts of a little-known television program funded by the army in 1987, *Phra Ko Phra Kuala,* to celebrate the virtues and contributions of the king and the queen.

37. Thanks to Michael Cullinane and Paul Hutchcroft, two colleagues who specialize in the Philippines and who knew nothing about Uthan, for their comments that were keys to solve the puzzles.

Chapter 10: Praxis of Memory

1. Phatcharapha 2013, 120.

2. For Seksan's speech in full, see *Phujatkan raiwan* (The Manager Daily), October 8, 1996.

3. Kanokrat Lertchoosakul mentions that the term in Thai has been used before, though she does not specify (2016, 1). Kasian confirms that the translation was his. He adds, "I chose the word 'Octobrists', whose lexical origin comes from the French word for October, i.e. Octobre, hence 'Octobrist' . . . By the way, I recall that the term 'Octobrists' had already been used in relation to a political party in Tsarist Russia. So, the term itself had existed before in the political vocabulary of Russia. That I chose it as an English equivalent of "*Khon duan tula*" was done with no political connotation whatsoever" (personal email communication in English, November 14, 2017).

4. Seksan's speech in *Phujatkan raiwan*, October 8, 1996.

5. Kanokrat 2016.

6. Seksan explains his intention for the words was to make people of the two Octobers inclusive because at the 1996 commemoration, the massacre was often set in contrast with the uprising in various aspects—defeat versus victory, forgotten versus celebrated (see *Matichon*, October 14, 2003).

7. Prajak 2005.

8. Thongchai 2008, 19–21; 2019, 286.

9. In a subsequent study, Kanokrat herself notes the diverse backgrounds of these radicals. Even the CPT's influence over the student movement remains debatable (see Kanokrat in Netiwit 2016, 178–181).

10. This plot of the story of deradicalization and the reconciliation with the monarchy was proposed by Somsak Jeamteerasakul (2007). It is influential among the scholars of later generations who are attracted by radicalism, thus seeing the surrender of radicalism by former radicals in negative terms. Apart from Kanokrat, the well-known one is Thikan Srinara (2009, 2012).

11. Kanokrat 2016, chapters 4–5.

12. See Anek 1992; LoGerfo 2000, 221–52; Ockey 2004, 151–171.

13. See Pasuk and Baker 1998, 2000.

14. The newsletter began in April 1996 as part of the commemorative year. It continued after October 1996, produced by the network, at different frequencies, from bimonthly to quarterly. The latest issue in my personal collection was published in 2003. I do not know when it stopped.

15. *Suebsan*, no. 22, July 2001. This is not to suggest that they should be able to find a collective agenda and the inability to find one was a failure. In my opinion, it was probably natural and fitting that they could not find one.

16. For their names, see Phatcharapha 2013, 118. Apparently the leadership group included no women.

17. Phatcharapha 2013, 119.

18. The monthly newsletter was available from December 2000 but became irregular in 2002.

19. This summary is based on the group's newsletters, *P x P*.

20. Kanokrat 2016, chapter 4–6.

21. For example, *Phujatkan raisapda* (The Manager Weekly), October 8–14, 2001. For a comprehensive account of the TRT-Octobrists, see Kanokrat 2016, chapter 6.

22. Kanokrat 2016, 97–100.

23. For an extensive account of Thaksin and his administration, see Pasuk and Baker 2009.

24. See the articles in *Phuchatkan raiwan,* October 8, 2003; *Krungthep thirakit,* October 14, 2003; and *Matichon,* October 13, 2003, respectively.

25. Kanokrat 2016, 226–250.

26. Analyses of Thailand crisis since 2006 are now abundant. See, for example, *Journal of Contemporary Asia* 38 no. 1 (2008) and 46, no. 3 (2016); see also Pavin 2014.

27. Kanokrat 2016, 235–245.

28. The network announced it on the Thai October website.

29. Sirote 2007, 83–103.

30. For the 2010 massacre, see Montesano et al. 2012.

31. Baitonghang 2010.

32. This is its English name. Its Thai name is different, literally translated as the People's Committee for Absolute Democracy with the King as Head of State.

33. Wat 2013. Many Octobrists shared his sentiment on Facebook, including Kasian Tejapira and Baitonghang.

34. Phatcharapha 2014.

35. Most in Thai, among them, Thikan 2012; Kasian 2006; Baitonghang 2010; Phatcharapha 2014; in English, see Kanokrat 2016, 284–287. Kasian's essay is also available in English in *Kyoto Review of Southeast Asia,* issue no. 8, 2007.

36. Seksan 2014.

37. Prajak 2010.

38. Khaen 2007.

39. Phichit Likhitkitsombun, Facebook post, February 23, 2018.

40. Seksan's letter, *Way,* no. 38 (2010): 9.

Epilogue

1. Wat 2016.

2. Attachak 2006.

3. Reiff 2016, 58, 101.

4. This is the Thai title of the art exhibit, "Flashback '76" (see Ing et al. 2008).

5. Facebook, "Manee has a chair" @maneehaschair, https://www.facebook .com/maneehaschair (accessed June 2, 2019). For an interview with the anonymous creators, see *Prachatai*, "Thammai mani tong mi chae" (Why must manee have a chair?), Dhewarit Maneechai interviewed," July 3, 2013, https://prachatai .com/journal/2013/07/47507 (accessed June 2, 2019). It stopped in July 2016 with the episode 139. It reappeared in late 2018 after a controversial rap song.

6. In later episodes, Mani also beats Chao To with many other materials— paper, a television, a sofa, an airplane, and so on—materials that implicitly recall the original folding chair. Some later episodes are more like a typical political cartoon, with verbal satires but without Mani beating the dog.

7. Sudarat 2010.

8. Hunt 2018. Among the thirty-one films he mentions, two are about other bloodshed in 1992 and 2010. One each was produced in 1985, 1991, and 2003. The rest (twenty-six) were produced between 2006 and 2018, perhaps in line with the proliferation of noncommercial filmmaking and short and documentary films in Southeast Asia due to the availability of affordable and convenient technology (see the works by Ariel Heryanto on popular culture, especially film-making in Indonesia and Southeast Asia).

9. Hunt 2018, 7.

10. Ibid., 3. The producer of this film is Tunsaka.

11. Ibid., 5.

12. The quotes are from an essay telling a behind-the-scenes story, published in *The Standard*, an online news site in Thai (https://thestandard.co/home, October 30, 2018).

13. Personal communication with the director.

14. A comment on the blog *Kon mong nang* (Movie watcher), October 6, 2016, https://konmongnangetc.com (accessed December 8, 2017).

15. The citation is part of the full text of the speech: "Stand Tall Ready for the Challenges," http://prachatai.com/journal/2016/10/68230 (accessed July 13, 2019). The speech was given at the commemoration at Thammasat University on October 6, 2016. For a report of this commemoration, see Haberkorn 2017.

References

ARCHIVES

AAGO. Archives at the Attorney General's Office, "The October 6 Trial," seventy-three boxes. In this study, I focus on boxes 17–19, 51, 69, and 71–73, which include more than three thousand pages of testimonies of the prosecutor's witnesses, supporting evidence and photographs, and autopsy reports.

TUA. Thammasat University Archives, *Ekkasan chut phak communit haeng prathet thai* (Documents on the Communist Party of Thailand), particularly Section A.1.3 News; Section A.1.6.1 Announcements by student leaders; Section B.1 Student activities; Section B.2 Educational materials; Section B.4 The October 6, 1976 incident; Section B.5 The October 6 trial.

Doct6. Documentation of October 6, digital archives, https://doct6.com.

Interviews

Bangkok Post editors and reporters	October 11, 2000
Commander of Patriotic goons (ISOC, a navy commander)	June 1 and August 15, 2016
Corporal-healer (an army intelligence officer)	June 14, 2006
Deputy police inspector	June 28, 2006
Dr. B (a former student leader)	June 26, 2006
Patriotic goons (six of them) and the commander	June 12, 2006
Phra Paisal Wisalo (Buddhist monk and scholar)	April 6, 2007
RG1 (a Red Gaur leader)	June 12, 2006
RG1, Kant, and Chup (Red Gaurs)	June 21, 2006
Intelligence sergeant (an army officer)	June 14, 2006
Sawat (a witness of the massacre)	June 27, 2006
Sermyot (former leftist, a prosecutor's witness)	June 18, 2006
Somsak K (a Red Gaur leader)	July 28, 2000
Spy journalist (a *Dao sayam* journalist)	October 12, 2000
Ulevich, Neal (an AP journalist)	September 1, 2016

| Uthan Sanidvongse na Ayuttaya (the broadcast master) | October 11, 2000 |
| Watthana (a Red Gaur leader) | July 2, 2006 |

NEWSPAPERS AND NEWS MAGAZINES

A-thit, October 11, 1978

Bangkok Post, several issues in October 1976, 1988, 1996, 1998, 2000, and 2008

Chatturat, June 29, 1976

Daily News, September 24, 1976, October 9, 1976, October 22, 1976

Dao sayam, October 5, 6, 9, 1976

Khaophiset, July 27–August 2, 1988

Krungthep thurakit, several issues in 1996, and October 14, 2003

Lak Thai, June 30, 1988

Matichon, several issues in 1978, 1979, 1980, 1981, 1982, 1983, 1988, 1996, 1999, and 2003

Matuphum, October 7, 1983

The Nation, several issues in 1976–1978, October 1996, October 1998

Nechan sutsapda

Phuchatkan raiwan, May 27, 1996, October 8, 1996, October 8, 2003

Phuchatkan raisapda, October 8–14, 2001

Prachatai, October 20, 2008, April 19, 2010, October 6, 2010

Sayammai, October 16, 1982

Sayamrath, several issues in 1976–1978

Sayamrath sapdawichan, October 9–15, 1977, September 18–24, 1988, October 29–November 4, 1989

Su-anakhot, no. 305, July 20 26, 1988

Thairath September 13–16, 18–20, 27, 1978

The Standard, October 30, 2018

Way, 37 (October 2010), 38 (November 2010)

BOOKS AND ARTICLES

Amnuaysat Hatsadin. 2001. "Samphat phiset amnuaysat hatsadin" (Special interview: Amnuaysat Hatsadin). *Nechan sutsapda* (Nation Weekly), September 10–16.

Amorn Suwanbuppha. n.d. *14 tula 16 wan mahawippayok thung 6 tula 19: chamra prawattisat khong chat* (From October 14, 1973, the day of extreme grief to October 6, 1976: clarification of the national history). Bangkok: Aphirak Chakri.

Anand Punyarachun. 1996. "Long Live His Majesty." *Bangkok Post,* May 26, 4–5.

Anderson, Benedict. 1977. "Withdrawal Symptoms: Social and Cultural Aspects of the October 6 Coup." *Bulletin of Concerned Asian Scholars* 9, no. 3 (September): 13–30.

Anek Laothammatas. 1992. *Business Associations and the New Political Economy of Thailand: From Bureaucratic Polity to Liberal Corporatism.* Boulder, CO: Westview Press.

———. 1993. *Mopmuethue: chonchanklang kap kan phatthana prachathippatai* (The mobile-phone demonstrators: middle-class and democratic development). Bangkok: Matichon Publishing.

Anuson sathan 14 tulakhom 2516 (The October 14, 1973, memorial place). 1998. "For the commemoration of the 25th anniversary of the 1973 uprising." Bangkok: Saitharn.

Atsiri Thammachote. 1981. *Khunthong chao cha klapma mua fasang* (Khunthong will return at dawn). Bangkok: Chao Phraya.

Attachak Satayanurak. 2006. *Mu thisam nai prawattisat kanmuang thai* (The third hand in Thai political history). English title, *Truth and the Dealing with Truth in the Context of the Third Party Culture, 1957 to Present.* Bangkok: Khop Fai/Obor.

Baitonghang [pseud.]. 2010. "34 pi 6 tula: thisut hang khwam saman" (The 34th anniversary of October 6: the utmost disgust). *Prachatai,* October 6, 2010.

Bergin, Bob. 2016. "Defeating an Insurgency—The Thai Effort against the Communist Party of Thailand, 1965–ca. 1982." *Studies in Intelligence* 60, no. 2 (June): 25–36.

Bowie, Katherine A. 1997. *Rituals of National Loyalty: An Anthropology of the State and Village Scout Movement in Thailand,* New York: Columbia University Press.

———. 2017. *Of Beggars and Buddhas: The Politics of Humor in the Vessantara Jataka in Thailand.* Madison: University of Wisconsin Press.

Brundage, W. Fitzhugh. 1993. *Lynching in the New South: Georgia and Virginia 1880–1930.* Urbana-Champaign: University of Illinois Press.

Bunchana Atthakor. 1982. *Banthuk kanpatiwat 1–3 mesayon 2524 kap khaphachao* (Memoir: the 1–3 April 1981 coup and myself). Bangkok: Bunchana Atthakor Foundation for Education and Research.

Chai-anan Samudavanija. 1982. *The Thai Young Turks.* Singapore: Institute of Southeast Asian Studies.

———. 1984. "Thailand: A Stable Semi-Democracy." In *Democracy in Developing Countries,* vol. 3, edited by Larry Diamond, Jonathan Hartlyn, Juan J. Linz, and Seymour Martin Lipset, 305–346. London: Adamantine Press.

Chai-anan Samudavanija, Kusuma Snitwongse, and Suchit Bunbongkarn. 1990. *From Armed Suppression to Political Offensive: Attitudinal Transformation of Thai Military Officers since 1976*. Bangkok: Institute of Security and International Studies, Chulalongkorn University.

Chaiwat Satha-anan. 1986. "Roidang kap khwam ngiap" (Stain and silence). In *Satcha thorayuk* (Truth in tyrannical era), edited by Bandit Thamtrirat et al., 151–154. Bangkok: Thammasat Student Government and the Students Federation of Thailand.

Chandler, David P. 2008. "Songs at the Edge of the Forest: Perceptions of Order in Three Cambodian Texts." In *At the Edge of the Forest*, edited by Anne Hansen and Judy Ledgerwood, 31–46. Ithaca, NY: Cornell Southeast Asian Program.

Charnvit Kasetsiri and Thamrongsak Petlertanan, eds. 2013. *Tula-Tula: Sangkhom ratthai kap khwamrunraeng thang kanmuang* (October to October: Thai state and society and political violence). Bangkok: The Foundation for Textbooks in Social Science and the Humanities.

Cho-chongkho [pseud.]. 1996. "Duangchai chao-ei ya loey loplum thongtham" (My dear friends, do not forget the just cause). In *Mahawitthayalai khong chan* (My university), 78–126. Bangkok: Thammasat University Union.

Connerton, Paul. 1989. *How Societies Remember*. Cambridge: Cambridge University Press.

Connors, Michael. 2007. *Democracy and National Identity in Thailand*. Copenhagen: NIAS Press.

Crane, Susan A. 1997. "Writing the Individual Back into Collective Memory." *American Historical Review* 102, no. 5 (December): 1372–1385.

Daniel, E. Valentine. 1996. *Charred Lullabies: Chapters in an Anthropology of Violence*. Princeton, NJ: Princeton University Press.

Dawes, James. 2013. *Evil Men*. Cambridge, MA: Harvard University Press.

De Beer, Patrice. 1978. "History of the Communist Party of Thailand." In *Thailand Roots of Conflict*, edited by Andrew Turton, Jonathan Fast, and Malcolm Caldwell, 143–157. Nottingham, UK: Spokesman Books.

Ettinger, Glenn. 2007. "Thailand's Defeat of Its Communist Party." *International Journal of Intelligence and Counterintelligence* 20 (August): 669.

Ferrara, Federico. 2015. *The Political Development of Modern Thailand*. Cambridge: Cambridge University Press.

Ford, Eugene. 2017. *Cold War Monks: Buddhism and America's Secret Strategy in Southeast Asia*. New Haven, CT: Yale University Press.

Friedlander, Saul, ed. 1992. *Probing the Limits of Representation: Nazism and the "Final Solution"*. Cambridge, MA: Harvard University Press.

Garland, David. 2005. "Penal Excess and Surplus Meaning: Public Torture Lynchings in Twentieth-Century America." *Law and Society* 39, no. 4 (2005): 793–833.

Gates-Madsen, Nancy J. 2016. *Trauma, Taboo, and Truth-Telling: Listening to Silences in Post-dictatorship Argentina*. Madison: University of Wisconsin Press.

Gawin Chutima. 1990. "The Rise and Fall of the Communist Party of Thailand (1973–1987)." Occasional paper no. 12. Canterbury: Center for South East Asian Studies, University of Kent.

Gillis, John R., ed. 1994. *Commemorations,* Princeton, NJ: Princeton University Press.

Girling, John. 1981. *Thailand: Society and Politics.* Ithaca, NY: Cornell University Press.

Gluck, Carol. 2007. "Operations of Memory: 'Comfort Women' and the World." In *Ruptured Histories: War, Memory, and the post-Cold War in Asia,* edited by Shella Miyoshi Jager and Rana Mitter, 47–77. Cambridge, MA: Harvard University Press.

Godoy, Angelina S. 2006. *Popular Injustice: Violence, Community, and Law in Latin America.* Stanford, CA: Stanford University Press.

Goldstein, Daniel. 2004. *The Spectacular City: Violence and Performance in Urban Bolivia.* Durham, NC: Duke University Press.

Haberkorn, Tyrell. 2011. *Revolution Interrupted.* Madison: University of Wisconsin Press.

———. 2015. "The Hidden Transcript of Amnesty: The 6 October 1976 Massacre and Coup in Thailand." *Critical Asian Studies* 47, no. 1: 44–68.

———. 2017. "The Anniversary of a Massacre and the Death of a Monarch." *Journal of Asian Studies* 75, no. 2 (May): 269–281.

———. 2018. *In Plain Sight: Impunity and Human Rights in Thailand.* Madison: University of Wisconsin Press.

Halbwachs, Maurice. 1980. *The Collective Memory.* Translated by Francis J. Ditter Jr. and Vida Yazdi Ditter. New York: Harper and Row.

———. 1992. *On Collective Memory.* Translated by Lewis A. Coser. Chicago: University of Chicago Press.

Handley, Paul. 2006. *The King Never Smiles.* New Haven, CT: Yale University Press.

Huebner, Thom. 2017. "Monument as Semiotic Landscape: The Conflicted Historiography of a National Tragedy." *Linguistic Landscape* 3, no. 2 (October): 101–122.

Hunt, Matthew. 2018. "Cinema and Politics: 6th October 1976." Accessed November 19, 2018. http://www.matthewhunt.com/6october.pdf.

Hyun, Sinae. 2014. "Indigenizing the Cold War: Nation-Building by the Border Patrol Police of Thailand, 1945–1980." PhD diss., University of Wisconsin-Madison.

———. 2017. "Mae Fah Luang: Thailand's Princess Mother and the Border Patrol Police during the Cold War." *Journal of Southeast Asian Studies* 48, no. 2 (June): 262–282.

Igarashi, Yoshikuni. 2000. *Bodies of Memory: Narratives of War in Postwar Japanese Culture, 1945–1970.* Princeton, NJ: Princeton University Press.

Ing Kanchanawanich, Wasant Sitthikhet, Suthee Khunwichayanond, and Manit Sriwanichaphum. 2008. *'Flashback' 76: History and Memory of October 6 Massacre*. Brochure in Thai and English for the art exhibition at the Pridi Banomyong Institute. August 2–23, 2008.

Jackson, Peter. 2004. "The Thai Regime of Images." *Sojourn: Journal of Social Issues in Southeast Asia* 19, no. 2 (October): 181–218.

Janjira Sombatphunsiri. 2016. "Santi withi khong puey" (Puey's nonviolence method). In *Puey kap sangkhomthai nai wikrit plianphan* (Puey and Thai society in the transitional crisis), edited by Prajak Kongkirati and Pokpong Janwit, 147–177. Bangkok: Foundation for Textbooks in Social Science and the Humanities.

JCA—Journal of Contemporary Asia 6, no. 4 (1976): 515–516; 7, no. 2 (1977): 263–267; 7, no. 3 (1977): 430–434. Translated documents and broadcast by the Communist Party of Thailand.

Jelin, Elizabeth. 2003. *State Repression and the Labors of Memory*. Translated by Judy Rein and Michael Godoy-Anativia. Minneapolis: University of Minnesota Press.

Ji Ungpakorn and Suthachai Yimprasert. 2001. *Atchayakam rat nai wikrit kanplianplaeng* (State crime in the crisis of changes). Bangkok: The October 6, 1976 Fact-finding and Witness Interviewing Committee.

Jory, Patrick. 2017. *Thailand's Theory of Monarchy: The Vessantara Jataka and the Idea of the Perfect Man*. Albany: State University of New York Press.

Kanokrat Lertchoosakul. 2016. *The Rise of the Octobrists in Contemporary Thailand*. Monograph no. 65. New Haven, CT: Yale Southeast Asia Studies.

Kanthima Wongwiangchan, ed. 2013. *Phrommin Lertsuriyadej: Phrom mai dai likhit* (Phrommin Lertsuriyadej: Not a fate). Bangkok: Matichon Publishing.

Kasian Tejapira. 1996a. "Nung prayok kao kham" (One sentence, nine words). *Phuchatkan raiwan* (Manager Daily), May 27, 8.

———. 1996b. "Rusuk haeng yuksamai" (The pulse of our time). In *Mahawitthayalai khong chan* (My university), 42–55. Bangkok: Thammasat University Student Union.

———. 1996c. "Banthuk naksuksa khunsaphap" (Memoir of a student returnee). In *Mahawitthayalai khong chan* (My university), 68–77. Bangkok: Thammasat University Student Union.

———. 2006. "Khwam taek salai khong udomkan duantula" (The collapse of the October ideology). *Matichon,* October 20.

Keyes, Charles F. 1978. "Political Crisis and Militant Buddhism in Contemporary Thailand." In *Religion and Legitimation of Power in Thailand, Laos and Burma,* edited by Bardwell Smith, 147–164. Chambersburg, PA: Anima Books.

Khaen Sarika [pseud.]. 2007. *Khon tula tai laew* (The Octobrists have died). Bangkok: Sarika.

Kobkua Suwannathat-Pian. 2003. *Kings, Country and Constitutions: Thailand's Political Development, 1932–2000*. London: Routledge/Curzon.

Kong Rithdee. 2016. "In the Eye of the Storm: Interview with Neal Ulevich." *Bangkok Post*, September 30.

Kulvadee Sastree and Suthachai Yimprasert, eds. 1996. *Rao mai lum jaruphong* (We do not forget Jaruphong). Bangkok.

LaCapra, Dominick. 2000. *Writing History, Writing Trauma*. Baltimore, MD: John Hopkins University Press.

Langer, Lawrence. 1991. *Holocaust Testimonies: The Ruins of Memories*. New Haven, CT: Yale University Press.

Lim, Samson. 2016. *Siam's New Detectives: Visualizing Crime and Conspiracy in Modern Thailand*. Honolulu: University of Hawai'i Press.

LoGerfo, James. 2000. "Beyond Bangkok: The Provincial Middle Class in the 1992 Protests." In *Money and Power in Provincial Thailand*, edited by Ruth McVey, 221–270. Singapore: Institute of Southeast Asian Studies.

Mallet, Marian. 1978. "Causes and Consequences of the October '76 Coup." In *Thailand Roots of Conflict*, edited by Andrew Turton, Jonathan Fast, and Malcolm Caldwell, 80–103. Nottingham, UK: Spokesman Books.

Manas Sattayarak. 1994. "Ramluk 6 tula; wan wangweng" (Commemorating 6 October: The sadden day). *Matichon Weekly*, October 7–13, 79–80.

McCargo, Duncan. 1997. *Chamlong Srimuang and the New Thai Politics*. London: Hurst & Co.

Montesano, Michael, Pavin Chachavalpongpun, and Aekapol Chongvilaivan, eds. 2012. *Bangkok May 2010*. Chiang Mai: Silkworm Books.

Morell, David, and Chai-anan Samudavanija. 1981. *Political Conflicts in Thailand*. Cambridge, MA: Oelgeschalager, Gunn & Hain.

Mulder, Neils. 1997. *Thai Images: The Culture of the Public World*. Chiang Mai: Silkworm Books.

Nakharin Mektrairat. 2006. *Phraphusong pokklao prachathippatai* (His Majesty who protects democracy). Bangkok: Thammasat University Press.

Naowarat Phongpaiboon. 2001. *Anuthin 14 tula* (The annals of the October 14). Bangkok: Kieo-Klao Publishing.

National Administrative Reform Council (NARC). 1976. *Khothetching 6 tula* (Facts about the October 6 incident). Bangkok: Public Relations Committee of the NARC.

Nations, Richard. 1976. "October Revolution–Part II" and "Thanom: the Unwanted Catalyst." *Far Eastern Economic Review*, October 15.

Nattapoll Chaiching. 2011. "Phra barami pokklao tai ngao insi: phaen songkhram chittawitthaya amerikan kap kansang sathaban kasat pen sanyalak haengchat" (The royal benevolence under the eagle's shadow: American's psychological warfare and the making of the monarchy as the national symbol). *Fa Diaw Kan* 9, no. 2 (April–June): 94–166.

———. 2013. *Khofanfai nai fan an luachua: khwamkhluanwai khong khabuankan patipak patiwat Sayam (2475–2500)* (To dream the impossible dream: The counter-revolutionary movement of the 1932 Siamese revolution). Nonthaburi: Sameskybooks.

Nelson, Robert S., and Margaret Olin, eds. 2003. *Monuments and Memory, Made and Unmade,* Chicago: University of Chicago Press.

Netiwit Chotiphatpaisan, ed. 2016. *Chula kap 6 tula* (Chulalongkorn University and the October 6 incident). Bangkok: The October 6 and Chula People Project.

Nguyen, Viet Thanh. 2016. *Nothing Ever Dies: Vietnam and the Memory of War.* Cambridge, MA: Harvard University Press.

Nidhi Eoseewong. 2006. *Pen and Sail.* Translated by Chris Baker and Pasuk Phongpaichit. Chiang Mai; Silkworm Books.

Nithatsakan 6 tula (The October 6 exhibit). 1996. Bangkok: The Committee for the Commemoration of the 20th Anniversary of the October 6 Incident.

Nora, Pierre. 1989. "Between History and Memory: *Lieux de Memoire.*" *Representations,* no. 26 (Spring): 7–24.

Ockey, James. 2004. *Making Democracy: Leadership, Class, Gender, and Political Participation in Thailand.* Honolulu: University of Hawai'i Press.

Paisal Wisalo, Phra, Sulak Sivaraksa, and Mo.tho. ko.189. 1996. *6 tula charuk khwamsongcham khwamwang lae botrian* (Inscribing October 6: memory, hope and lesson). Bangkok: Komol Khimthong Foundation.

Pasuk Phongpaichit and Chris Baker. 1998. *Thailand's Boom and Bust,* rev. ed. Chiang Mai: Silkworm Books.

———. 2000. *Thailand's Crisis.* Chiang Mai: Silkworm Books.

———. 2009. *Thaksin,* 2nd ed. Chiang Mai: Silkworm Books.

Pavin Chachavalpongpun, ed. 2014. *Good Coup Gone Bad: Thailand's Political Development since Thaksin's Downfall.* Singapore: Institute of Southeast Asian Studies.

Payne, Leigh. 2008. *Unsettling Accounts: Neither Truth nor Reconciliation in Confessions of State Violence.* Durham, NC: Duke University Press.

Peleggi, Maurizio. 2017. *Monastery, Monument, Museum: Sites and Artifacts of Thai Cultural Memory.* Honolulu: University of Hawai'i Press.

Penn, Michael. 2003. "Noise from the Edge of Silence." *On Wisconsin,* summer issue, 30–33, 62. Madison: Wisconsin Alumni Association.

Phatcharapha Tantrachin. 2013. *Khwamkhit thang sangkhom kanmuang khong seksan prasertkul* (Social and political thoughts of Seksan Prasertkul). Bangkok: Praphansan.

———. 2014. "Su mai thoi kap 40 pi khwamfan duan tula" (The song 'Relentless Struggle' 40 years of the October dream). An article in five parts. *Nechan sutsapda* (The Nation Weekly) May–June: 1144–1148.

Phillips, Herbert. 1987. *Modern Thai Literature with an Ethnographic Interpretation.* Honolulu: University of Hawai'i Press.

Phutthapol Mongkholworawan. 2003. "Klum phalang faikhwa lae sathaban phramahakasat nai hetkan 6 tulakhom 2519" (The right-wing groups and the monarchy in the October 6, 1976 incident). In *Ruam botkhwam thang wichakan yisip-ha pi hok tula nai boribot sangkhom thai* (Collected articles: twenty-five years of the October 6 incident in the context of Thai society), edited by Suthachai Yimprasert, 177–208. Bangkok: Hok Tula Ramluk.

Pitch Pongsawat. 2016. "6 tula 2519 kap u-domkan khonrunlang 6 tula" (The October 6 incident and the ideology of the post-1976 generation). In Netiwit 2016, 195–231.

Prajak Kongkirati. 2005. *Laelaew khwam khluanwai ko prakot: kanmuang watthanatham khong naksuksa lae punyachon kon 14 tula* (Thus, the movement appears: Cultural politics of students and intellectuals before the October 14, 1973 event). Bangkok: Thammasat University Press.

———. 2006. "Counter Movements in Democratic Transition: Thai Right-Wing Movements after the 1973 Popular Uprising." *Asian Review* 19:101–134.

———. 2010. "Song khontula khao non" (Sending the Octobrists to bed). *Way* (Thai magazine), no. 37, October: 49–58.

Pratimanuson 6 tula 2519 (The October 6, 1976 monument). 2000. Bangkok: Thammasat University.

Puangthong R. Pawakapan. 2017. "The Central Role of Thailand's Internal Security Operations Command in the Post-Counter-Insurgency Period." *Trends in Southeast Asia 2017 no. 17.* Singapore: ISEAS Yusof Ishak Institute.

Puangthong R. Pawakapan and Thongchai Winichakul. 2018. "Kan thamrai sop mua 6 tula" (Desecration of the corpses in the October 6 massacre). *Fa Diaw Kan* 16, no. 2: 42–64.

Puey Ungphakorn. 1977. "Violence and the Military Coup in Thailand." *Bulletin of Concerned Asian Scholars* 9, no. 3 (September): 4–12.

———. 1981a. "Khwamrunraeng lae ratthaprahan 6 tulakhom 2519" (Violence and the coup on October 6, 1976). In *Annuangmatae 6 tulakhom 2519* (On October 6, 1976). Bangkok: Komol Khimthong Foundation.

———. 1981b. *A Siamese for All Seasons: Collected Articles by and about Puey Ungphakorn.* Bangkok: Komol Khimthong Foundation.

———. 1993. *Khamhaikan khong dr. Puey Ungphakorn karani hetkan 6 tulakhom 2519* (The testimony of Dr. Puey Ungphakorn regarding the 6 October 1976 event), 4th printing. Bangkok: Komol Khimthong Foundation.

———. 2000. *Khunnahap chiwit patithin haeng khwamwang chak khanmanda thung choengtakon* (Quality of life of a South East Asian: a chronical of hope from womb to tomb), 4th printing. Bangkok: Komol Khimthong Foundation.

Rao khu phu borisut (We are the innocent). 1978. Bangkok: Klum Naksuksa Kotmai.

Reiff, David. 2016. *In Praise of Forgetting: Historical Memory and Its Ironies.* New Haven, CT: Yale University Press.

Rousset, Pierre. 2009. "The Rise and Fall of the Communist Party of Thailand." *Links International Journal of Socialist Renewal.* Accessed June 23, 2017. http://links.org.au/node/1247.

Rudee Reungchai [pseud.]. 1996. "Hetkan 6 tula yuthinai nai prawattisat" (The place of the October 6 incident in history). In *Tulakan* 1996, 313–328.

Saithan duan tula (Streams of the Octobers). 1990. Bangkok: Committee for the Construction of the October Memorial.

Samokao [pseud.]. 1977. "Nithatsakan hetkan 6 tula" (Exhibition on the October 6 incident). *Nawikkasat* 6, no. 1 (January): 27–65.

Sa-nguan Nittayarumphong, ed. 2003–2005. *Pum prawattisat mahidol phua prachathippatai* (Historical records of Mahidol for democracy), 3 vols. Bangkok: Alfa Millenium.

Sanphasiri Wirayasiri. 2001. *Phom pen khonkhao khonnung ko khaenan* (I am a journalist, just that). Bangkok: Phakkhathat.

Sarakhadi (Feature Magazine). 1996. Special issue on the October 6, 1976 incident.

———. 1999. Special issue on Puey Ungphakorn (1916–1999).

Scott, James C. 1992. Domination and the Arts of Resistance: Hidden Transcripts. New Haven, CT: Yale University Press

Seksan Prasertkul. 2014. *Khwan fan duan tula* (The October dreams). Bangkok: Samanchon Publishing.

Sila Khomchai [penname]. 1996. *Lao khwam ching: khabuankan nuksuksa ram-khamhaeng yukton 2514–2519* (Telling the truth: the Ramkhamhaeng student movement in the earlier period 1971–1976), 2nd printing. Bangkok: Mingmitr.

———. 1997. *Patiwat bao bao* (Revolution lite). Bangkok: Mingmitr.

Sirote Khlamphaibun. 2007. *Prachathippatai maichai khong rao* (Democracy is not ours). Bangkok: Open Books.

———. 2013. *Prawattisat batphlae duantula lae duan phrutsapha* (The traumatic history of October 1973 and 1976, and May 1992 and 2010). In Charnvit and Thamrongsak 2013, 380–395.

Somsak Jeamthirasakul. 2001. *Prawattisat thi phoeng sang* (History that was just created). Bangkok: 6 Tula Ramluk Publishing.

———. 2007. "*Chaichana khong panyachon sipsi tula (tonthi 2: kan plian praden khrangyai)*" (Victory of the 14th October intellectuals: Part 2: major shifts in their thinking). In *Ratthaprahan 19 kanya* (The 19th September coup), edited by Thanapol Eawsakul, 400–403. Bangkok: Sameskybooks.

Sondhi Limthongkul. 1975. "Nawaphol: khrai—a-rai—thinai—yangrai (Nawaphol: who-what-where-how." In *Songthai* (Looking at Thais), edited by Cholthira Kladyoo, 349–357. Bangkok: Suksit Sayam Publishing.

Steedly, Mary. 1993. *Hanging without a Rope*. Princeton, NJ: Princeton University Press.

Stern, Steve. 2004. *Remembering Pinochet's Chile*. Durham, NC: Duke University Press.

Streckfuss, David. 2011. *Truth on Trial in Thailand: Defamation, Treason and Lese Majeste*. London: Routledge.

Suchit Bunbongkarn. 1987. *The Military in Thai Politics, 1981–1986*. Singapore: Institute of Southeast Asian Studies.

Sudarat Musikawong. 2010. "Art for October: Thai Cold War State Violence in Trauma Art." *Positions: East Asia Cultural Critique* 18, no. 1 (Spring): 19–50.

Suebsan (Carry on). 1996–2003. Newsletter of the October Network.

Sun khomun prachachon (Peoples' Information Center). 2012. *Khwam ching phua khwam yuttitham: hetkan lae phonkrathop chak kansalai kanchumnum mesa-phrutsapha 53* (Truth for justice: The April-May 2010 crackdown). Nonthaburi: Sameskybooks.

Surachat Bamrungsuk. 2017. "41 pi hang kaukhluanwai: rung a-run hang itsaraphap" (41 years of movement: the dawn of freedom (final episode). *Matichon Weekly*, December 29, 2017–January 4, 2018.

Surin Matsadit. 1979. "Chotmai phra surin" (Letters from Phra Surin). In Thawatchai 1979, 454–460.

Suthachai Yimprasert. 2015. *Nām pā: banthuk kāntǭsū nai khēt pā thǔakkhao Banthat* (Jungle stream: Memoir of the guerilla war in the jungles on the Banthat mountain). Bangkok: Aan.

Sutham Saengprathum. 1979. *Phom phan hetkan 6 tulakhom madai yangrai* (How I have been through the 6 October event). Bangkok: Daohang Publishing.

Swearer, Donald K. 1991. "Sulak Sivarak's Buddhist Vision for Renewing Society." *Crossroads: An Interdisciplinary Journal of Southeast Asian Studies* 6, no. 2: 17–57.

Tambiah, Stanley. 1992. *Buddhism Betrayed? Religion, Politics, and Violence in Sri Lanka*. Chicago: University of Chicago Press.

Thamrongsak Petchlertanan. 2008. "Anakhot khong 6 tula" (The future of the October 6). *Prachatai* (online newspaper), October 20.

Thawatchai Sucharitworakul, comp. 1978. *Khadi prawattisat: Khadi 6 tulakhom* (The historic trial: The 6 October trial), vol. 1. Bangkok: Bophit Kanphim.

———. 1979. *Khadi prawattisat: Khadi 6 tulakhom* (The historic trial: The 6 October trial), vol. 2. Bangkok: Bophit.Kanphim.

Thikan Srinara. 2009. *Lang 6 Tula* (After October 6). Bangkok: 6 Tula Ramluk Publishing.

———. 2012. *Khwamkit thang kanmuang khong 'panyachon faikhan' phailang kantoktam khong krasaekit sangkhomniyom nai prathetthai 2524–2534* (Political thought of the "Opposition Intellectuals" after the decline of the socialist ideas in Thailand 1981–1991). PhD thesis, Chulalongkorn University.

Tho. Krating [pseud.]. 1975. *Waek-ok kradtingdaeng phua khwamkhaochai andi nai sangkhomchaothai* (Exposing the Red Gaurs for the better understanding in Thai society). Nonthaburi: Arunkit Printing.

Thongchai Winichakul. 1994. *Siam Mapped: A History of the Geo-Body of a Nation*. Honolulu: University of Hawai'i Press.

———. 1996. "Duantula chao wanphut" (October, Wednesday morning). In *Sarakhadi* 1996, 122–128.

———. 1999. "Achan puey kap khwam ngiap nai tangdaen" (Peuy and his silence abroad). In *Sarakhadi* 1999.

———. 2002. "Remembering/ Silencing the Traumatic Past: the Ambivalent Memories of the October 1976 Massacre in Bangkok." In *Cultural Crisis and Social Memory: Modernity and Identity in Thailand and Laos,* edited by Charles F Keyes and Shigeharu Tanabe, 243–283. London: Routledge/ Curzon.

———. 2008. "Toppling Democracy." *Journal of Contemporary Asia* 38, no. 1: 11–37.

———. 2016a. "Thailand's Hyper-Royalism: Its Past Success and Present Predicament." *Trends in Southeast Asia 2016, no.7.* Singapore: ISEAS Yusof Ishak Institute.

———. 2016b. *6 tula lum maidai cham mai long* (October 6: Cannot forget, Cannot remember). Nonthaburi: Sameskybooks.

———. 2019. "Thailand's Royal Democracy in Crisis." In *After the Coup: The National Council for Peace and Order Era and the Future of Thailand,* edited by Michael J. Montesano, Terence Chong, and Mark Heng, 282–307. Singapore: ISEAS Yusof Ishak Institute.

Todorov, Tzevtan. 1996. *Facing the Extremes: Moral Life in the Concentration Camps*. Translated by Arthur Denner and Abigail Pollak. New York: Henry Holt & Co.

Trouillot, Michel-Rolph. 1995. *Silencing the Past*. Boston, MA: Beacon Press.

Truth for Reconciliation Commission of Thailand (TRCT) (Khana kammakan issara truatsop lae khonha khwamching phua kanprongdong haeng chat). 2012. *Rai-ngan chabap sombun* (The final report). Bangkok: TRCT.

Tulakan (In October). 1996. Bangkok: The Coordinating Committee for the 20th Anniversary of the 6 October Event.

US Department of State. 1994. "Thailand Human Rights Practices, 1993." Report. Washington: Government Printing Office. Accessed June 2, 2019. https://www.refworld.org/docid/3ae6aa541c.html.

Uthan Sanidvongse na Ayutthaya: Cremation volume. 2014. Bangkok: Family of Uthan Sanidvongse na Ayutthaya.

Wandee Santiwutthimethi. 1996. "Khamhaikan khong khon run 6 tula 19" (Testimonies of people of the 6 October 1976 generation). *Sarakhadi,* no. 140: 133–174.

Wanit Charungkit-anan. 1988. "*6 tula*" (October 6). *Matichon,* July 18.

Wanrak Mingmaninakhin, ed. 1996. *80 pi achan puey: chiwit lae ngan* (80th anniversary for Professor Puey: life and works). Bangkok: Thammasat University.

Wat Wallayangkun. 2001. *Dinso dome thammasat den susuk* (The dome of Thammasat stands tall in battle). Bangkok: Friends of 6 and 14 October Group.

———. 2013. "Daodaeng" (Red star). *Matichon*, June 17.

———. 2016. "Pak" (Mouth) in *Thoithuan haeng a-rayatham* (The coarse words of the civilization). Bangkok: Aan Publishing.

Wattanachai Winichakul, ed. 1988. *Samutphap duan tula* (A photo collection of the October events). Bangkok: Student Federation of Thailand.

Weinrich, Harald. 2004. *Lethe: the Art and Critique of Forgetting.* Translated from German by Steven Rendall. Ithaca, NY: Cornell University Press.

Wong, Ka F. 2006. *Visions of a Nation: Public Monuments in Twentieth-Century Thailand.* Bangkok: White Lotus Press.

Yoneyama, Lisa. 1999. *Hiroshima Traces: Time, Space, and the Dialectic of Memory.* Berkeley: University of California Press.

Yukti Mukdavijitra. 1996. "6 tula sanyalak khong khwam runraeng, khwam runraeng khong sanyalak" (October 6: The emblem of violence and violence of the emblem). *Ratthasatsan*, 19, no. 3: 50–67.

Zimmerman, Robert. 1976. "Reflections on the Collapse of Democracy in Thailand." Occasional paper no. 50. Singapore: Institute of Southeast Asian Studies.

Index

Page numbers in **bold** indicate figures.

About the Author

Thongchai Winichakul is emeritus professor of history at University of Wisconsin–Madison and Senior Researcher at the Institute of Developing Economies (IDE-JETRO), Japan. His first book, *Siam Mapped* (University of Hawaiʻi Press, 1994), was awarded the Harry J. Benda Prize from the Association for Asian Studies in 1995. The Japanese edition (2003) won the Grand Prize from the Asian Affairs Research Council (Japan) in 2004. The journal *Sojourn* (April 2009) recognized it as one of the "most influential books of Southeast Asian studies." The book was also translated into Thai (2013), Chinese (2016), and Korean (2019). A recipient of the John Simon Guggenheim Award in 1994 and many other fellowships, Thongchai was elected to the American Academy of Arts and Sciences in 2003 and served as president of the Association for Asian Studies in 2013. His main interests are in cultural and intellectual transformation to modernity in Siam under the semicolonial conditions (1880s–1930s). He also published seven books and numerous articles in Thai, including many political and social commentaries. A student leader in Thailand during the tumultuous 1973–1976 period, he is a survivor of the massacre he has written about in this book.